The First Century
of the Detroit Auto Show

Robert Szudarek

INTERNATIONAL®
Society of Automotive Engineers, Inc.
Warrendale, Pa.

Library of Congress Cataloging-in-Publication Data

Szudarek, Robert.
  The first century of the Detroit Auto Show / Robert Szudarek.
    p. cm.
  Includes index.
  ISBN 0-7680-0502-7
    1. North American International Auto Show (Detroit, Mich.)--History. 2.
  Automobiles--Michigan--Detroit--Exhibitions--History I. Title.

  TL7.U62 D477 2000
  629.2'074'77434--dc21
                                                                    99-052130

SAE Order No. R-281

Table of Contents

Introduction

The First Automobile on the Streets of Detroit

A steam carriage came to Detroit as part of Spalding and Rogers' Great Ocean Circus in 1864. It was described as a family steam carriage for common roads (roads without rails). Upon arrival it was driven through the principal streets then displayed in full operation at scheduled performances in the circus ring. It could attain a speed of 30 mph, and needed only a periodic bucket of water and a handful of twigs to burn. Thus, by stretching one's imagination, it could be considered as the first automobile show in Detroit.

Sylvester Hayward Roper of Roxbury, Massachusetts, built this "family steam carriage." He began experimenting with steam carriages in 1859, and is considered to be in the forefront of steam carriage development. The March 1864 issue of *Scientific American* reported Roper's invention as a vehicle weighing 650 lb., powered by a 2-hp engine making it capable of 25 mph. Roper built ten vehicles in the next 20 years, and also fitted steam engines to bicycles when they began to become popular in the 1880s.

W.W. Austen of Lowell, Massachusetts, was billed as "Prof. Austen," with the newly invented "family steam carriage." Actually, he was Roper's agent, and his ethics are still in question as to the omission of Roper's name on the advertising handbills. Austen was killed in 1894 after colliding with another steam carriage, which was probably the first two-car collision in U.S. history.

The First Detroit Automobile Show

In 1899, there were at least six automobile inventors reportedly at work in Detroit, including Henry Ford, Barton Peck, James Rogers, and C.W. Koch. As a carriage builder for many years, Koch explained why the horseless carriage was bound to come to Detroit, saying that some large wagon companies were making only 16 cents per wagon. One Detroit company was boasting of making $1 on a $50 cart, and work was done in a slipshod manner, with very few good workers coming into the trade. The coming of the electric car and the bicycle helped ruin the trade further, and rubber tires took more work away. He felt the horseless wagon would revive the trade and that was why many blacksmiths and wagon makers were experimenting with the horseless carriage.

William Metzger felt the time had come and, along with Seneca G. Lewis, who was connected with the sporting goods department of the Fletcher Hardware Company, organized the Tri-State Automobile and Sporting Goods Association. The Detroit Light Guard Armory was leased for showing sporting paraphernalia and automobiles. The show consisted of bicycles, firearms, fishing tackle, and sporting goods. One of the exhibits, which was put on display for attracting the public to the show, was a collection of animal heads bagged in Africa, donated by Oren Scotten and Colonel Seyburn Wesson. With Metzger being the only automobile dealer in Detroit, the exhibit also included a display of two steam Mobiles and two Waverly electrics, produced by Pope Company factory in Indianapolis. The public at this time was very skeptical as to the possibilities of motor vehicles and Metzger arranged to give a visible illustration of what they were capable of using a set

Groundbreaking for the Detroit Light Guard Armory took place on May 31, 1897, headed by Col. H.M. Duffield, C.P. Taylor, with nickel-covered shovels, and R.A. Bissel with a nickel-plated pickax. A hollow square was formed and an old dirt wagon was glorified with elaborate decorations of flags and bunting, and the driver was masqueraded as Uncle Sam. Col. Lum, the captain of the company during the Civil War, lifted the first earth with a spade loaded by Commander David R. Pierce. The armory was officially opened with a ceremony on October 18, 1897. (Reprinted with permission of the Burton Historical Collection of the Detroit Public Library.)

For over half a century the Light Guard was prominent in the social and civic life of Detroit. In 1911 a reorganization was effected by which the Light Guard and the Detroit Light Infantry were merged in the first regiment of the Michigan National Guard.

of rollers with dials. Once every hour during the four days of the show the steam and electrics would alternate in spinning the rollers and agitating the dials to the wonder of the skeptical public. The show attracted 200 sportsmen from all parts of the country which was deemed a howling success. The promoters of the show were so elated they threw a banquet at the old Russel House where practically all the profits were absorbed.

In September, a horseless carriage manufactured by the Still Motors Company of Montreal was used for a mail collection trial in Detroit. The trip took 1 hour and 13 minutes versus the normal horse carriage time of 2 hours and 15 minutes. The National Master Horseshoers Association convened to discuss the adverse effects of the horseless carriage on their trade.

William E. Metzger

S.G. Lewis

View of the Drill Hall. The Armory was designed by the most-famous American architect of the time, Henry Hobson Richardson. He used one of his favorite motifs: large, round arches and a number of small panels.

The Speedonome was the first dynamometer. Two Mobile "Steamers" are shown racing. (Courtesy of the National Automotive History Collection, Detroit Public Library)

1900

Model Year

The first "recognized" automobile show in the United States was held in New York in November 1900, with the assistance of William Metzger. There was no buying public to speak of and its main purpose was to enlist dealers. In this way the manufacturers were afforded the chance to engage potential dealers from all over the country; franchises could be signed on the spot. It was sponsored by the National Association of Automobile Manufacturers (NAAM), and the Automobile Club of America (ACA). The annual shows in New York became the most important, with the shows in Chicago a close second.

The Detroit show was repeated in 1900 with a display of blooded dogs added as a special feature, causing visitors considerable discomfort since the livestock was billeted in the gallery. Later in the year, William Metzger jumped into the automobile game head-first and joined William Barbour, Jr., and G.M. Gundeson in organizing the Northern Motor Car Co. in Detroit.

The first New York Automobile Show lacked enough exhibits to fill the floor of Madison Square Garden, so a flat oval track for showing cars in motion was built around the floor. An incline was erected on the roof to show the hill-climbing capabilities of the machines. (Courtesy of the National Automotive History Collection, Detroit Public Library)

1901

Model Year

In Detroit in 1901, the Light Guard Armory continued holding conventions, shows, and plays. The Tri-State Automobile and Sportsman Show featured new car dealerships of J.P. Schneider with the Milwaukee Automobile, and the White Sewing Machine Co. with the White Steam Carriage. William Metzger boasted a new two-story building on Jefferson Avenue and Brush Street, leased from Henry B. Joy (president of the Packard Motor Car Company). It contained a showroom on the first floor and offered automobile accessories on the second floor. Later in the year, Metzger helped organize an automobile race in Grosse Pointe, where Henry Ford beat Alexander Winton.

Mrs. L. Oakley Bunce of Detroit, with her son at the controls, is pictured at an automobile dealer in Detroit. The car is a Waverly electric built in Indianapolis under the sponsorship of the Pope conglomerate.

In 1901 William Metzger leased a building from Henry B. Joy and opened his own showroom on East Jefferson at Brush (across from where the Renaissance Center entrance is today). Later, the Detroit Auto Club (which eventually became part of AAA) would hold its meetings on the second floor.

The first annual Tri-State
Automobile and Sportsman's Show

DATE: February 26 - March 1, 1902

SPONSOR: Tri-State Automobile
& Sporting Goods Association

BUILDING: Detroit Light Guard Armory

ADMISSION: 25 cents to all

DECOR: The building was gaily decorated with bunting, moss, trees, and festoonings of vines. The general decorations were the finest ever attempted in the armory; special wiring was arranged for by the management, and the electrical effects of the signs were the most extensive ever attained in Detroit. The main floor of the armory was laid out in blocks of booths with aisles between them. The heavier goods such as gasoline engines, automobiles, and a launch were positioned around the walls. In the blocks of booths in the middle of the floor were many of the bicycle displays and parts such as chains, wheel appliances, and brakes. There were guns, fishing poles, punching bags, baseball supplies, pictures, and mounted head skins—everything for a sportsman or his friends.

ENTERTAINMENT: Finney's famous orchestra furnished concert and solo performances nightly. The Sportsman's Art Gallery showed masterpieces of famous sportsman artists, with a Mr. Osthans and other famous artists in attendance. Much interest was given to the revolver and rifle contests.

J.P. Schneider's exhibit at the automobile show. Like Bill Metzger, he sold bicycles before automobiles.

The Russel House was torn down and replaced by the Hotel Ponchartrain, which was later replaced by the First National Bank Building.

INSIDE THE SHOW: William Metzger dominated the displays at the Automobile Show with: the Waverly, Baker, Fanning, and Columbia electrics; Mobile and Toledo steam cars; Winton, Oldsmobile, Knox, and Silent Northern gasoline cars. Other makes included the Elmore, Peerless, Geneva, International, Henry Ford Co., Milwaukee, National, Toledo, Waltham, White, and Winton.

The show was headed by William E. Metzger, the president of the Tri-State Automobile & Sporting Goods Association. He had an able coadjutor in the Association's secretary and treasurer, Seneca G. Lewis, a director in the Fletcher Hardware Company and manager of its sporting goods department. There were ten dealers listed in the Detroit city directory for 1902; at that time, the Metzger establishment on the northwest corner of Brush Street and Jefferson Avenue was the largest automobile dealership in the U.S.A.

One of the most popular attractions was R.D. Camp's rollers with dials. It was then known as the "Speedonome," and used every evening for contests between electric, steamer, and gasoline vehicles. The Speedonome had attracted large crowds as expected; on March 1, the last night of the show, the Geneva and White vehicles were expected to take a fall out of the victorious Toledo. The Toledo had beaten an Elmore in five miles in 11:36, and in the gasoline competition the Olds machine made five miles in 11:31. This was the last year of the "Speedonome" for the automobile show. It was subsequently sold to the Olds Motor Works for vehicle testing.

The "horseless carriage" was becoming extinct, in fact it had the "horse wanted" effect. Vehicles were being made with engines mounted in front and concealed with a hood. They were referred to as an "automobile." This concept was originated in France which was the pre-eminent automobile producer in the world. The placing of the engine under the hood, instead of under the carriage, distributed the load more uniformly and gave better access to the same. It reduced vibration or jarring effect compared to the rear undercarriage location. Most important, there was a general demand for vehicles of the French type. It was evident in the Peerless.

The natural development of a fully enclosed car was also beginning. Entirely closed driver's seats were impractical in horse-drawn rigs for centuries because of the necessity to converse with an outside element with voice, rein, or whip. The limousine pattern of automobile with a front glass to partially protect the driver and a completely enclosed hood to protect passengers was becoming

William Metzger is pointing to one of the first Cadillac automobiles. The driver, Alanson Brush, put the car "through the paces" at the Grosse Pointe, Michigan, horse-racing track. The car was shipped to New York for the 1903 Auto Show where Metzger, Sales Manager for Cadillac, received down payments for over 2000 Cadillacs.

popular. Still, the automobile was stored away for the winter. This precipitated the strategy for the manufacturers to use the fall season for the beginning of the new model year. Thus, when purchased in the fall it was a new model and driven until winter, and still new the following spring when it was taken out of storage. New models brought out in January would not sell due to lack of passable roads.

NOTE: There were few roads beyond the city. Nor were there signs, garages, gas stations, or road maps. In order to venture any distance, vehicles usually toured in "packs." The first attempt to improve these conditions was made in 1902 when William Metzger formed the Automobile Club of Detroit. He became its first president with a membership of 30, with quarters in the second floor of his store on Jefferson and Brush. Charter members included Charles A. DuCharme, Henry B. Joy, Russel A. Alger, and John and Truman Newberry.

DATE: February 9-14, 1903

SPONSOR: The Tri-State Automobile
and Sporting Goods Association

BUILDING: The Detroit Light Guard Armory

ADMISSION: 25 cents to all

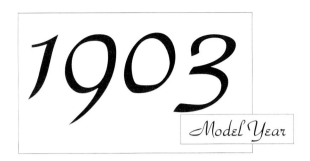

1903
Model Year

DECOR: The optic nerves of the visitors were stimulated by the profusion of the strong national colors of American flags artistically draped from the steel arches of the roof, almost hiding the iron girders. From the center was a festoon pendant of flags, while a blazing arc lamp crowned the device. Railing draperies around the booths incorporated harmonious combinations of colors. Purple and white, green and white, black and yellow were some of the combinations. The electrical sign work was also a prominent feature, including an enormous sign extending all across the east end of the main hall above the balcony that read "Cadillac Automobiles Go All the Time." The north wall was relieved of its barrenness by the skillful hanging of numerous private collections of trophies of the hunt—moose, elk, deer, bear, and other stuffed heads, game birds, fish, and many skins. In general, exhibits of tires and lamps, rifles and other sportsman's small goods, and phonographs occupied the open center of the main floor. Automobiles and marine motors and launches were shown in spaces along the north wall, under the balcony at each end of the drill hall in the basement. The dogs were arranged in temporarily constructed stalls in the gallery.

ENTERTAINMENT: The Metropolitan orchestra and solo artists, located on the south end of the gallery seated under a canopy of American flags, rendered a program nightly and also at the special matinees for ladies and children on Wednesday and Saturday.

OPENING: The opening night show was called "Press Night," followed on Tuesday by "Society Night."

INSIDE THE SHOW: Starting at the left by the entrance, the Oldsmobile exhibit was first. "Billy" Rands, now city agent for the Olds factory, was in charge of the big booths. Next came William Metzger's exhibit taking in several booths. The Cadillac, Waverly, Winton, Columbia, Toledo, and Baker were found in all their forms. John P. Schneider had the Elmore, Peerless, Marr, and Northern. The Geneva Steamers came next, and then at the corner W.H. Weber was showing Ramblers, Orients, Searchmonts and Conrads. The White Sewing Machine Co. had its ordinary rig of the 1903 model along with a new touring car. The Sandusky, Kirk, Chelsea, Flint, and Ide-Sprung-Huber automobile companies with rigs or engines occupied center spaces. Max Dingfelder had one of his roadsters there and the Jackson steam car was shown in the basement.

THE SECOND ANNUAL TRI-STATE
AUTOMOBILE AND **SPORTSMAN'S SHOW**
Week of February 9, **Light Guard Armory**
The Bench Show of 250 Dogs
Fifty 1903 Model Automobiles
Fast Gasoline Launches
Finest Shot Guns and Rifles
Fishing Tackle That Will Catch 'Em
Exhibit of Taxidermy
Many Novel Features
SEE
25c—Admission to All—25c
METROPOLITAN ORCHESTRA and SOLO ARTISTS
nightly and Wednesday and Saturday Matinees

15

Notice there are two Wheeler automobiles (built in Detroit) at the 4 o'clock position in the photograph.

The year 1903 was considered as the real beginning of the automobile industry in Michigan. Oldsmobile was well established at the time. Cadillac had started in 1902, and William Metzger took over 2000 advance orders for $10 apiece at the January 1903 New York Auto Show. The Ford Motor Company was incorporated in June of 1903. Henry B. Joy brought the Packard Motor Car Co. to Detroit in 1903, and Buick was chartered the same year.

At the Detroit Auto Show it was considered a novelty to pay one price at the outer gate for the entire exposition. It took a person all the way through and brought him out pinned full of badges and pockets bulging with souvenirs. The Olds booth was always crowded and W.C. Rands, Roy Chapin, and James Brady were kept busy. Fred Smith and Ransom Olds predicted that "the horse is passing."

A feature of the Northern exhibit was the rejuvenated runabout that Jonathan Maxwell was racing in October 1902 at Grosse Pointe when he struck Winton's Bullet and turned a somersault resulting in a providential escape from death. W.H. Weber's Orient Buckboard came in for lots of attention. The White automobiles were all painted white as usual; they reported their first sale of their new touring car to H.S. Pingree, son of the late Governor of Michigan. The Jaxon steamer was a clever car reflecting a great deal of credit to Byron J. Carter, its designer, who was in attendance. Tom Cooper's "999" was shown and always had a curious crowd around it.

The Wheeler touring car.

Automobile accessories were well represented, including Hussey Auto & Supply, with tilt steering wheels and radiators, and Briscoe Mfg. Co.'s radiator coils and tanks. Gas engines and launches were shown by Charles A. Strelenger Co., Blomstrom Launch Co., M. Dingfelder, and L.C. Steers. Numerous arms companies and the Fletcher Hardware Co. showed sporting goods.

The dog show was said to be one of the best ever held in the city, but there was a distracting din made by the 250 canines that were yelping, howling, and barking, in addition to the cracking of rifles and ringing of bullets against metallic targets.

"The Biggest Little Show in the Country" (Metzger and Lewis)

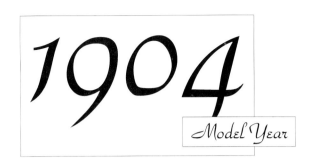

1904
Model Year

DATE: February 16-22, 1904

SPONSOR: Tri-State Automobile and Sporting Goods Association

BUILDING: Detroit Light Guard Armory

ADMISSION: 25 cents to all

DECOR: The main floor was divided into booths and it was necessary to plat part of the gallery. In all there were 56 booths for 80 manufacturers. The automobiles were on the main floor, and the exhibition featured not only Detroit automobiles but also some famed outside vehicles including some of the machines from France. The booths wore a profusion of colors and many electrical signs set off the little enclosures. The armory itself was elaborately decorated in festoons of colored bunting running from the dome to the side walls.

ENTERTAINMENT: Finney's Orchestra was in its prime and provided such programs as "The Belle of Bohemia," "Dat Gal of Mine," "When Johnnie Comes Marching Home," and "Der Freishutz."

INSIDE THE SHOW: Detroit had become the principal automobile manufacturing center of the world and local companies attracted the most attention. Detroit had the advantage of being the first place where the standard models of 1904 cars were exhibited. Many changes were made in some since the New York show and manufacturers saw room for improvement earlier in the year at Chicago.

The list of automobile exhibitors included: Cadillac Automobile Co.; Olds Motor Works; Pope Motor Car Co., Indianapolis; Electric Vehicle Co.; Packard Motor Car Co.; Autocar Co.; Ford Motor Car Co.; White Sewing Machine Co.; Hammer-Sommer Auto Carriage Co.; Pope Motor Car Co., Toledo; Haynes-Apperson Co.; Reid Manufacturing Co.; American Darracq Automobile Co. (this was the first foreign car at a Detroit automobile show); Chelsea Motor Car Co.; Reliance Gas Engine Co.

The only new car at the show, the Little Four, was a very lightly constructed steam runabout by McLachlan & Brown, Detroit. W.A. Russel & Co. carried the Winton, Darracq, Berg, and Woods electrics. The Wheeler Mfg. Co. had the Detroit touring car, fitted with double opposed engines. The Wayne Automobile Co. showed their double-cylinder 16-hp car. The Ford Motor Co. showed for the first time their new four-cylinder touring cars. The Commercial Motor Vehicle Co. showed a 600-lb. electric runabout, fitted with a 12-cell battery generating 1.5 hp. The Reid Mfg. Co. showed the Wolverine. William Metzger staged exhibits of the Cadillac Automobile Co., Packard Motor Car Co., Autocar Co., Pope Motor Car Co., Toledo Electric Vehicle Co., and Waverly, all occupying eight spaces extending nearly across one side of the large armory. While automobiles were the principal things on the main floor, there were also large displays of accessories as well as a number of light and powerful boats. Metzger also exhibited a full line of accessories, automobile clothing, and bicycles, which were becoming something of a novelty at a time of infrequent bicycle displays. He had the Cleveland, Tribune, Crescent, Regal, Stearns, and Yale motorcycles.

Mason and Kalin designed four additional stories of William Metzger's automobile store, with construction completed in 1904. It was the largest and best-equipped, exclusively automobile establishment in the U.S.A.

If the armory had been larger, it is probable that additional booths would have been rented. A plaint was made by the Sintz Gas and Engine Co. saying they were unable to secure a space in the armory and they were obliged to display their exhibit elsewhere. Consequently the Pungs-Finch light touring car, manufactured by the Sintz Co., was exhibited at the W.A. Russel & Co. salesroom at 248-252 Jefferson.

During the 1903 show, the howling of the canines interfered with conversation; the animals, despite their "blue blood," did not know how to behave. As a result the management turned the big drill hall on the lower floor into a kennel. Their barks were muffled and caused no annoyance in the cellar. The bench show of 200 dogs was held the first four days. Hunting dogs were judged the first day and non-sporting dogs the next three days. Judge Spacklin of Windsor judged the dogs and unearthed several surprises in the way of unknown animals defeating champions. In the Cocker Spaniel class the champion Mark Hanna was defeated for the blue ribbon by Little Pickpania. The champion pit bull Montage had to surrender first honors to Vondoteka. The Michigan Cat Club, with fine displays, took over the last two days. There was a public rifle and revolver range in the east gallery with prizes for both kinds of small arms. There was also a live bird and target shoot at the Rusch house under the auspices of the show.

At the end of the show it was estimated that 200 cars were sold—hardly a start on the number which would undoubtedly be sold later when the warm weather gave the demonstrators a chance to take contemplative purchasers for rides about the boulevard and the island. One of the features of the last evening of the show was the announcement by J.P. Schneider of the sale of eight Northern touring cars in a bunch. It was the first club sale in Detroit and, as far as it is known, in the business. The Silent Northern did extremely well at the show and was the only machine on the floor permitted to run all through the show, its noiselessness and freedom from vibration securing its owners this privilege.

A final salvo of automobile horns, mingled with the old automobile classic "Hail, hail, the gang's all here," broke out in the armory just before the close of the most successful automobile show ever held in Detroit.

20

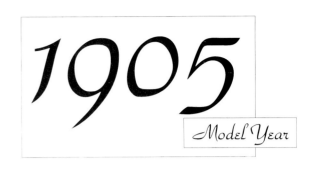

DATE: February 13-18, 1905

SPONSOR: The Tri-State Automobile and
Sporting Goods Association

ADMISSION: 25 cents to all

DECOR: The decorators departed from the usual strong colors such as reds, purples, and oranges. To give the show a look of delicate beauty, which had never before been attempted, the exhibitors generally used corn color and white or pale blues, greens, and pinks. These, in the sheen of thousands of light bulbs, made a marvelous effect. The ceiling bore corn-color bunting stretched across the arched room. This canopy was divided into squares and from the outline of the squares drop-folds of white bunting made the effect look dainty, giving it an air of brightness and concealing the wood and iron. Scores of incandescent arcs lit up the bunting, while hanging from it and lower down were the electric signs spelling out in blinding light the names of the various automobiles and their dealers. The main floor was platted into spaces for automobiles alone. The only way in which the whole floor could be given up to the whiz wagons was by finding other space for the accessories. This was solved by converting the gallery into smaller spaces than on the main floor. This was seized with avidity by the trade and all 36 spaces were sold.

The drill hall on the floor below was again used to bench over 200 dogs. The general sentiment of visitors was: "I can't afford an automobile, but I can buy a dog." Around the walls of this room were scores of mounted deer heads, elk, groups of game birds, and other suggestions of the hunt afield and afloat.

ENTERTAINMENT: Finney's Orchestra was secured for the entire week with selected programs each afternoon and evening. Some of the better selections included "Yankee Patrol," "Adlyn," and "Rigolette."

INSIDE THE SHOW: As one entered the hall and turned right, the Pungs-Finch Motor and Gas Engine Co. was in front of the partition of the hallway inside. On the right entrance was the E.R. Thomas Co. exhibit showing the Thomas Flyer and chassis.

The Reid Manufacturing Co., with the chainless Wolverine, was on the left entrance. Next to the Reid exhibit on the south side of the hall, the Blomstrom Motor Co. had a neat little space showing the output of this local factory. Adjoining it was the Stirling Auto Co. showing the Pierce and the Studebaker electrics.

Then right before the observer were the Wayne in the center, the Olds on one side, and the W.H. Weber & Co. exhibit of the Rambler and Mitchell cars on the other. The middle space was divided into six squares of equal size with three directly behind and were occupied by the White on the left, the Young and Miller, with the Elmore and Yale cars occupying one half of the right, and the Reliance Motor Co. and the Hammer Motor Co. each with a quarter square.

The Ford cars were in the center with the prettiest exhibit at the show marked by graceful white columns topped with electric balls. The whole west side of the floor was given to the Packard Motor Car Co. and the Cadillac Automobile Co. Metzger had roomy stalls for the Cadillac, Northern, Waverlys, and a Pope-Toledo. Other automobiles shown were the Buick Co. of Jackson, Maxwell,

General view of the show.

Peerless, Autocars, Columbias, Welch, Wayne, REO, Pope-Hartford and Pope-Tribune. High tariffs limited foreign companies to the Renault with just enough room to squeeze in a chassis. The Auto-Bi was the only motorcycle at the show, located near the front entrance with one of the winning cars at the 1904 Grosse Pointe car race.

Twelve degrees below zero in the moonlight was what 2,000 automobile enthusiasts had to face in visiting the Automobile and Sportsman's Show the first night. A sort of nervous excitement was in the air as men and women hurried from one stand to another in search of the information that would finally result in placing an order. The armory was a blaze of light, and society folk were there in body-length fur automobile coats. The crowd strolled up and down the aisles and thronged the booths, and sat on expensive divans and carved chairs to the ruination of the upholstery because everyone was covered with snow. They examined machines and when the bonnet was raised they reached inside with their white gloves to see the whys and wherefores. People learned more in half an hour lounging about the Packard Pavilion and listening to those people discussing the various makes than they could all the rest of the evening put together. These people did not care whether the

Appreciation for the exhibitors was shown by the Motor Club of Detroit and the Tri-State Association by a blow-out given in Harmonie Hall for $200 a plate. Vaudeville performers lent to the festivities. A new march called "Motor Club," composed by Seneca G. Lewis and dedicated to the Club, was premiered by Finney's Orchestra.

car had a limousine body or a patent footwarmer. They wanted to see if it had a new carburetor, a novel make-and-break ignition, and to see the handsome machine work on the chassis parts.

The coats came off when the heat became oppressive, and the beautiful dresses met at every turn and evening suits for the men seemed to portend that the show was becoming distinctly a society event. Up in the gallery, a lady near the Standard Oil booth yelled out: "I want to see Mr. Rockefeller"—but he wasn't there because he had missed his train.

DATE: February 12-17, 1906

SPONSOR: Tri-State Automobile and
Sporting Goods Association

BUILDING: Detroit Light Guard Armory

ADMISSION: 25 cents to all

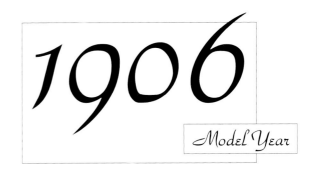

1906

Model Year

DECOR: Surrounded by darkness and gloom, within the armory was a blaze of lights, big arcs, thousands of incandescents, and the shining machines and rakish-looking touring cars with glistening brass and polished steel. There were polished limousines with Pullman-like interiors, fitted with every imaginable convenience from heaters for cold days to electric cigar lighters and speaking tubes.

And up in the gallery were all the incidentals such as engines, radiators, carburetors, wheels, spokes and artillery spokes, tires, horns, mud guards, and goggles.

ENTERTAINMENT: Music was furnished by Finney's Orchestra, with programs that included "Spares and Strikes," "Plantation Melodies," and "Dainty Dames." A special electrical display was added for the Thursday evening program. The Aerocar Co. had the Clef Quartet from the Hotel Metropole render a musical program every evening, and every lady visitor was given a carnation as a souvenir.

INSIDE THE SHOW: Opening night broke all records and the crowd was enough to have filled a building twice the size. The need was felt for an adequate building to do justice to this growing enterprise. Society was represented by ermine furs and silk hats who seemed to enjoy the event which was as informal as a country fair. Chaperones were helplessly buffeted by the surging

The Cadillac Hotel in Detroit, where many of the show's visitors stayed. The LeLand Faulkner Co. started out by building a steam engine for the Cadillac Hotel. Henry LeLand later became the first manager for the Cadillac Car Co., which started in 1902.

A 1907 model of the Northern Motor Car Company, shown on Bell Isle in Detroit.

crowds when they tried to follow the talkative young people from booth to booth. Entering the show the dazzling lights and swarms of people congregating about each car were bewildering. People talked of the relative merits of two- and four-cycle engines, the merits of water- and air-cooled engines, transmissions, gears, sparkers, clutches, controls, brakes, and motive forces. While the ladies stood looking at the machines they were discussing what style of auto coats and what colors of veiling would do to match the peculiar tints of the automobiles. "Isn't that perfect dear," one was heard to remark. "And wouldn't that color just match my hair. Oh I am so glad I came." You soon realized the motor car had a place in the national pastime right up there with baseball.

At the REO exhibit throngs of people clung about the cars taking their last looks until April or May, when deliveries would be made. The Northern exhibitors drew a great share of the patronage and praise. The Aerocar demonstrators were kept busy all week handling the crowds that packed around the big vehicles and studied the air-cooled motors. John P. Schneider's exhibits of Columbias, Pierce-Arrows, and Pope-Toledos resulted in one steady and unending question: "When can we get our cars?" The Grant Bros. were happy with their exhibits of Buicks and Thomas Flyers. The Ford runabout was a hub of humanity and the number of sales made the agents happy. The "Doctor" special, shown by Cadillac, was well received by doctors and ladies. More orders were taken for the Soules delivery vehicle and the Welch touring car than were ever dreamed of. The Walker runabout was causing a lot of comment, and the Waverly people showed their handsome electric coupe which was much admired by the visitors. On the north side of the armory at the Paragon exhibit was a crowd that never was less than five deep; built to go over any roads was the lowest-priced car at $375. Agents of the White Sewing Machine Co. reported six vehicles, and sales at Olds broke the Detroit record. The Cartercar was shown in the basement by the Motorcar Co., which drew more than its share of attention. Homer Warren, well-known baritone singer and Detroit realtor, purchased a big Queen touring car which would be seen touring the countryside in the spring.

Gasolines, steam cars, and electrics had attained such a high state of simplicity and reliability that the dealers said there was little more to look for in motor car construction beyond mere simplification of parts and the working out of details here and there.

NOTE: William Metzger left the Cadillac Motor Car Company in 1906 and joined the Northern Motor Car Company in Detroit as their head of sales.

DATE: February 11-16, 1907

SPONSOR: Tri-State Automobile and
Sporting Goods Association

BUILDING: Detroit Light Guard Armory (and
salesrooms on Jefferson Avenue)

ADMISSION: 50 cents to all

DECOR: Bunting with festoons from the ceiling was colored maze and blue of the University
of Michigan. The colors of the commonwealth floated everywhere, and the exhibitors showed it as
much as possible. This with the brilliant electric signs made a nice setting for the cars. The main
floor of the armory was platted so the cars could be cleverly shown. The new Detroit cars were in
the drill hall and the accessories were in the gallery. There was everything in the way of tops, hoods,
horns, lamps, tires, and other articles.

ENTERTAINMENT: Finney's Orchestra was constantly in attendance situated in the upper
east gallery. The music floated to the main hall in a most pleasing manner, never too loud to distract

General view of the show.

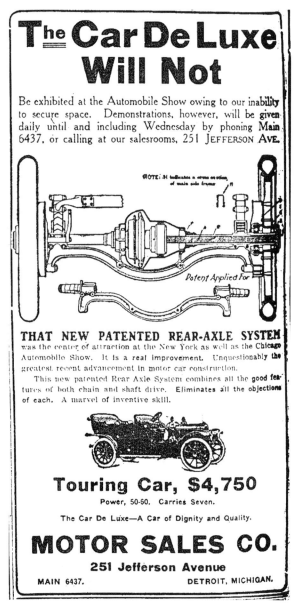
customers or agents. Many times the crowds remained silent and immovable during the rendering of some selections, only to burst into applause when the number was finished.

OPENING: Detroit's Mayor Thompson turned on the lights and opened the show with a flourish of praise for the automobile. The United States was now the leading automobile producer in the world, having produced a total of 98,000 cars since 1900. Detroit was the largest car-producing city in the United States, and Mayor Thompson was the only big-city mayor that did not own a car, although he was chauffeured around in a Mitchell. When asked why he didn't own a car he replied: "I have eight children; I dare not."

INSIDE THE SHOW: There were 33 makes of vehicles at the show, and nearly half of them were made in Detroit, including those from four new companies. The Brush runabout had a one-cylinder engine, solid tires, coil springs on all four wheels, and a clockwise rotating engine, making it safer to hand crank when starting. Economy of fuel and lubricating oil was guaranteed for 10 years with intelligent usage for the little car. The Kermath runabout, the Blomstrom 30, and the Fee-American with a two-cycle engine were also newcomers.

Because of lack of space, several cars of local make as well as several foreign-built machines that had applied for space were not in the show. The local cars were fortunate to have salesrooms convenient to the armory. The Queen line was exhibited in the salesroom of that local factory, on Jefferson Avenue, just around the corner from the show. The Car De Luxe was also shown with the Queen, as they were the city agents for this new make. The Ford Motor Car Co. said they were out of the auto show business and exhibited their cars at their Jefferson salesroom also.

To the auto enthusiast there were many attractions at the show. For instance, thousands of people were curious as to what constituted the Cartercar friction drive. One of the vehicles was stripped and powered with an electric motor so everyone could see the entire mechanism. Similarly, Cadillac had a "transparent chassis" with a sectional motor to reveal the inner workings. The White display was doing some of the best business in the building. The big steam cars were handsomely equipped and elicited remarks of admiration. One gentleman asked one of the attendants: "What is the price of that big car?" The salesman told him $3,700. "What?" the man cried. "$4,370? Say, have you got time to show me that car? It looks like about $6,000 to me." The Maxwell-Briscoe-McLeod Co. had a busy booth. There was a large case filled with trophies of the many races that instantly created interest in the famous Maxwell. Beyster-Thorpe was showing the new air-cooled Aerocar. The largest booth at the show was J.P. Schneider, with a Franklin, Pope-Toledo, and a Stevens-Duryea chassis, Pierce, and Columbia.

A Pope-Toledo in front of J.P. Schneider's showroom. Schneider is in the left-front seat. Potential customers were taken on demonstration rides.

A considerable feature was the gathering of motorcycles in the basement. For some reason they failed to make an impression on the local trade but the dealers were now booming them with unusual ardor. One lone bicycle, a National, was exhibited by John B. Trossel and formed an eloquent commentary on bygone days.

Show #1
"Harmony"

1908
Model Year

DATE: December 9-14, 1907

SPONSOR: Detroit Automobile Dealers
Association (DADA)

BUILDING: Riverview Park (formerly Wolf's Park)

ADMISSION: 50 cents to all
$1.00 society night only

The Detroit Auto Dealers Association had its beginning in the winter of 1907-08. With 16 firms merchandising individual transportation, they figured it was time to run a show of their own, under their own rules and regulations. They originally chose the Light Guard Armory for their show but found out the Tri-State Automobile and Sporting Goods Association had a contract which prevented any other automobile show. Just who discovered the merits of Riverview Park for the automobile show has never been divulged but it fitted the purpose nicely and was ample in dimensions. Henry Ford played an important part in the show by lending his advertising manager, E. LeRoy Pelletier, to become manager of the show. The only local dealer not represented at the show wasn't there because he deemed it a matter of personal dignity not to associate his cars with a building that was once a dance hall.

DECOR: The show was situated right in the middle of the "Coney Island" section of the city, and the exterior of the buildings illy prepared the spectator for the first glimpse of the show inside. One blaze of green and gold met the eye. Banners, streamers, pillars, and rafters were artistically draped. Most prominent in the decorations was a frieze of 24 immense 7 x 16-ft. canvas poster-cartoons, the work of Detroit's leading newspaper artists, singly and in series, completely encircling the hall. And beneath, covering the floor space except for two long aisles that trisected the hall longitudinally and formed the sole method of travel, motor cars were so close together that even adept, white-shirted attendants had difficulty moving about. There were no booths whatsoever: a little line of molding, nailed to the floor, provided a line of demarcation between cars. A coterie of little boys garbed in show colors acted as floor pages, splashing an additional bit of color on the scene.

SEASON 1907-8
D·A·D·A
AUTO SHOW
Souvenir Book of
CARTOONS

The show committee insisted on providing the illumination, though that cost the loss of the electric signs which usually had flaunted themselves in the eyes of the optically wearied spectator. The vehicle locations were advertised by modest little signs, bearing only the name of the exhibiting firm, suspended from a standard comprised of three spears, also in show colors. The sundry vendors and barkers were not represented on the floor and the smallest cardboard sign had to be approved by the management before it could be posted. Although, one enterprising distributor located in the center of the hall used a stepladder to discern any real heart-to-heart conversations elsewhere, thereby laying himself open to the charge of spotting live ones. Gasoline and acetylene were rigidly prohibited. Horns were shown as parts of cars fully equipped but their reeds were carefully removed. Exits were kept clear at all times and there was no smoking inside the hall.

ENTERTAINMENT: At the extreme end of the hall was the stage for Finney's Orchestra. With the entire show on one level, the strains could reach the most remote corner of the place.

The original members and exhibitors in the first DADA shows, assembled outside the show building, just before the exhibition was opened to the public.

OPENING: Members of the Automobile Club of Detroit were allowed into a special showing at 2:00 p.m. Monday. On Monday evening the exhibitors had the privilege of inviting their friends. Chauffeurs, factory testers, and other branches of the trade all rubbed shoulders with the general public. A "stag" lunch was held Tuesday night for the dealers, at Harmonie Hall, an appropriate location to reinforce the show's slogan "Harmony." Wednesday evening was "society night" for the city's fashionable people.

INSIDE THE SHOW: As a general rule the public looked upon this show as an advertisement of the wares exhibited rather than an amusement enterprise. They were interested in the development of the machines. There were few families in Detroit in which some members did not either own an auto or work in a place where they were manufactured or sold. In that way the development of the industry and advancements in the mechanisms became topics of common interest. Of 30 different makes shown comprised of 76 machines, 22 were gasoline-propelled, seven were electrics, and one was a steamer (the White). There were no freak cars—the management felt the public had no interest in such things. Prices ranged between $500 and $6,000 per machine. A large portion of the sales were expected to be made to farmers who were beginning to realize that the auto was just as useful in the country as in the city.

The Ford Motor Co. had a display of sixes, runabouts, and a light touring car. A new Ford taximeter cab, with a four-cylinder motor, was accompanied by the gathering of a crowd so big as to block its way in the hall for some minutes. William F.V. Nueman & Co. had a big center space to show the Welch, REO, and Rauch & Lang electric. This booth also featured a Stoddard-Dayton, with cylinders cross-sectioned and blazing with tiny electric lights, which formed one of the principal centers of interest to the spectator as it went through regular operations, actuated by an electric motor. A newcomer to the Detroit trade, the Anderson Electric Agency, distributor of the Detroit Electric manufactured by the Anderson Carriage Co., was located next to the east wall. A feature of the Detroit Electric was that it incorporated a Yale lock and was the only electric car that required a key to start it. They also showed the American Simplex, a machine of the famous Mercedes model. This was the first time the American model of the great German car had ever been shown in Detroit. In spite of the fact that William Metzger was the president of the Tri-State show and would conduct an auto show later in the winter, the Cadillac local branch utilized the DADA show to the limit, with a large space in the center of the hall filled with the latest productions of the Cadillac factory.

The feminine visitor at Riverview rarely mistook a phaeton for a high-powered roadster with a rumble, and she could distinguish a six-cylinder machine from a steam car without looking at the nameplate. A well-known Detroit society leader was responsible for an expression that bidded fair to become famous in automobile advertising. Speaking of her Thomas-Detroit car and the beauty of its outlines, she exclaimed: "It's worth your while to be in style," then went on to explain how satisfying it was to ride in a car that was so distinctly superior with regard to elegance and equipment, as was her Thomas-Detroit.

Two of the biggest sales at the show were credited to the J.H. Brady Auto Co. They involved $6,000 for a four-cylinder Peerless limousine and a $6,000 six-cylinder Peerless roadster; both purchased by Willis Buhl. Two Peerless machines had finished with a perfect score in the 1907 Glidden tour. "Reliability is the keynote to success of any business," said Jack Brady, "and particularly is this so in reference to the automobile business." Improvements for the Peerless included the power and riding qualities, and springs were still made with steel imported from Lemoine, France.

Show #2

DATE: February 10-18, 1908

SPONSOR: The Tri-State Automobile and
Sporting Goods Association

BUILDING: The Detroit Light Guard Armory

ADMISSION: 50 cents to all

DECOR: The walls, rafters, ceiling, and gallery were completely covered with the color scheme of maroon and white. Every car that was not finished in plain black was either of maroon finish or of maroon and white, the same colors as the bunting. There was one notable exception—a runabout finished in lavender, which looked to be just the confection for a cooing couple to slip away on a honeymoon trip, but otherwise a little too dainty for any ordinary use.

ENTERTAINMENT: Instead of having an orchestra, the show was divided into special days: Monday was "Governors Night"; Tuesday was "Automobile Club of Detroit Night"; Wednesday was "Society Night"; Thursday was "Good Roads Night"; Friday was "Board of Commerce Night"; Saturday was "Question Club Night." A number of distinguished visitors attended the exhibition on the feature days named in their honor.

OPENING: On Monday night, welcoming addresses were made by Governor Warner and Mayor Thompson in behalf of the state and city, respectively. Both speakers were introduced in the gallery by Fred Castle from the Continental Tire booth, which had been handsomely decorated with palms and cut flowers. The Governor called attention to the fact that more than 50% of the automobiles made in the United States were built in Michigan, and the mayor referred more particularly to the importance of the automobile industry to Detroit, and Detroit to the automobile trade. The show was practically in full running order when Mayor Thompson declared it open.

INSIDE THE SHOW: Whereas in former years it was frequently necessary for exhibitors to display only one type of car, this show was advertised as the most diverse and complete show ever held in Detroit. This was attributed to the reduction of exhibitors due to the DADA show in December 1907.

Many well-known cars were missing at the opening due to their presence at the DADA show or use of their own salesrooms. Cadillac, Northern, Aerocar, Brush, Packard, Elmore, Pope-Waverly, Wayne, Oakland, and Reliance participated in both shows. The Regal, a new Detroit product, and the International Harvester Co.'s high-wheeled buggy were displayed for the first time. In all, there were 27 gasoline makes and six electric makes at the show presented with a larger variety of types and patterns. A glance at the 1908 auto field showed little difference over the 1907 models. There were some new wrinkles in style, in shape of the body, in cut of the rumble box seat, and in rich lines for the big touring cars and limousines.

In addition to the suppliers located in the gallery, the drill hall contained the good roads exhibit, which was arranged as an educational feature. It gave those who didn't study the subject an idea of

Typical apparel for riding in an automobile.

what was being done for the betterment of the highways, and how it was being done. This exhibit drew the most interest than any other in the show, inasmuch as good roads were a matter of vital interest to those who owned an auto or rode a horse, either for pleasure or a beast of burden, as well as to the cyclist. There were some new features in the way of miniature delivery vans and other adaptations of bicycles and motorcycles. William Metzger had an exhibit that occupied three spaces in the basement showing the Indian with chain or gear transmission and the Racycle with a Thor motor. Yale cushion frame bicycles were also exhibited.

NOTE: Whether there would be one or two shows the following year was not known. It appeared that two shows would continue, one for the dealers and one for the manufacturers. There was also talk of an amalgamation of the two associations. The two shows indicated that February was a better month than December for a local show, which was all Detroit could give with the facilities at hand. Metzger and Lewis had already retired from the conduct of the show as Metzger had found that his duties for Cadillac had taken up a great deal of his time, and Seneca Lewis was also branching out into other endeavors. In June 1908 William Metzger helped form the Everitt-Metzger-Flanders Company (E-M-F), manufacturer of automobiles, leading to the dissolution of the Tri-State shows.

"The Spirit of the Motor Car"

1909
Model Year

DATE: February 15-20, 1909

SPONSOR: DADA (This was the first show under the management of the DADA after its incorporation in November 1908.)

BUILDING: Wayne Hotel (casino) pavilion

ADMISSION: 50 cents to all
$1.00 society night only

DECOR: A contract for the interior work of the show was awarded to Hugo V. Buelow under whose direction a whole set of artists, sculptors such as Frederic Wagner, staff workers, and artisans were employed. Over 5,000 lights illuminated sculptures and cars, and thousands of yards of plush and other cloth were used for drapes. There were no bunting, flags, banners, or streamers—everything was the best.

Every inch of floor space was occupied, though there were no railings between the booths and sharp demarcation was not attempted. The greater part of the lower hall was devoted to the motor cars. The exhibits were marked by luminous signs against the wall, and fringing the entire background was a series of oil paintings, depicting familiar scenes which were readily recognized by the motorists.

A wide stairway led to the upper floor. Ascending, one was struck by the majestic work of the sculptor's art which, displayed in a mellow red light, adorned the top of the stairway. "The Spirit of the Motor Car" was the title, consisting of a motor car at full speed, pursuing an eagle. A woman in the car had just reached out and pulled a feather from the noble bird's wing. The spirited conception was further emphasized by a cloud effect, giving the illusion of the car in transit through a roadway of mist, through which the wheels and framework were but faintly traceable.

The Wayne Hotel opened in 1887. Located on 3rd Street on the Detroit River, it was a popular place and the only hotel in a city of 300,000 with the combined advantages of being a resort and a commercial hotel.

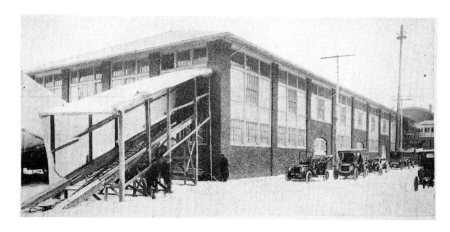

View of the pavilion on the waterfront. Vehicles had to be pushed up the runway by hand.

The upper floor with high ceilings and vaulted roof gave the designer fine facilities for his art. The centerpiece was a majestic staff fountain, reached on either side by a parallel row of pergolas, covered with smilax. Thousands of partly hidden electric lights shed their radiance through the crevices in the fountain. A circular path surrounded the fountain, on either side of which were upholstered seats forming a highly prized resting spot for the weary.

Signboards denoting the location of various exhibits were placed on massive-looking pillars, which lent an air of substantial permanence to the whole. The staff workers demonstrated their faithful attention to detail in these pillars by frescoing conventional motoring designs on the four sides. A lamp, a horn, and similar representations were seen at every turn.

ENTERTAINMENT: The music of 2,000 canaries mingled with the notes of an orchestra at one end of the big hall.

View of the second floor of the pavilion set up for a publicity photograph.

Automobile clubs were an important part of the still-new automobile industry. They helped prove to the public that automobiles could be reliable. Tours were made throughout the country and the Glidden tours were well-known. The AAA sponsored a Glidden tour from Detroit to Denver in April 1909 and chose the new E-M-F "30" as the "offical pathfinder."

OPENING: The opening arrived simultaneously with the hardest snowstorm of the season, but the hall was filled. In the absence of Mayer Breitmeyer, the show was formally opened by his secretary, Fred Van Vleet, who delivered a short address.

INSIDE THE SHOW: Detroit employed 45,000 people in the manufacture of motor cars and accessories, and ranked first in cars owned in proportion to population. It was said that Detroit folks knew an automobile like a Kentuckian knew a horse. They enjoyed looking at them and reveled in studying the mechanics and the fine points of design. The Detroit show was given by the dealers for the auto-buying public, in contrast to the big shows in New York, Paris, and London, which were manufacturers' shows for the trade in which the buying public was really a secondary consideration.

The rule requiring full evening dress from all exhibitors and employees was observed to the letter. There were exactly 200 motor cars on exhibit, including four varieties of trucks and delivery wagons, two makes of steam-propelled cars, and a liberal sprinkling of electrics.

J.P. Schneider, Detroit's pioneer distributor, was absent from the show for the first time, though he was well represented in the exhibits. He collapsed on the way to the Chicago auto show and was recuperating in a Kalamazoo sanitarium. The Chalmers-Detroit stole a march on its competitors by placing one of its cars in the window of the Wayne Hotel directly on the corner at which the show visitors disembarked from the Woodward Avenue streetcars. At the exhibit a Chalmers "30" chassis was displayed with portions of the cylinders and housings cut away, with a small electric motor to enable everyone to see just how every part of the mechanism of the car operated.

One of the points of interest was the Hupmobile runabout, a car that made its debut at the Detroit show. The American Simplex on display traveled 35,000 miles on the worst roads in the country, and sometimes at full speed. The spieler whispered that the car's top speed was nearly 80 mph, and the car ran so quietly and so smoothly that you would wonder if it had a motor at all! The $1,600 Mitchell was an imposing-looking car with an all-metal body, with the engine housed under a big, handsome hood. There were no foreign cars at the show.

In addition to the truck displays, the most imposing array of motorcycles ever gathered under one roof in Detroit included the Indian, Excelsior, N.S.U., Reading-Standard, and New Era. A complete range of auto parts manufacturers also exhibited their wares.

DATE: January 24-29, 1910

BUILDING: Wayne Gardens pavilion

ADMISSION: 50 cents to all
$1.00 society night only

DECOR: The show was held in Wayne Gardens, then the largest building in the city for the purpose, with a total of 30,000 sq. ft., exclusive of aisles. The upper and main floors had a general scheme of an Italian garden, and had no marked divisions for displays. Ivory and gold were the prevailing color tones, with green for the floor, while the roof was covered by an illuminated glass dome. The ceiling was a latticework of white bunting, in which were festooned immense quantities of southern smilax and thousands of paper roses. From interstices in the foliage gleamed many colored electric lights. In the center was a fountain, fancifully sculptured with figures appropriate to the occasion. The water at the foot of the fountain was filled with goldfish and the reservoir was surrounded by a circular seat, deeply upholstered, offering an inviting resting place. The pillars of the hall, as well as the entrance to the stairway, were embellished by hollow panels of stained glass, lit from within. On the walls were displayed the white and gold of the DADA and the escutcheon of the association's staff. The same general plan prevailed on the lower floor, with spaces divided by aisles formed by green latticed posts set with a pattern of green stained glass above and lit by incandescent bulbs. The aisles were covered with trellises, which supported the vines and roses.

ENTERTAINMENT: The one great defect of the show was that it was radically cut in half with the two floors, a feature doubly emphasized by the necessity of two orchestras. On the second floor, a troup of fierce-looking lions, upholding a golden cord in token of their bondage, guarded the bandstand.

OPENING: The exhibition's opening was preceded by a banquet at the Wayne Hotel for local and visiting newspapermen, at which Detroit's Mayor Breitmeyer, himself a member of the Anhut Motor Car Co., a Detroit motor car manufacturer, presided.

There was no official opening ceremony; the crowd stormed the doors of the show, more than 12,000 people within the first two hours. The crowd jammed the aisles, invaded the exhibits, and simply ran riot. The dealers and salesmen were swept off their feet.

INSIDE THE SHOW: The 1910 show was comprised of 312 motor cars from 57 different

Exterior of the Detroit Auto Show.

Interior of the Detroit Auto Show. (Archives of Labor and Urban Affairs, Wayne State University)

42

The E-M-F display.

factories, exhibited by 44 manufacturers of whom 23 were members of the DADA. Every manufacturer kept his displays shrouded in tarpaulins until the minute the show opened, and guarded their new models with extreme security measures. Many 1910 models came equipped with the top, windshield, speedometer, lamps, and fenders. No accessories were allotted space and motorcycles were also barred.

The west side of the lower floor was for the display of commercial vehicles, the most prominent being the Rapid. Immediately opposite were the Stoddard-Dayton Torpedo and other Stoddard models. The Torpedo body had a full-height front door and streamlined design from the cowl back. Not far away was the Chalmer's display. Other motor cars on the first floor were the Thomas, Herreshoff, Cartercar, Elmore, and a considerable number of newer cars.

The upper floor was devoted largely to the older dealers of the DADA. Ford had several of its model T cars. The Mitchell and Krit were at the head of the stairs with a grouping of light runabouts, along with the Hupmobile and Paige-Detroit.

Among the 14 newcomers were the Dearborn-Detroit with a torpedo body, Van Dyke, Abbott-Detroit, Warren-Detroit, Beyster-Detroit, and Templeton-Dubrie. Also noteworthy were the Anhut Six, named after one of its backers, Michigan Senator John Anhut. The only automobile not produced in Detroit, the Patterson "30," was noteworthy because all working parts were enclosed and protected from the effects of dust and dirt.

The crowd's enthusiasm was increased during the week when Lozier, Hudson, and Maxwell announced plans for the erection of new large factories. Several times the hall was crowded almost to the danger point, and even on "Society Night," with the admission increased to $1.00, there was a good crowd.

The 1910 automobile chassis consisted of 1,400 to 2000 different parts, and Michigan led the world in the manufacturing of these parts, mainly due to the fact that the larger companies made their own. Michigan had 42 automobile assembly plants, followed by Indiana with 31 and Ohio with 29, for a total of 20 states with 116 plants.

Auto Week poster for 1910 making the point of automobile growth and the demise of the horse as a mode of transportation. (The hotel pictured in the background is the Ponchartrain.)

NOTE: In 1910, four women claimed to have been the first to drive a car in Detroit; Mrs. Russel Alger, Mrs. Wilson Mills (Hazen Pingree), Mrs. Henry B. Joy, and Mrs. Florine Smith Stoddard.

The average life of a tire in 1910 was 1000 miles. An automotive writer predicted that by 1960 roads would be made of an artificial rubber and cars would have iron tires.

DATE: January 16-21, 1911

SPONSOR: DADA

BUILDING: Wayne Gardens pavilion

ADMISSION: 50 cents to all
$1.00 Society Night only

DECOR: Contractor Hugo V. Buelow, who was in charge of decorating, prepared an entirely new setting for the show. A rose garden, abounding in trellises over which climbed a riot of bloom, surrounded the glittering 1911 motor cars. The upper floor was transformed into a giant rose bower. Countless hundreds of yards of white bunting, torn into strips of uniform width, were employed to give the walls and the ceiling a lattice effect. Intertwined among the latticework were 40,000 artificial American Beauty roses and carloads of smilax. The roof of the rose-covered bower was in the form of a half circle, conforming to the roof of the pavilion. In the intervening spaces were hundreds of red and green incandescent lights which constantly flashed on and off by automatic switches, giving the effect of twinkling stars as viewed through the foliage. A fountain played constantly in the center of the upper floor, giving another refreshing touch to the general effect. The exhibits were arranged along the side walls. There were no railings or posts separating one from another. Each exhibit was marked by a uniform sign above the center of the space. Anyone who had subscribed to the view that romance and the automobile business were no longer kin was forced to revise his opinion after a visit to the DADA show of 1911.

OPENING: The opening of the show was auspicious. When Manager Walter Wilmot gave the word to let down the bars, there was a ready response from the waiting public, eager to see the magnificent spectacle for which its curiosity had been whetted by the glowing advance descriptions in the local press; they were not disappointed. It was general opinion that the decorations alone were well worth the admission fee of 50 cents, to say nothing of the exhibits. The crowd on opening night simply choked the show and made progress through the aisles and the ends of the stairway a matter of great difficulty. More than 5,000 people passed through the stiles, overflowed into the exhibits, clambered over the

The most brilliant display of Motor Cars ever assembled will be seen at

The D. A. D. A. Automobile Show

Thirty-six of the city's most prominent dealers will show over 200 Motor Cars of every known variety. Doors open Monday evening at 7:30 and the show continues daily at the

WAYNE GARDENS
Jan. 16th to 21st

A musical program of rare merit by two orchestras and high class singers will contribute to the entertainment.

Society Night Thursday
TICKETS ONE DOLLAR

A brilliant assemblage will greet this most artistic auto show ever prepared anywhere.

Doors open Monday night at 7:30 and daily thereafter from 10 a. m. to 11 p. m.

Admission 50 Cents

Inside the Wayne Gardens pavilion.

cars, and asked questions so fast that each salesman wished for a thousand tongues and a pair of ears to go with them.

Thursday evening was set apart as "Society Night," and Detroit's 400 were out in force.

INSIDE THE SHOW: There were automobile shows and then there was the type which Detroiter's came to know. Motordom contained only one Detroit. In the matter of motor-wisdom all other cities were still in the kindergarten stage. The Detroiter in his motor show had the same at-home sensation as a Goucester man in a fishing schooner, as an Iowa farmer in a cornfield, as a Seattle lumber baron in a pine forest.

The Abbott-Detroit was built in Detroit from 1909 to 1915, then moved to Cleveland, Ohio, from 1915 to 1918.

The Hudson was built in Detroit from 1909 to 1954, then moved to Kenosha, Wisconsin, and merged with Nash to become American Motors Corp. until 1987, when the Nash and Hudson nameplates were dropped.

One of the sales managers of a non-Detroit company stood inside one of the exhibits and watched his experts vainly endeavoring to answer the questions which a motor-wise coterie of men were pouring in. "I'll have to fire my salesmen and hire a bunch from the crowd, I guess," he stated. "It looks as if everybody here knows more about cars than we do." Yet those salesmen had been through a New York show with credit and were veterans at their trade!

The DADA show of 1911 contained no exhibits aside from completed motor cars and chassis. The exhibits could have been divided up into three types: the runabout 20-hp or less; the light touring cars of approximately 30 hp; and the large, luxurious type with accommodations for seven and a power of 40 hp or more. Motor cars were becoming increasingly alike. There was less variety than ever in the location and plan of the control system. In fact, one standard system evolved that made it possible for someone familiar with any type approaching the popular to drive any other car without difficulty: pedals for the clutch and service brake, side levers for the gearshift and emergency brake, hand levers on the steering wheel for spark and throttle, and an accelerator between the foot pedals. There was still some lack of uniformity in the location of the driver's seat. The great majority of manufacturers still preferred the right side, with right-hand levers, but there were notable recruits to the left-hand drive. A new development was the inauguration of several new models with left-hand drive with control levers located between the passengers on the front seat. The prevailing feeling was that this was the most logical.

The largest exhibit was that of the United Motors line, which, in various parts of the two floors, showed practically every model made at its large group of plants. Upstairs they showed the Maxwell, Brush runabout, and the Alden-Sampson, made at the new factory in Hamtramck. The Buick exhibit was located at the head of the stairs on the second floor. Always a center of interest was a brightly lit chassis cut out in several places to show the operation of the mechanism. Next to Buick was the exhibit of the Cunningham Auto Co., distributors for the E-M-F Company. This firm showed the E-M-F "30" and the Flanders "20."

In 1910 the Ford Motor Co. showed the Model T in coupe and touring model. For 1911, they added a roadster, two-passenger torpedo, and a roadster with a rumble. One of the most attractive exhibits was by Craig Auto Co., which showed a number of Abbott-Detroits in various hues and body designs. The stage which formed the end of the upper floor was assigned to the J.H. Brady Auto Co. and John P. Schneider, both veterans of the local retail field.

The Brady exhibit featured the Hudson "33" in various forms, along with the Peerless. Mr. Schneider's exhibit featured the Alco, which was one of the most admired cars in the show. Built by the American Locomotive Co., it won two successive Vanderbilts, driven by Harry Grant.

Regardless of the size of the average spectator's pocketbook, it took a tremendous amount of moral courage to get him past the north side of the upper floor where nearby were grouped the offerings of the Oldsmobile and Packard companies. The Haynes was shown on the left side of the grand stairway and on the opposite side was the Lion "40."

"Overflow Show"

DATE: January 16-21, 1911

SPONSOR: United Automobile Dealers
and Manufacturers Association

BUILDING: Regal Motor Car Co. factory

ADMISSION: Free

DECOR: Although the show promoters could not go in for elaborate decorations, a prominent Detroit decorator was secured for several days to install 70,000 yds. of red, white, and blue bunting artistically draped around the posts and between the exhibits. Uniform signs, conspicuously posted, enlightened the visitor.

ENTERTAINMENT: The services of Boos' Orchestra was secured for the entire week. The catering for the United show was by the Ponchartrain Hotel Co., and the M.A. Lafond & Co. maintained a cigar stand. One of the features of the show was the use of a quarter-mile track alongside the show building for demonstrator cars. Another Regal building was made available to house the demonstrators.

INSIDE THE SHOW: There was no conflict between the management of the two shows. The officers of the DADA regretted exceedingly that there was not enough room and expressed themselves as pleased that the disappointed dealers and makers were able to find a way out of their difficulty. With the 32,000 sq. ft. at the Wayne Gardens pavilion and 60,000 sq. ft. of uninterrupted space on the second floor of the Regal factory, no fewer than 318 cars were on view at the combined shows. There were 83 exhibitors, including a score of accessory manufacturers and dealers at the United display, while the DADA show was confined exclusively to cars.

Detroit had 19 companies manufacturing gasoline pleasure cars, three companies manufacturing electric pleasure vehicles, and 15 manufacturing commercial cars. These were not all separate concerns, however, as some manufactured both pleasure and commercial cars. Allowing for duplications, there were 31 individual corporations in Detroit. In addition, an aeroplane from Toledo, Ohio, was exhibited.

Inside the auto show at the Regal factory.

The Regal display, including a racing car (No. 20).

J.P. Schneider's showroom on the right (with the tall facade). In 1911, there were over 30 manufacturers of automobiles in Detroit, 107 manufacturers of accessories, 136 dealers, with 38,000 people employed.

DATE: January 22-27, 1912

SPONSOR: DADA

BUILDING: Wayne Gardens pavilion
and annex

ADMISSION: 50 cents to all

1912

Model Year

DECOR: The chief interest was centered on the second floor of the pavilion, with its high arched ceiling, fountain, and the Wayne Gardens cafe at one end of the building overlooking the Detroit River. In studying the decorations, the onlooker was impressed with the dignity and refinement throughout the entire display. The ceiling of the upper floor was a work of art. The material used for covering the 19,600 sq. ft. of space was called Abersheen, invented by J.L. Hall of Minneapolis, who was the designer and contractor for the show. In the center of the ceiling was placed a 20-ft.-diameter circle which represented an auto wheel. Between the spokes was a series of mural panels painted in oil and illuminated, giving the effect of stained glass. A duplicate wheel hung against the east wall, at the far end of the auditorium above the stage. Directly under the ceiling, following the curves of the arches, was a series of electric lights in green, giving a mysterious

General view of the show.

The Miller Car Co. display. The Miller was manufactured in Detroit from 1912 to 1914.

atmospheric effect. Along the center of the ceiling were ten great candelabras on chains and decorated with curved globes. Uniform signboards marked off respective spaces and these were of the same material as the walls and the ceilings. The floors throughout the entire show were covered with green denim, which harmonized with the general decorative scheme. The Gray Bros. Electrical Co. installed over 11,000 incandescent lights throughout the show.

The staircase arch was decorated with plaster ornaments. On the sides were a series of panels showing a classic decorative forest effect and producing an appropriate background for the automobiles. A border of leaves and flowers encircled the room, topping the panels. The lower floor and vestibules were in keeping with the upper floor decoration.

The demand for floor space was so large that it was necessary to secure a permit from the city to close Front Street, allowing construction of an additional building on the lot in back of the Wayne Hotel. This additional building, which was torn down five days after the show, was known as the "annex" and covered a space 165 ft. long by 108 ft. wide, to create a total of 50,000 sq. ft. for the entire show. It was decorated in purple and white bunting and American flags, and a complete steam heating system was installed.

INSIDE THE SHOW: This was the first of the so-called local shows whose circuit covered over 230 cities and lasted until April. The officers and members of the Wolverine Auto Club did much to aid in the success of the DADA show as well as promote what was best for motoring in Detroit and the state. It was claimed that no exhibition in the country would cover as much territory or include as many exhibits as the Detroit show. There were 73 makes of pleasure and commercial cars, trucks, and motorcycles, shown by 62 manufacturers or dealers; and the accessory booths were operated by 25 exhibitors. With the single exception of the Auburn, every car was manufactured or handled in Detroit.

George Grant, of the Grant Bros. Auto Co., whose Everitt sixes were always thronged, said: "This show convinced me beyond any doubt that the six-cylinder car has come to stay." The bigger engines were getting extremely hard to hand-crank, and about one-half of the display vehicles

The Century Electric Motor Co. display. The company was founded in 1912 by five people, including Phillip Breitmeyer, who was mayor of Detroit. The Century was built in Detroit until the company went out of business in 1915.

featured a self-starter. There were several types including compressed air, exhaust gas (Winton), and electric, which was featured by Cadillac. That the self-starter was a desirable thing was well known by anyone who had to jump into the mud or snow to crank a car, and it was a great boon to anyone who did not want to do any unnecessary work. (Self-starters were also finding their way into race cars which were becoming difficult to start due to their high-compression engines. There were already several cases where cars couldn't be started in time to make it to the starting line.)

The Packard Motor Co. bragged that its mighty Packard Six could go 1,000 miles without an oil change. Usually with that much driving, the crankcase had to first be flushed with kerosene before changing oil. Pierce-Arrow urged that the owner oil six items each day. And every 100 miles there were another 20 parts to be lubricated. On the 2,000th mile that the car was driven, the owner was urged to perform 143 different oil and greasing chores and to wash out the crankcase with kerosene.

Five new makes made their appearance at the show, including three electrics and, remarkable to say, one steamer—a truck. One of the electrics, the Colonial, featured a cut-out switch located in front of the rear seats, which was provided with a Yale lock and key. This was designed to prevent unauthorized use of the car. The E-M-F "30" had the unique distinction of being the oldest car in the show. This claim was not made for the individual models in the exhibition. The slogan applied to the design of the car itself, in which all essential features were identical to the earliest E-M-F "30" produced.

The Belmobile, just brought out by the Bell Motor Co. of Detroit, attracted more than passing attention in spite of the fact that it was necessary to display it outside the pavilion for lack of space within.

NOTE: The self-starter was responsible for women's hemlines rising from just above the top of their shoes so they could operate the floor pedals. In turn, silk/cotton stockings gave way to nylon hosiery. The self-starter also affected women's dresses because corsets and the hourglass look were incompatible with driving a car with any degree of comfort.

Detroit's First
National Auto Show

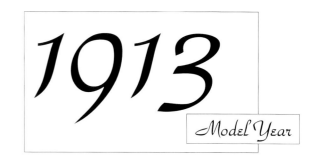

DATE: January 27 – February 1, 1913

SPONSOR: DADA and NAAM

BUILDING: Wayne Gardens pavilion and annex

ADMISSION: 50 cents to all

DECOR: The decorations by J.L. Hall were on a more elaborate scale than ever before and the show was given a most beautiful setting. A hand-painted canvas 250 ft. long covered the ceiling of the second floor of the casino. To decorate the streamers of lights for the several pergolas, almost 1,000 lb. of Alabama smilax was used. In the center of the second floor was a fountain, comprised of seven figures, which typified the progress of art of the Motor City.

An annex was erected, covering not only the lot in back of the Wayne Hotel, but extending across the street.

INSIDE THE SHOW: The Detroit Auto Show was sanctioned by the National Association of Automobile Manufacturers, giving it a position on the national circuit, along with eleven other cities, for the first time. Michigan was producing three-quarters of all autos in the U.S.A. The remainder were made in Ohio (10%), Indiana (8%), and Wisconsin and the Northeast.

There were 66 exhibits at the Detroit show, with 42 gasoline pleasure models totaling 300 cars alone. Commercial, steamers, electrics, and automobile accessories made up the rest. "Putting on the show" was the way many car manufacturers spoke of their exhibits at the big automobile show.

"The show is for the dealer and his assistants," said H.R. Radford, manager of the Cartercar Co. At the beginning of every show he called his men together and told them how to make sales, how to demonstrate the cars, and how to display them.

Each man had a regular time to be on the floor and the shifts were arranged to have at least two men on hand at all times to receive the visitors. The cars were displayed so that the "star" of the line was given the most prominence, and the rest of the cars were given the best possible arrangements. In going about it in a real business manner, Radford said: "We have gotten far better results from our exhibits than ever before. We have been able to interest many more agents and make a better impression all around."

Practically every carmaker showed a six-cylinder engine. Chevrolet had a starting system consisting of an English air compressor. The Oldsmobile was new

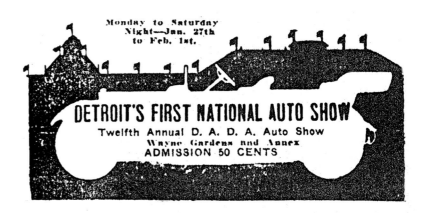

Monday to Saturday
Night—Jan. 27th
to Feb. 1st.

DETROIT'S FIRST NATIONAL AUTO SHOW
Twelfth Annual D. A. D. A. Auto Show
Wayne Gardens and Annex
ADMISSION 50 CENTS

View of the interior showing the lighting effects. This was the last show at the Wayne Hotel.

in every respect. The toolboxes, which formerly ran the length of the running boards, were gone, and in their place two lockers were positioned beneath the frame and out of the way, leaving the running boards perfectly clear. Another feature, which attracted attention to this car, was the way all of the control elements, other than the levers, were placed on the cowl dash close to the driver. The Hupmobile was the first car constructed with a pressed steel body.

Buick told its owners that trouble was generally the result of negligence, inexperience, or carelessness on the part of the operator. They also advised operators to keep on their side of the road. The eminently sensible bit of advice to owners of the Ford Model T was to throw away your cigar when filling the fuel tank.

One of the novel features of the auto show was the exhibition by the Punctureless Tire Co. of a sleigh which once belonged to Napoleon. The ancient sleigh was especially built for the great leader by A. Ehrier of Paris in 1795. A pretty story belonging to the sleigh runs as follows: Before his marriage to Josephine, Napoleon promised his bride-to-be a ride in the royal sleigh on a certain date and on the day mentioned there was no snow on the ground. But Napoleon wasn't daunted. Rather than disappointing Josephine he had three thousand barrels of salt strewn in the courtyard and the promised ride was taken.

DATE: January 17-24, 1914

SPONSOR : DADA

BUILDING: Ford branch building

ADMISSION: 50 cents to all
$1.00 society night

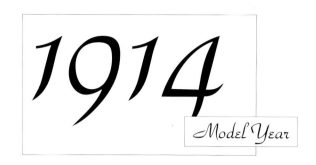

DECOR: The show was set in splendid surroundings, and the decorations more elaborate than in previous years. The director, J.L. Hall, was entitled to much credit for planning the grand entryway to the show building with electrically lighted columns supporting the roof as well as the general decorative scheme, which created wide and favorable comment. Needless to add, the bare walls of the Ford building were behind the usual variety of decorations and draperies, with strings and bunches of glowing lanterns that almost literally turned night into day.

Each of the gaily decorated floors featured an orchestra. The Schmemann band, familiar to all Detroit people, was on the show's first floor. The Ben Shook orchestra enlivened matters on the second floor, and the third floor was made pleasant and musical by Frankenstein's band, along with a restaurant. In addition to the orchestra music, vocal selections by prominent singers of Detroit and elsewhere were heard nightly.

A scheme was borrowed from the New York auto show: using elevators to take people up but not take them down. Forcing visitors to walk down ensured they would see most everything that was seeable, to coin a word.

OPENING: Previous shows opened on a Monday night, but the DADA decided the show would be opened, as was the custom in other cities, on Saturday night.

INSIDE THE SHOW: All told, there were 73 exhibitors of vehicles and accessories, 37 of whom showed 41 different brands of gasoline pleasure cars, not counting six makes of commercial vehicles, 19 of whom showed accessories, with one motorcycle exhibit. The only newcomer that made an appearance was Robert C. Hupp's "Monarch."

The six-cylinder car had come into its own for 1914. Electric lighting and cranking was another great development. Beauty was now becoming a primary consideration in the design of the American body, and streamlined bodies deserved to be well up toward first place in consideration of the most significant development since the 1913 models. The majority of the touring cars were equipped with side and storm curtains, and

OFFICIAL PROGRAM

Detroit
Automobile Dealers
Association

Thirteenth Annual
Automobile
Show

Ford Motor Company Branch Building

Woodward and Boulevard

JANUARY 17-24, 1914

Program Published Under the Auspices of the Detroit Automobile Dealers' Association

The swastika was the emblem for a car manufactured in Detroit from 1909 to 1915. The car was named after its designer, Ken Crittenden. The owners of the company spelled the name "Krit" and used the swastika because for many centuries it was considered a good-luck sign. The photograph shows a Krit in a showroom in Brooklyn, NY. The window was too small for a turntable so the car sat on a mirror.

there was evidence that the body designers were giving thought to finding a place where the owner could store baggage while on tour.

There were no bank loans for cars and some of the dealers would accept property as a down payment on a new car, after having it carefully appraised. Some dealers took in just about everything for trade-ins, including livestock, diamond stickpins and jewelry.

The Lozier with a new four-cylinder block motor was available in both five- and seven-passenger models. The steering was on the left with center control. A cowl board was used with the gages and switches within easy reach of the operator. The Detroit display had the distinction of housing a parcelcar, the newest type of delivery vehicle. The car was mounted on a Rocket cyclecar chassis with the drive seat in front. There were a number of cyclecars at the show. These were small cars with a narrow tread which could pass through an ordinary door, and equipped with a motorcycle

Detriot's Auto Show Home

The Ford sales office as it appeared for the Auto Show.

View of the second floor.

engine. The most prominent cyclecar on display was the La Vigne, along with the Hawk, Mercury, and Saxon, and the Car-Nation. Several of the cyclecar makers were obliged to stay on the outside because they could not find space.

View of the third floor.

DATE: January 16-23, 1915

SPONSOR: DADA

BUILDING: Detroit Lumber Company

ADMISSION: 50 cents

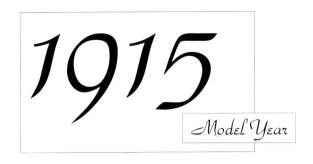

1915
Model Year

DECOR: Utilizing buildings erected for lumber mill purposes and located in the far west section of the city among mills and factories, the DADA event drew thousands daily from every section of Detroit. The Detroit Lumber Co.'s new buildings were spacious, well-lit, and constructed of the best materials. With 68,000 sq. ft. of floor space, there wasn't a display booth vacant.

From West Jefferson Avenue, a wide sidewalk with a canopy led to a one-story frame building 210 x 136 ft. Inside, commercial vehicles, gas engines and launches, and a 1915 model aeroplane were shown. Art Smith, who turned somersaults in the air show at the November 1914 state fair, gave exhibitions during the show, flying far over the river and showing how bombs were dropped by aviators in the European wars.

The decoration of the commercial building was purple and gold and yellow with an abundance of wisteria. A passageway, having murals resembling a grotto, led to the automobile display building 30 ft. away.

The automobiles and accessories were located in a 210 x 138-ft. building with two floors that size. The first floor resembled a Japanese garden, with creeping vines, flowers, and birds. Like the commercial building, light was furnished by thousands of lamps and was the best ever provided at a local show. The second floor was what might be termed the Lincoln Highway, as the walls were covered with 40 panels, 18 x 14 ft., representing various scenic features which the traveler along the route would encounter in the different states from coast to coast.

The third floor of 210 x 40 ft. was given over to the café and cabaret in one end and dancing in the other. The idea of promoting the social end made the show a desirable place for all who succumbed to the lure of the dance.

OPENING: At a dinner given by the DADA prior to the opening of the show, the need for a convention hall was brought out by W.E. Scripps. Mayor Marx took up this topic also, pledging his aid to secure a hall adequate to care for conventions and other like gatherings.

INSIDE THE SHOW: All told there were 203 cars and chassis on the three floors, with, perhaps, the

JOHN J. COMERFORD
DETROIT
VICE-PRESIDENT DETROIT LUMBER CO.

A general view on the second floor looking northwest. This floor was decorated with panels that represented various scenic features which a traveler would encounter while driving coast to coast, and was referred to as the Lincoln Highway floor.

most conspicuous features of the show being a twelve-cylinder Packard and an eight-cylinder Cadillac. The cyclecars were being replaced by the so-called "small car," which was a real motor car differing only in size, weight, and price from the larger cars. The Dodge Bros. did not exhibit their "mystery car" of 1914 at the Detroit show, although it attracted a great deal of attention at the New York show at the beginning of the month. The Dodge was exhibited during DADA week at Thomas Doyle's salesroom, Jefferson Avenue and Brush Street.

An innovation at the show was the motor car museum. Pioneer automobiles from 10 to 15 years prior to the show were on deck, along with other relics of bygone ages in automobiledom. They included the first Oldsmobile built in 1895, the first Hudson built in 1908, and the first Packard built in 1899.

It was a typical "show me" crowd at the exhibits. Everybody wanted to know just what the claims for each car were and just how one model differed from another. It kept the salesmen on their toes to answer all the queries that came to them and there were generally a half-dozen people listening for each answer as it was given.

There were pretty girls at the show, and lots of them. Some paraded up and down the aisles and others (an innovation of up-to-date managers) sold accessories and gave out catalogs. Of course there were self-starters, clutches brought all the way from Kokomo, and radiators from Racine. But visitors admitted that the motor girls beat them all.

NOTE: There were 40,000 license tags issued in Detroit from the Secretary of State located in the Magestic Building. An example tag number read C0660: One hundred thousand, six hundred and sixty vehicles in Michigan. In 1915, Rose Diamond was the first woman to get a driver's license in Michigan.

William Metzger was elected president of the Auto Parts Manufacturing Co., when A.O. Dunk resigned.

Packard armored motor car display.

The oldest cars that could be found were lined up in the "Motor Museum" at the Auto Show. The first Oldsmobile, the first Hudson, the first Model A Packard made in 1899, the first Buick, and the Detroit Electric were in the display.

DATE: January 15-22, 1916

SPONSOR: DADA

BUILDING: Riverview Park

ADMISSION: 50 cents

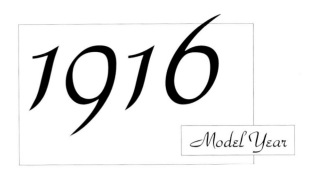

DECOR: There were three buildings at Riverview Park to house cars: the Palace Auditorium, Palais de Danse, and the Pier, which was the scene of the welcome mid-winter fixture. Wide, well-lit corridors connected the three buildings, and electric signs at the two entrances blazed forth the fact that the show was there.

George W. Graves, the architect who conceived the decorative scheme of the show, used four colors producing a remarkable effect. All the rules in decorating were set aside and Mr. Graves evolved a scheme that was a common topic of discussion for the visitors. Straight lines were used exclusively, particularly a bar effect.

At the Pier, where admittance was gained through the main entrance, crimson and white decorations covered the walls and the ceilings. Colored spheres on a white background were used in the auditorium along with thousands of incandescent lights. In the Palace, the decorative effects were the most unusual. Mr. Graves had a black and white checker scheme with a French poster effect.

All buildings were inspected by the fire marshal and the decorations were fireproof. Several fire extinguishers were distributed among the three buildings.

ENTERTAINMENT: Music was provided each afternoon and evening.

OPENING: Just prior to the opening all the members of the association attended a banquet at the Hotel Griswold. Frank N. Sealand, president of the DADA, hosted and Mayor Marx gave a speech. Turning an electric button Saturday night, Mayor Marx officially opened the show. The three buildings with 183 cars and chassis on the floor were flooded with light. Of the 183 cars and chassis in the booths, 115 were passenger cars and 16 chassis, 30 were commercial cars and 12 chassis, and 10 were electric cars.

INSIDE THE SHOW: The auto show was now becoming an important fountainhead for educating the general public. Originally the shows were mostly for the purpose of bringing together an army of dealers and men who showed symptoms of inclining toward the distribution of motor cars as a business. The value of the show was measured by the number of new dealers who

DETROIT

Auto Show

January 15 to 22

———

Three Big Buildings Linked Into One
Palace Auditorium, The Pier,
Palais de Dance

—EAST JEFFERSON, near the BOULEVARD—

Two Buildings of Pleasure Cars
One Building for Trucks and Accessories

Open Daily, from 10 a. m .to 10:30 p. m.

Admission, 50 cents

———

Under Auspices of D. A. D. A.

Home of the 1916 DADA Auto Show.

General view of the exhibits in the Palais de Danse building.

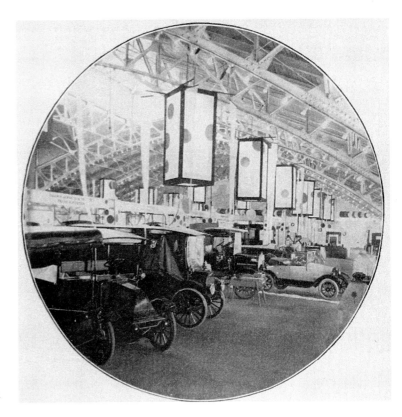

The commercial exhibit in the Palace Auditorium.

scratched their names in the lower right-hand corners. By 1916, shows were no longer necessary to get dealers because most of the makers had widespread organizations of dealers, who in turn had their sub-dealers. While additional dealers were still being taken on at the shows, the visiting public, whether buying or window shopping, had become an element of importance.

An increase in popular interest in automobiles exceeded the floor space at the show and it was impossible to stand still long enough to look at a new model. A multitude of enthusiasts slowly swung around the circles in each of the big three exhibition buildings, and the only thing to do was to swing along with it. Probably the most striking thing about the 1916 show was the great increase in the numbers of cars for the "everyman." There was a wholesale slashing of prices of medium-priced cars over the last year, to below $1,000. In addition, a new class of fully equipped cars was created that sold for $500 to $700.

To increase people's ability to afford an automobile, the Maxwell Co. initiated a "pay as you ride" idea. It was first offered to its own retail branches and some of its selected and most powerful dealers, and was now extended to all Maxwell dealers. Since the pay-as-you-ride plan went into force, thousands of Maxwell cars were sold. There was no report of one single car on which payments were not kept up. A spokesman said: "Undoubtedly the time is coming when automobiles will be generally sold like real estate, pianos, expensive phonographs, and other purchases of large value."

Wayne County Roads were featured at the show, including the chairman of the Good Roads Committee, William E. Metzger.

DATE: January 20-27, 1917

SPONSOR: DADA

BUILDING: DADA Auditorium

ADMISSION: 50 cents (In the former shows
almost anyone could get in for
free, but the "free paper" was
done away with and most visitors paid their way in.)

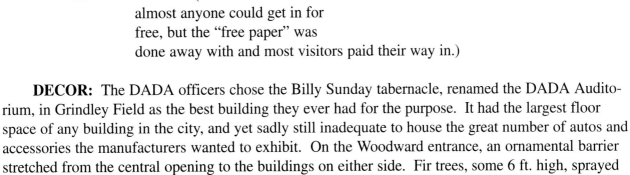

DECOR: The DADA officers chose the Billy Sunday tabernacle, renamed the DADA Auditorium, in Grindley Field as the best building they ever had for the purpose. It had the largest floor space of any building in the city, and yet sadly still inadequate to house the great number of autos and accessories the manufacturers wanted to exhibit. On the Woodward entrance, an ornamental barrier stretched from the central opening to the buildings on either side. Fir trees, some 6 ft. high, sprayed with white paint and sprinkled with mica, formed a background against which tall white poles, festooned with veri-colored fabrics, lanterns, banners, and electric lights, guided visitors to the main walk leading to the building. This wooden walk, 20 ft. wide, was bordered with the decorated poles and lined with trees.

The walk led directly to the main entrance at the center of the building, where it joined a similar walk from Cass Avenue, from which a driveway was constructed for motor cars. Immediately within the entrance were two booths where change could be obtained for deposit at the turnstiles when entrance was gained from the lobby.

The tabernacle's proportions were such as to allow a big scheme of decorations and its quadrangular shape provided the greatest efficiency in laying out the exhibits. A steam heating plant was installed with the boiler in another building to reduce the possibility of fire. Architect Graves was commended for making such an excellent show place out of the tabernacle. There was a Japanese garden scheme of decorations selected with an ideal blending of gay colors and the quaint nature of

Billy Sunday, the evangelist, had a tabernacle erected on the former site of the Detroit Athletic Club, which the DADA renamed the DADA Auditorium and used for the Auto Show. The photo shows the building from the Cass Avenue side.

The Hudson display.

the scenic backgrounds using 12,000 lights. The carpet on the floor required 15,000 yds. of denim, while the same amount of white goods went on the ceiling.

INSIDE THE SHOW: Not all of the cars manufactured in Detroit or in Michigan were exhibited due to space limitations. There were 60 different makes with more than 200 different styles. The floor was laid out with large aisle room for the thousands of visitors, and crowding was not as noticeable as in previous shows. There was a heavy snow during the week of the show and the snow began to melt on the roof, not from the external, but from the internal heat. The roof gave way to buckets of water, snow, and slush on Tuesday night, while salesmen were working on prospects. The holes in the roof were patched up with much cleverness and speed. Despite this, with the interior all dressed up like a Japanese garden, this was the most beautiful of all Detroit exhibits.

Manufacturers were beginning to send their "show cars" to the Detroit show. Usually they sent their "show jobs" first to New York and then Chicago, giving Detroit only stock cars. In recognition of Detroit as the growing important market as well as manufacturing center, the big makers turned out more of their special cars. In addition, most manufacturers were abolishing yearly models due to cost. Tooling for pressed steel, for example, was too expensive to change every year.

The Doble steam car got more than its share of attention from the crowds. One chap in a fur coat, who was quite willing to air his knowledge, looked the car over and then remarked in a disgusted tone: "Why, the danged thing ain't got no self-starter."

Thomas J. Doyle, the Dodge distributor, lured a new salesman for the show. The "green" salesman was more than pleased when, in the first hours of the exhibition he observed a big power-

The sign above the open car door is actually in Chinese and reads "Good Luck."

ful, blond chap who seemed to take an extraordinary interest in the Dodge car. With true salesman's instinct, he froze onto that prospect, explained every mechanical detail, and was just getting his order blank out when Mr. Doyle happened along and stretched out his hand to the visitor. "How do you do, Mr. Dodge?" said Doyle. The salesman slipped behind a car as John F. Dodge talked things over with Mr. Doyle.

The Series 18, the most expensive motor car ever built, was displayed by Studebaker. The six-cylinder, seven-passenger touring car, with a distinctive Victoria top, was standard in every detail with the exception of its brilliant gold and glistening white finish. About 100 oz. of 24-carat gold were used in finishing the "gold car."

The convertible was the most popular body style at the show, but Alexander Winton forecasted that it would become an oddity and would be taken over by the closed car. He said the folding top was the last link between the automobile and its forerunner, the horse and buggy. All of the early machines had regulation buggy tops, modified to a degree, which were the only reminder of the buggy ancestry of the motor car. The Detroit Weatherproof Body Company, one of the exhibitors of the show, reinforced this. They produced detachable tops designed in accordance with the design of the car, that gave comfort and protection, and also preserved the beauty of the car.

DATE: January 19-26, 1918

SPONSOR: DADA

BUILDING: Willys Overland garage

ADMISSION: 50 cents to all

DECOR: The 1918 show came at the trying period of the United States' entrance into World War I. Being hard-pressed for a place to hold the show, the dealers accepted an offer from Guy O. Simmons, the Overland distributor, to use his five-story service station building for their display. The first three floors were used, with trucks and accessories on the first floor and automobiles on the second and third floors. Upon entering, visitors proceeded to the third floor then descended to the second and first floors for the utmost convenience in inspecting the entire show. The stairways had wide doors and aisles as a guarantee against crowding.

The Linsell Company Studios of Detroit attended to the decorating and studied the Overland building for weeks before they set to work. The visitor, upon entering the building from Willis Avenue, passed through handsome doors, beautifully paneled walls and into a garden. The spirit and color of old Italy, the Italy of Raphael or Michelangelo and Dante, opened before him. Every booth for automobiles was a bower amid clusters of beauties of another variety. The whole interior of the building was transformed to imitate a Roman garden, with antique stone walls, flanked by huge vases, which stood in relief to the distant blue skies. The walls were flower-covered, giving a perfect garden effect. The huge columns which supported the floors of the building were papered and tinted in soft gray tones, causing them to blend harmoniously with the general, out-of-doors, decorative effect. The lighting, which was one of the most appealing features of the exhibition, was plain, with the light coming from white globes, giving a glow of pure light. To enable the on-looker to see the displays at the best possible advantage, natural light was excluded from the building entirely to prevent confusion of natural and artificial lighting.

INSIDE THE SHOW: When the date of the show arrived, the government made a drive to save foodstuffs and fuel. The show was forced to close for several periods during the eight days of the exhibit to comply with the government's requirements of "lightless" and "heatless" days, but the show was able to carry on and almost equaled the prior year's attendance. This was the largest exhibit in Detroit's auto show history. There were a total of 100 exhibitors, with 50 automobile companies showing 234 different models.

Changes and improvements over the 1917 models were designed to attract mechanics and women. The

The Willys Overland building, scene of the Auto Show.

mere male who did nothing but say yes and pay for the car was almost slighted by the manufacturers. There were comparatively few changes of bodylines, but a riot of color in body paint and upholstery greeted the eye of the visitor on the second and third floors. The exhibits were subdued and business-like. The dealers had "show jobs," but not the freaks of the past years. They had a little extra polish and finished with a little extra care, but they were truthful representations of the different lines. Practically every salesman at the show was armed to the teeth with facts and figures to show that his car was a better product, mechanically, than ever before, and ready to prove that the rising price in gasoline was more than offset by an increase in engine efficiency. A chassis was finished in white and nickel to show the new mechanical features; an overhead camshaft acting directly on the valve stems was a unique feature of this car.

The first floor, assigned to trucks.

The second floor, assigned to passenger cars.

The first floor, assigned to trucks.

The second floor, assigned to passenger cars.

DATE: March 1-8, 1919

SPONSOR: DADA

BUILDING: Crosstown Garage Building

The so-called national shows in New York and Chicago were discontinued for 1919, and Detroit was looked upon to have the most comprehensive display of the year. The Crosstown Building was leased, making possible the largest show ever offered in Detroit. This required the cooperation of 400 motorists, who had to find other quarters for their cars for a period of two weeks.

ADMISSION: 50 cents plus war tax of 5 cents

DECOR: A temporary entrance was built across a vacant lot from the rear of the garage to Woodward Avenue. A facade on the entrance had plastic medallions in bold relief, and brilliant electric lighting. A long entrance corridor or foyer was faced on either side by solid massing of natural foliage, brightened by the systematic use of national colors. This provided a well-protected entrance for over 200 ft. from Woodward Avenue. Approaching the exhibition hall proper, the visitor entered a rotunda, the dome of which was draped down in delicate colorings, divided by ribs of electric lights (installed by William Rothman who had the electrical contract), while a gigantic ball studded with electric lights formed an imposing centerpiece. The frieze of pendant crystals was the most striking and beautiful feature, illuminated in colors.

To the right of the rotunda was a reception room. There were beautiful rugs and furniture, and the walls were covered with scenic paintings by the most famous people in America. In the center of the room, a prismatic fountain, changing colors every few minutes, lit up a sparkling stream; to make it more complete, real ferns banked up the natural lake at its base. A feature for art lovers was a balustrade surrounding the fountain. It was a reproduction of a 12th-century balustrade measured and detailed from the original in Venice, Italy, by the builder of the show, while touring Europe in 1913.

A novel treatment was given to the great number of steel columns that supported the girders. Each one was encased in a Nubian marble panel 6-ft. high with molded corner beads of the finest workmanship. Above this was a four-sided enclosure of decorative fretwork. On opposite sides of the column, held in by the ornamental center of the open work, were American and Allied flags.

Draperies in Parisian blue were hung from the girders and extended from post to post, giving a light

The Crosstown Garage. A lobby entrance was built for pedestrian traffic on the Woodward Avenue side.

and airy appearance. A finely molded portico was erected between the columns, flanked by two posts 8 ft. high. The framework was left entirely open and the bars forming the apertures were made more effective by dainty traceries of vines and flowers.

Finely molded pieces of statuary were placed on the side columns supporting signs giving the name of the car exhibited. Festoons of flowers completed the ensemble.

Instead of closing the five light shafts and entire ceiling, beautiful and spectacular effects were devised by the designer. Each light well was a dome in itself—with vari-colored bands and colored electric lights forming a continuous series of charming art pictures. Sixteen arches that spanned the aisles were covered with vines and flowers.

ENTERTAINMENT: Saturday featured the Ford Motor Co. band; Sunday the Maxwell Motors band; Monday the Oakland Motors band; Tuesday the Willys-Overland band; Wednesday and Thursday the Dodge Bros. band; Friday the Packard Motor Car Co. band; and Saturday the Packard Motor Car Co. band.

OPENING: Mayor Couzens threw the electric switch at 7:30 Saturday evening to open Detroit's 18th Annual Auto Show, with the largest amount of floor space under one roof than the dealers ever had.

INSIDE THE SHOW: The show was held (just 60 days after the Armistice) in March for the first time for several reasons: The manufacturers who were bending every effort toward war work couldn't get back in regular production and have their new models ready for the market in time for a January show. Second, the thousands of men and boys returning from foreign shores would be back in large measure by March, and a good share of them would take keen interest in the show. In addition, it was felt that people were most ready to purchase a car in March with the approach of spring, whereas in January the public was interested but wasn't buying in large quantities. There was much discussion among the dealers as to the advisability of holding the show open on Sunday, but the majority favored the idea.

With 50,000 sq. ft. of floor space, the show included 350 cars and trucks, comprised of 45 different makes of passenger cars, 33 different makes of commercial cars, 3 different makes of tractors, and 25 accessory exhibits. An aeroplane was to have been shown, but the government refused to sanction the display. Instead, the automobile that broke the mile speed record shortly before the show was displayed.

The war probably did more than anything else to eliminate novelties. The experience gained by the motor car manufacturers during the war, when production had to be exact, certainly put them on guard when something radically new was offered to them for incorporation in their tried-out product.

There was an estimated shortage of 700,000-800,000 cars in the United States, as well as a big foreign business in prospect. Besides the returning military men, hundreds of thousands of women whose husbands, brothers, and fathers went into the Army and Navy became proficient automobile operators and would no longer be satisfied riding as passengers. They wanted cars of their own, or to be able to make use of the family car while the male members of the family were at work, creating at least half a million new candidates for car sales.

Closed Car Salon

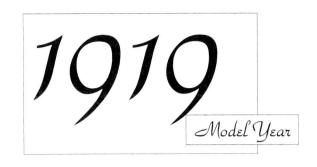

DATE: October 6-11, 1919

SPONSOR: DADA

BUILDING: Arena Gardens

ADMISSION: $1.00 (war tax included)

BACKGROUND: The closed body was a specialty and mainly a custom-job affair before World War I. People feared to ride behind glass—many did not like the conspicuousness of the "showcase on wheels." Excessive cost was a big factor as well as the inability of the early body builders to construct a body sufficiently light, strong, and silent. Also, of course, in the early days the motor car was more of a sporting proposition, and comfort was a secondary consideration.

Wooden body construction was the single largest factor. Hand-fashioning wooden parts, including wooden paneling, was formerly done by one high-priced craftsman who would virtually build one job complete, taking months to do it. The building of a closed body was a fine job of cabinet work. The glass was in a wooden frame and held in the closed position with leather straps, resulting in severe rattles and squeaks. They often came loose due to sudden jarring and exposure of the wooden frame to the elements.

Stamped metal parts enabled the manufacturer to simplify the design and progressively assemble the body, resulting in appreciable cost reduction. Windows were sandwiched between metal panels, which allowed them to be lowered or raised to any height with a mechanical regulator, obviating the rattles and squeaks.

In the years 1919 through 1927 the sale of closed cars increased by 10%, 17%, 22%, 30%, 34%, 43%, 56%, 72%, and 85%, respectively.

The DADA blazed a trail for other cities by producing the first closed car salon ever held. The classic, which was much smaller than the annual mid-winter show, was a high-class exhibition and it attracted many leaders in the industry who were enthusiastic over its success.

DECOR: The decorations and settings were superior to those furnished for the annual automobile shows. The salon was as dignified and as handsome as any of the exclusive shows that were staged for years in New York and Chicago by the importers of foreign cars, and was even superior in that all of the cars were closed.

OPENING: Mayor James Couzens switched on the lights and formally opened the first annual Closed Car Salon of the Detroit Auto Dealers Association. He made a close inspection

The Arena Gardens, opened in late 1918, was located on the northwest corner of Woodward and Hendrie (which later became I-94), which made it the most accessible auditorium in Detroit with splendid parking facilities and superb acoustics and dance floor. (Reprinted with permission of the Burton Historical Collection of the Detroit Public Library.)

of all the models on the floor, joining the hundreds of fans who were standing in line at the Arena Gardens, anxious for a glimpse of the show.

INSIDE THE SHOW: There were 75 cars displayed at the show including all types of bodies. There were sedans, limousines, coupes, town cars, laundelets, victorias, suburbans, and electric coaches. One noticeable feature of the display was the conservativeness of the closed cars' color schemes. The cars were done in sedate colors, and the upholstery and appointments were in keeping with their finish. The upholstery ranged from whipcord to silk plush, with a few of the cars upholstered in Spanish leather.

Walter L. Judd of the Miller-Judd Co., Liberty distributor, was particularly proud of his exhibit. Three models were upholstered in soft-toned silk velour. The town car model was finished in blue with gray upholstery; the sedan in Liberty green with gray upholstery; and a coupe in gun-metal gray with gray upholstery.

Jay E. Morehouse, Scripps-Booth distributor, had one of the novelties of the salon and coupe model. The extra seat to bring the capacity up to four was not a folding affair. Taking their cue from the Caterpillar tractor, the engineers mounted a rigid seat on a track in the floor which permitted it to be pushed forward under the cowl when not in use. The coupe was finished in maroon, with black top, fenders, hood, and white wire wheels and was upholstered in gray whipcord.

A general view of the exhibits.

View of the stage with a Paige automobile in the foreground.

DATE: February 14-21, 1920

SPONSOR: DADA

BUILDING: Fisher Body Building
(former Ford Branch Building)

DECOR: The former Ford service garage had passed into the hands of the Fisher Body Co., and the dealers were fortunate to obtain the use of the structure for their auto show.

All five floors, totaling 160,000 sq. ft., were used to create a show that was over twice as large as any previous two exhibits combined. In outdoing all previous efforts the management employed a different scheme on every one of the five floors. A corps of noted Boston architects and artists were specially engaged for the decoration schemes. Under their direction, a small army of decorators, carpenters, electricians, and laborers transformed the interior of the building into a veritable palace. Floors were covered in adamant. The brick and cement walls were camouflaged with backgrounds from which thousands of incandescent lights shed their brilliancy. The cars were surrounded by vernal blossoms, rich landscape coloring, and tree-like columns.

For the first floor the general effect was a rural spring scene, backed by green trees and bright touches of smilax, the green of hemlock and the bloom of holly; hocks predominated with decorative shields of bronze designating the respective exhibits, with trucks and commercial cars on display.

The second floor was a garden of real vines and foliage, together with large quantities of imported Japanese wisteria blooms of realistic workman-
ship. Columns were entwined with vines and foliage; scenic pieces and side walls were paneled with brightly colored flowers and vines. Commercial cars, together with accessories, were displayed.

Florentine design was the general motif of the third floor with strings of incandescent lights, columns encased in hand-decorated brocade and finished in tapestry, surmounted by dull gold medallions which served as brackets for massive chandeliers in the shape of a flam-
beaux. Above all that was a grouping of smilax and highlights in flowers overlooking the passenger cars.

The fourth floor also housed passenger cars. A pleasing contrast was furnished by the introduction of an old English rose garden, complete with lattices and rose vines in profusion. The columns were framed in lattices, foliage and roses ensconced in fret-work boxes with trellises.

The fifth floor was a picture of rich apple orchard in full bloom and columns were covered with bark to the height of 11 ft. From these, branches extended profusely covered with fresh green leaves. This idea was also

carried out on the side walls, which portrayed a fine perspective of apple trees in bloom, distant scenery, and flower-laden landscape.

The fifth floor held passenger cars and light delivery cars. Elevator service at the show aided the management in handling the crowds, as the big freight elevators carried 25 at a load and did not return any to the lower floor. An extra stairway was built by the DADA in an elevator shaft to "handle the traffic" for those going up. There were refreshment booths on all floors, and a restaurant and a lunch room on the fourth floor. Telephone stations were located at the west end of the building on all floors.

ENTERTAINMENT: Four miniature symphony orchestras, both imported musicians and the best Detroit knew, were located on the upper four floors. Selected hits of both popular and classical numbers were rendered during the afternoon and evening sessions. On Sunday afternoon an orchestra on the third floor gave a special concert and blocked the aisles for many yards.

OPENING: Various days were designated for special attention to particular phases of the show. Chief among these was the truck section: In view of the tremendously increased interest in the development of highway transportation, Tuesday night was designated "Ship-by-Truck."

INSIDE THE SHOW: There were 180 separate displays set up within the 150,000 sq. ft. of floor space. There were 70 different makes of passenger cars and 27 commercial cars, trucks, and trailers.

One of the unique exhibits was that of the International Mack truck. One of the monster "beasts of burden" was turned on its side to show the prospects the mechanism. The lower half of the crankcase was removed to allow exploration of the engine.

The Victor Tire Co. was one of the few accessory firms that gave away souvenirs: a rubber heel and toe pad for the driver with the firm's slogan "mileage hogs" in raised letters.

The Stanley Steamer made its initial appearance in Detroit and was a novelty to the thousands of visitors. All of the 1920 cars featured the straight-line effect. Many cut-away engines, electrically operated, revealed improvements. Accessibility was a paramount feature of chassis design. The engines were notable for their simplified block construction, with all wires, pipes, and additional equipment that usually appeared between cylinders eliminated. Radiators were high and so were the hoods. Better grades of leather upholstery, with stronger springs, and deeper cushions prevailed. Tops appeared to be lower and generally had a snappier appearance.

NOTE: On a day when the traffic was abnormal, during the United Railway strike in Detroit, an average of 18,424 cars passed the corner of Woodward and Michigan Avenues in ten hours. This eclipsed New York's Fifth Avenue and 42nd Street, which was averaging 16,900 cars in ten hours, giving Detroit the dubious honor of having the busiest intersection in the nation.

Carriage makers were on the wane; in 1909, the Detroit city directory listed 48 manufacturers. In 1920, there was only two listed: Columbia and Wilfred Parent.

The Hotel Ponchartrain closed on January 31, 1920, in accordance with the plans of the First and Old National Bank, for erection of a 24-story office building. The final meal was served on the last Saturday of the month, with no further guests allowed to register.

DATE: March 19-26, 1921

SPONSOR: DADA

BUILDING: Morgan and Wright factory
and annex

ADMISSION: $1.00

1921

Model Year

DECOR: The second floor, with 150,000 sq. ft. allotted for the show, permitted a splendid decorative motif. A giant welcome sign was hung over the entrance and by means of giant reflectors powerful lights were directed onto the sign and the facade of the building. A phalanx of poles flying the Stars and Stripes insured the visitors that the show was an American institution.

Architectural thought of the Pompeiian era was applied to the circular first floor lobby, further emphasized by the use of mural decorations, boxwood trees in wall niches, and cast Greek vases. A canopy in deep blue covered the lofty ceiling area, and suspended therefrom were silk drops decorated with dancing girl silhouettes and fringed with tassels. Divans and lounge chairs provided convenient resting places.

Within the exhibit hall proper was the suggestion of spring fever, lazy days, long smooth roads, and easy-riding, swift-moving vehicles of an era rightly called "The Age of Transportation." Mellow light was cast over colorful drapery, flowers, palms, and potted plants. Panels of soft, silken materials and huge light shades decorated with dancing girl impressions, tasseled and corded, concealed the otherwise cold ceiling. Seven-foot columns, emerald green, orange-striped frieze, a background of blue and coral-colored vases filled with blossomed foliage completed the general decorative scheme. Shadows which often defy careful inspection of cars through faulty lighting were eliminated by the lights and positioning of the cars.

ENTERTAINMENT: Musical programs were arranged so as to greatly enhance the pleasure of the visitors, and at the same time detract as little as possible from the business at hand—that of examining and buying and selling cars.

The new Morgan and Wright building was built on seven acres with a frontage along the river of 420 ft. The Auto Show was held on the second floor with more exhibit space than the show ever had. Morgan and Wright became a unit of the U.S. Rubber Corp. which consolidated into Uniroyal in 1914. The small building to the left was an automobile factory for the Hupmobile, then later the King automobiles.

The Pierce-Arrow exhibit can be seen at the center. Walter P. Chrysler, Executive Vice-President of the Willys Corp., stated that it was the best auto show he ever attended.

OPENING: Each day was given significance by a formal designation: Saturday was "Opening Night"; Sunday was "Automotive Equipment Day"; Monday was "Manufacturers' Day," which featured factory representatives not only from Detroit but also from a wide area; and Tuesday was "Ship-by-Truck Day." At noon a parade of every known variety of motor trucks formed at Canfield and Woodward and proceeded south to Jefferson and then east to the show building. A brass band headed the procession. Once inside the show, movies showed the variety of uses for trucks. The pictures also demonstrated how trucks could help the railway to speed up business in America. Wednesday was "Michigan Day," Thursday "Detroit Day," Friday "Buy Your Car Day," and Saturday was "Old Timers' Day."

As usual, a city official presided at the opening and delivered a brief address, to which President A.L. Zeckendorf of the DADA responded.

INSIDE THE SHOW: The show date was the most opportune time to bridge the gap between winter and spring, with 300 passenger cars and 100 commercial vehicles on display.

The fear that the post-WWI recession would have a depressing effect on both attendance and sales prompted the distribution of thousands of opening-night tickets by manufacturers and dealers. At the same time, dealers took buyers into their confidence and orders were dated March 19 so they would be listed as "opening sales" at the show. Many improvements were found in the 1921 models. Notable among them was a reduction in engine vibration, with hardly any perceptible difference being noted between the motor's highest and lowest speeds. This was accomplished by better balancing of the crankshafts.

Two cars were brought out in public for the first time at the Detroit show—the Kess-Line Eight, made by Kessler Motor Company, Detroit, and the Freind Light Four, made by the Freind Motors Corporation, Pontiac, Michigan.

The Maxwell and Briscoe exhibits. The decorative setting depicting the Pompeian era furnished a telling background.

The art of "carosserie" (the French term for elite coach building) was displayed strikingly by the Packard, McFarlan, Cadillac, Pierce-Arrow, Lincoln, LaFayette, Marmon, R. & V. Night, Roamer, Peerless, and Paige exhibits.

Many striped chassis, which were rushed to Detroit from the Boston show, attracted crowds, especially those of the LaFayette and the Locomobile.

Crowds were also surging in and out of the annex which housed passenger cars, trucks, trailers, tractors, airplane exhibits, and accessories. There were 65 exhibitors of automotive accessories. Commodities ranged from special bodies, California tops, and small garages down to spark plugs and cotter pins.

A salon was held at the Hotel Statler, where several makers had space for showing special jobs. A series of twelve oil paintings by some of the country's best-known artists was shown at the Detroit Athletic Club. Each canvas depicted its creator's conception of "The Spirit of Transportation."

The prize-winning painting shown at the Detroit Athletic Club.

Enclosed Car Week

DATE: October 10-15, 1921

SPONSOR: DADA

BUILDING: Dealers' showrooms

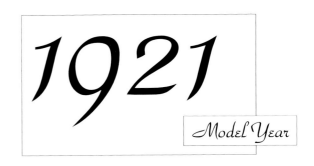

1921

Model Year

INSIDE THE SHOW: New car models were introduced each year in January, while Buick was an exception and displayed its new models in August, four months ahead of everyone else. A show was held for the 1921 models in October, as cold weather approached, to help educate the public on the virtues of the all-season enclosed car. Complete lines of body types were on display in showrooms that were specially decorated for the occasion.

In October 1921, Cadillac and Franklin headed the list of enclosed car production with 50% of their total output each. The Pierce-Arrow and Lincoln were at 40%, and Buick and Hudson each produced 30% of their output with the enclosed bodies.

When the motor car manufacturers first turned their attention to building enclosed bodies, such cars were all called limousines. With the development of a variety of all-season closed types, new names were necessary. Closed car body styles generally derived their names from the designations of horse-drawn carriages, except where a manufacturer twisted a name to get added distinction for advertising purposes. There were six basic names applied to closed motor cars: limousine, sedan, coupe, cabriolet, brougham, and landaulet.

Enclosed Car Week
October 10-15

Convenience and Comfort

DATE: January 21-28, 1922

SPONSOR: DADA

BUILDING: Morgan and Wright factory

ADMISSION: $1.00

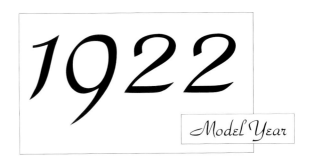

DECOR: After weeks of research and inspections of various buildings there was a dearth of adaptable structures for the 1922 show. Some buildings could be obtained, but the show would have been scattered over three to ten floors without elevators. The DADA laid its problems before the president of Morgan and Wright, and the United States Tire Co., and were again accorded the privilege of using the second floor for the show. This meant that the installation for the heavier machinery for the manufacture of tires on the main floor had to be halted and several of the monster machines removed. It also meant the installation of lighter tire-building machinery on the second floor had to be stopped and the machinery removed, which set back production 60 days. As soon as the machinery was removed, a small army of men scrubbed the floors and walls of the second floor and constructed a lobby on the first.

Upon entering, the visitor found himself in a spacious lobby, treated in the fashion of a rotunda in a hotel. The lobby was 200 ft. long with a promenade effect by the arrangement of 80,000 yds. of drape material to the entrance gates.

In the exhibit hall, vivid tones of blue and gold were the predominating colors for the side walls and columns, while the ceiling was done in transparent plaques of varied colors, with hundreds of parchment shades bearing fantastic designs. The main lighting effect was obtained from several hundred chandeliers carrying high candlepower lights, each with gold silk.

Attention was given not only to the interior but to the exterior as well, with blue and gold as the official colors. Strings of lights on Jefferson Avenue illuminated the exterior of the building.

ENTERTAINMENT: Two orchestras gave concerts each afternoon and evening. Refreshment booths were located at north and south ends of the building.

OPENING: Various days were given a distinctive significance: Saturday night was "Opening Night"; Sunday was "Old Timers' Day," in honor of the veterans of the industry; Monday was "Auto Equipment Day," which was marked with a convention of the accessory men in the state at the Hotel Statler; Tuesday was "Ship-by-Truck Day"; and Wednesday was "Michigan Day."

INSIDE THE SHOW: The vast 150,000 sq. ft. of floor space contained 300 passenger cars, 75 commercial

cars, and 100 accessory exhibits. Salesmen were sanguine over the prospects of good business during the year, particularly over business developed as a result of the show. There was wholeheartedness in their treatment of a visitor, and in their interest in seeing him buy right (one of their cars). Also there was no tendency to knock "the car you are driving now." It was believed that cars would be purchased on the basis of value and not list price alone.

Four new cars that excited national interest made their debut at the Detroit show. They were the Rickenbacker, Durant, Gray, and Detroit Air-Cooled. Practically every exhibit had its open chassis. The Willys-Overland Knight exhibit had an open chassis under which was mounted a telephone amplifier through which a demonstrator in a distant booth described the mechanism while it slowly revolved. A number of exhibits had their prices mounted on imitation Michigan license tags, which were bright red.

The Ford exhibit was missing, with an explanation given in the newspaper that congestion about the booths in former years had prevented individual attention to the visitors. Instead the Ford dealers staged exhibitions in their sales rooms which were said to have borne good results.

The premier position in the accessory exhibits went to the "stop" light, whose blinking signal of warning was placed on thousands of cars since its invention only a few months before the show. Next in line for favorite honors was the headlight lens to reduce glare. An automatic windshield cleaner was exhibited that operated from exhaust gas and was set in motion by a mere press of a button. An accessory exhibit which attracted the attention of the ladies was a small 6-lb. vacuum cleaner.

Closed Car Show

DATE: October 17-21, 1922

SPONSOR: DADA

BUILDING: General Motors Building

DECOR: The fourth floor of the General Motors Auditorium was designed for show purposes and lended itself to a pretentious decorative scheme. The riot of color was necessary to properly show the closed models, for the trend in all-season motor cars was for the more somber shades. The side walls of the auditorium were treated with panels in bright colors; almost every shade of the spectrum was used. The panels were separated by hand-painted silks which covered the lower ends of arched beams. The panel material was poplin. The ceiling treatment was classic festooning for the arched steel beams; they were fashioned of gold and silver cloths with kindred colors.

The location of various makes of cars on the show floor was designated by 14-ft. pillars, with an ornate base and the name of the car in an artistic panel at the top of the pillar.

Due to heavy demand for space, the entire annex adjoining the auditorium was also obtained. The ceiling treatment of the annex differed materially from the auditorium, but the same general color scheme was carried out in that section.

INSIDE THE SHOW: Entrance to the closed car show was by elevator from the main lobby off Grand Boulevard and through a specially constructed lobby on the fourth floor, leading back to the auditorium. There were 105 closed models and all-season cars ranging in price from $600 to $14,000 (for a Rolls-Royce limousine). As evidence of the increasing popularity of the closed cars the country over, a Hudson-Essex dealer in Ohio reported that 46 of the 47 cars sold as of September were closed cars.

The GM Building on West Grand Boulevard was completed in 1922.

DATE: January 20-27, 1923

SPONSOR: DADA

BUILDING: Detroit Municipal Building

ADMISSION: $1.00

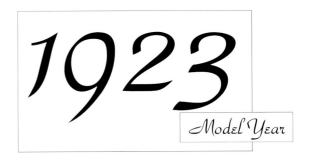

DECOR: The decorations were constructed by the Detroit Art and Craft Studios, Inc., under the direction of Charles Charpair. An Egyptian atmosphere was created throughout. At the entrance an Egyptian arch, copied from the ruined temple of Karnak in the Nile valley, was created. Down the lobby proper were hung draperies carrying out the decorative scheme, bordered above and below in Egyptian designs. It was lighted by numerous fixtures in imitation of the Egyptian pot lamp.

On entering the main salon the show visitor saw winged Egyptian figures mounted on the pillars, with the name of a product lettered in gold on one spread wing, denoting the various exhibits. Each pillar was covered with soft brilliant materials with an Egyptian border about 4 ft. from the floor and surmounted by a capital. The square cap above the capital of the pillar was artistically draped with soft material in harmony with the remainder of the column.

Between these caps of the pillars the ceiling was hidden by the use of oriental-looking striped material hanging as a canopy and interspersed with a myriad of highly colored lamps. The booths in the automotive accessory section were constructed in harmony with the Egyptian scheme.

ENTERTAINMENT: There were two large orchestras each afternoon and evening, one in the forward portion of the building and another in the truck section. A lunch counter with increased capacity, soft drink booths, and smoking rooms were available, and for women visitors at the show a number of cozy corners.

OPENING: While opening night on Saturday was given over mainly to the Detroit public, a grand concert was given. A vanguard of salesmen and outside manufacturers was on hand assisting DADA officials to give an auspicious start to the vast enterprise. Sunday was identified as "Old Timers' Day," and the doors to the show were thrown open to the public at noon. Special invitations were given to state and municipal officials of various cities in Michigan to attend the show on Monday. Tuesday was for automotive and equipment manufacturers and dealers. Wednesday was when the Michigan Trade Association had its annual convention in connection with the show. The convention was held in the Hotel Tuller, with a banquet in the evening. Thursday was known as "Detroit Day," with city and county officials as guests of the show, while special arrangements were made to entertain the public. "Manufacturers' Day" was observed Friday, and Saturday was known as "Buy a Car Day."

INSIDE THE SHOW: The building was rectangular in shape and extended from Jefferson Avenue back to Woodbridge Street, occupying one half block. Entrance to the show was from Jefferson Avenue on the second floor at ground level, with a main aisle extending the length of the building. A wide and commodious cross aisle was located at right angles to the head of the lobby and two other aisles were parallel to the center promenade. Another cross aisle extended across the rear of the show floor.

The exhibits included 250 passenger cars by 43 manufacturers and dealers, embracing practically every new model brought out for the 1923 trade. There were also 50 trucks displayed by 12 manufacturers, and 46 manufacturers of accessories. Passenger cars were located along three long aisles, with the truck and trailer displays across the rear of the building. The automotive equipment division was located on both sides of the entrance lobby in the customary booths.

The day of the "ginger bread" special for show purposes was on the wane and practically every exhibitor showed standard models, relieved by a stripped chassis to give the motor-wise and the mechanically inclined an opportunity to study the mechanisms at close range. One of the features of the show was the chassis of the new copper-cooled model of the Chevrolet family that was based on a major discovery for welding copper to iron. (This engine did not live up to expectations and was later cancelled.)

The electrically operated cut-away chassis of the new Willys-Knight model 64 was another attraction. All closed models were upholstered in cut velour, and the seven-passenger model 57 was finished in Japanese Purple Lake. The Ford Motor Company had three displays: the Lincoln Division, with models painted in cobalt blue, thistle green, maxine blue, and a green-gray limousine; the second exhibit was for the "universal car"; and the third for the one-ton truck and the Fordson tractor. Oldsmobile had the largest display with 14 passenger and three commercial car models.

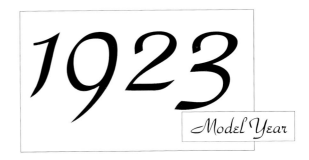

Closed Car Show

DATE: October 6-13, 1923

SPONSOR: DADA

BUILDING: Convention Hall

ADMISSION: 50 cents

DECOR: The Detroit Flag and Manufacturing Co. decorated the show building with scenery borrowed from the west. The side walls of the building gave the visitor a vista of broad smooth lakes with a background of snow-capped mountain peaks, while the foreground was set off with a stone wall surrounded by urns filled with flowers. Along the scenic background was a blue valance while the ceiling was masked in white. Thousands of electric bulbs dotted the ceiling and threw a flood of light on the cars.

ENTERTAINMENT: Two orchestras furnished music.

INSIDE THE SHOW: The show was held at the new and commodious Convention Hall, formerly the John H. Thompson Arcade. The building was divided into two wings with a total of 180,000 sq. ft. of floor space. The south wing was used to display 38 makes of automobiles with more than 200 models.

The new 1924 Haynes sedan was displayed and "equipped with all the interior niceties that are incorporated in fine motor cars." The seats were upholstered in genuine mohair. The car was equipped with a heater, roof ventilation, and an adjustable windshield. An interior dome light of exquisite design, smoking and vanity cases, curtains on quick-acting rollers, a clock on the dashboard, and a sun and vision visor were also included.

The president of the Oakland Motor Car Co. prophetically announced that the closed model was the car of the future.

Shown for the first time, the Packard single eight was the first big production car to use four-wheel brakes as standard equipment. The Rickenbacker, Buick, and Oakland also made their debut with four-wheel brakes. Some people feared that front brakes could cause a car to flip over forward, like a bicycle. The REO Motor Car Co. refused to be stampeded into the

CLOSED CAR
SHOW
Convention Hall · Cass and Forest
OCT. 6-13
Convention Hall · Woodward and Forest

First comprehensive exhibit of latest Closed Body Models in Detroit's wonderful new Exhibition Building. The beauty show of the Automotive Industry

ADMISSION FIFTY CENTS
Including Tax

DETROIT AUTO DEALERS ASSOCIATION

The show was held at Convention Hall located on Grindley Field, the same location as the 1917 show. Robert M. Grindley enlarged the building, spanning from Cass to Woodward Avenues with 90,000 sq. ft. of space. The Closed Car Show was the first event held at Convention Hall. The Cass Avenue side of the building is shown.

adoption of four-wheel brakes, and feared they would be a speed teaser and promote reckless driving. They retained rear brake and advised "when in danger push with both feet."

A view inside Convention Hall.

DATE: January 19-26, 1924

SPONSOR: DADA

BUILDING: Convention Hall

1924

Model Year

DECOR: The show could be entered from either Cass or Woodward Avenues. Each entrance had a canopy with 55 powerful nitrogen lamps. Over each stone archway were blue lamps, and projecting from the building at each entrance was a large sign, also done in nitrogen lamps.

Upon entering the building the visitor was struck by an oriental theme. The decorator used *mah jongg* for his theme. The bare steel girders were hidden behind a ceiling painted in the colors of the orient.

The north wing had signs, in English, inscribed on mah jongg tiles that identified the location of the passenger cars, automotive equipment, and motor boats on the Woodward side, and commercial cars on the Cass Avenue side. The oriental decorative scheme made it possible to cover the bare walls with combinations of bright colors.

The south wing was given over entirely to passenger cars, and was clothed in conventional black and white, providing a striking background for the products of the coach maker and shiny enamel of quality production products. Thousands of yards of white fabric hid from the eye the bare walls and girders, and the flatness of the white was relieved by the judicious use of black patent leather for panels and signs. The exhibits were denoted by black patent leather, with iridescent metal names.

ENTERTAINMENT: Four orchestras were grouped in the center of the building along the north and south walls. Refreshment booths and lunch counters were located at the four corners of the building.

OPENING: Acting Mayor Joseph A. Martin threw the switch and sent the electric current through throbbing wires, flooding the mammoth Convention Hall with lights from thousands of incandescent lamps. The four orchestras then struck up "America" and hundreds of people who had been awaiting the opening pressed into the Hall.

INSIDE THE SHOW: Practically every family in Detroit was interested in the Auto Show. The families that did not own cars were interested because they aspired to own their individual units of transportation. On hand were 329 passenger cars, 87 commercial cars, and 110 automotive equipment exhibits. The most comprehensive motor boat displays in the history of the

DETROIT AUTO SHOW

JANUARY 19 to 26

CONVENTION HALL

WOODWARD AT GARFIELD   CASS AVE. AT PRENTIS

TWENTY THIRD ANNUAL EXHIBITION

Detroit show drew much attention. The famous Belle Aisle Bear Cat, the new Dodge Water-Car, and Chris Smith's Chriscraft from Algonac were among the displays.

There were three new cars, which had already premiered at the New York show. The Chrysler was the most talked of in New York and the public's interest was such that it was impossible to even approach the Chrysler models on display. In the Detroit show, 2,000 sq. ft. were devoted to show ten cars on display so all the visitors had the opportunity to closely inspect Detroit's newest contribution to the industry.

The Eagle six, one of William Durant's new products, was exhibited by the Detroit-Durant Company, along with the Flint six, Locomobile, the Durant four, and the Star. The Rollins four was a new product from the firm organized by Rollin White, in Cleveland, Ohio.

A feature of the show week was that the Society of Automotive Engineers (SAE) held their annual convention in the General Motors Building in Detroit, whereas it was held in New York for the previous ten years. Balloon tires and four-wheel brakes were the big topics. One of the most interesting features of the sessions was an address by Henri Perrot, who pioneered four-wheel brakes in Europe and whose pattern was widely being used in the U.S.A.

DATE: January 17-24, 1925

SPONSOR: DADA

BUILDING: Convention Hall

1925

Model Year

DECOR: The Atlantic Decorating Co. of Boston, directed by F.W. Campbell who was considered one of the best decorators in the country, took care of the decoration scheme. Hundreds of additional lights were added on both the inside and the outside over the entrances and a springtime motif provided an added touch for the show visitors coming in from a chilling fog and muddy snow. Splendid accommodations were added in the entrance lobbies, making it possible to handle the immense throngs with little delay or confusion.

The show was exceptionally well arranged with wide aisles and ample room around the exhibits to make it possible to see everything comfortably. Bunting lowered and obscured the girded ceiling, and the blank stone walls were covered with tastefully painted panels. Curved, painted arches over the several wide aisles added further to the beauty of the ensemble.

ENTERTAINMENT: Music by four orchestras in various parts of the show helped make the visitors forget it was winter.

OPENING: Mayor John W. Smith clutched the lever to the master switch, jabbed it into place, and the great show place was flooded with light. Long lines of people were standing at the Woodward and Cass entrances, and the crowd entered so rapidly the enormous building was filled before the attendants fully realized the show was under way.

Saturday was "Opening Day"; Sunday was "Old Timer's Day"; Monday was "Accessories Day"; and Tuesday was given over to the Society of Automotive Engineers; Wednesday was "Michigan Day" and was marked by the fifth annual convention, held at the Hotel Statler, of the Michigan Automotive Trade Association. Since 1917, when the custom of having "Society Day," with the show visitors in formal attire, was abandoned, Thursday had become known as "Detroit Day." Friday was "Manufacturers' Day" and the final day of the show, Saturday, was "Buy Your Car Day."

INSIDE THE SHOW: There were 317 passenger cars and 84 commercial cars exhibited, along with 106 automotive equipment exhibits. The number of closed cars on display increased over the prior year, and balloon tires, or the semi-balloon type, were shown on almost all of the expensive car makes.

The new Chevrolet created a sensation with many features never before offered on a car in its price class.

JAN. 17-24

24TH ANNUAL

DETROIT

AUTO SHOW

CONVENTION HALL

WOODWARD AT FOREST

103

In the foreground, the Chevrolet display is on the right and Nash is on the left. (Courtesy of the National Automotive History Collection, Detroit Public Library)

Besides having a full streamlined body, a new dry disc clutch completely enclosed with the flywheel was offered.

REO introduced the new T-6 series E roadster painted Pyramid Gray above the body belt and Desert Sand below the belt. The two-tone effect was distinctly new among American manufacturers. It featured a compartment immediately behind the front seat for carrying golf sticks and other equipment.

Olds showed nine body styles, four open and five closed, finished in Duco, with rich blue the standard color for most models. The open model line was upholstered with fabrikoid, and the sedans were upholstered with genuine mohair.

Besides the more common varieties of trucks, capacious and comfortable motor buses, funeral cars, and conveyances for use in factories were exhibited. There were also interesting and extensive exhibits of accessories and an array of high-powered and smart-lined speed boats and cabin cruisers.

Amos L. Beatty of the Texas Co. predicted cars would get 50 miles per gallon by 1935 due to refining and auto design improvements.

The Silver Anniversary Auto Show

1926
Model Year

DATE: January 23-30, 1926

SPONSOR: DADA

BUILDING: Convention Hall (with new annex)

DECOR: The Atlantic Decorating Co. of Boston took care of the work of beautifying the building. The Director, F.W. Campbell, said he would give the Detroit show a decorative setting that would ensure it being the most beautiful show of the year.

A brilliant setting greeted the visitor upon entering, and no stone was left unturned to display the cars to the best advantage. Hundreds of additional lights were installed both inside the building and over the entrance, and were so brilliant they were discernable for many blocks in both directions. Splendid accommodations were provided in the entrance lobbies, making it possible to handle the immense throngs with little delay and confusion. In keeping with the fact that this was the 25th Annual Auto Show, the decorative scheme consisted largely of silver, which provided a striking background for the brilliantly painted exhibits.

ENTERTAINMENT: Four orchestras gave concerts both afternoon and evening.

OPENING: On Saturday evening, Mayor John W. Smith threw the switch and turned on the lights in the vast auditorium.

Many special events were arranged for show week, principal among them was the annual convention of the Society of Automotive Engineers. Tuesday was SAE day at the show and all the delegates were guests of the DADA. The sixth annual convention of the Michigan Automotive Trade Association was held at the Book-Cadillac Hotel, where Mayor Smith welcomed the 500 members of the MATA to the convention.

INSIDE THE SHOW: The addition of an annex increased the building to 200,000 sq. ft. of floor space. There were 340 passenger cars, 95 commercial vehicles, 76 automotive equipment exhibits (ranging from dust caps for tire valves to special bodies), tractors, buses, motorboats, and an airplane.

Entering the show from Woodward Avenue, the visitor found on the right the exhibit of the new Pontiac six along with the Oakland, both General Motors products from the

SILVER ANNIVERSARY
DETROIT
AUTO SHOW
JANUARY 23rd to 30th, 1926
CONVENTION HALL

The sixth annual convention of the Michigan Automotive Trade Association was held on Wednesday at the Book-Cadillac Hotel. Mayor Smith formally welcomed all members.

Pontiac, Michigan factory. Immediately in front of the entrance were the Dodge Bros. and the Studebaker Corporation, and at the extreme left of the entrance, the Hupmobile and Will Ste. Claire exhibit. Also on the north wall were the exhibits of the Buick, Chevrolet, and Jordan, and the displays of several equipment manufacturers.

Lower chassis, lighter reciprocating parts, four-wheel brakes, oil reclaiming and purifying devices, greater convenience in control, better finish, and a general cleaning up of the details of appearance characterized the exhibits.

Probably the most spectacular of the new cars was the Stutz straight-eight with worm drive. The car was so low that a 6-ft. man standing on an ordinary curb could look over the top of the coupe body.

Chrysler was also one of the interesting features of the show. The engine was mounted on a rubber support and rubber shock insulators were used for the connection between the frame and springs, the rubber blocks taking the place of the usual shackle connections.

Another exhibit that received much attention was the Powell racer aeroplane, shown by the University of Detroit. It was built by C.H. Powell, P. Altman, and senior students in the department of aeronautics. Although it was only 16 ft. wide and 14 ft. long it won three first prizes in the international air races in New York the previous October.

The Italian Garden.

DATE: January 22-29, 1927

SPONSOR: DADA

BUILDING: Convention Hall

1927

Model Year

DECOR: The building was converted into a baronial castle. On entering and leaving the show the visitor found massive stone gates with attendant towers and minarets at each entrance and exit. The six large units of the Hall had the bare walls covered with rich hangings of gold and silver fabrics, velvets and tapestries, pieces of art, the armor of knights of medieval ages, and other accoutrements of stately dignity which were associated with the castle of the days "when knighthood was in flower."

Another feature of the decoration was the method of displaying the names of the cars and trucks on exhibit. Those signs were illuminated for the first time in the history of the Detroit Auto Dealers Association, and the car or truck name was cut in a shield surmounted by a plume and suspended over the exhibits and along the aisles.

The passenger car exhibit was colorful because the almost universal use of cellulose finishes made it possible for the carmaker to turn out his merchandise in almost every shade of the spectrum, many with two-tone motifs. Instead of blacks, blues, and greens, they now ranged from somber blacks and greens to pure white, delicate grays, and sand shades.

ENTERTAINMENT: Four of Detroit's well-known orchestras gave concerts each afternoon and evening, with special radio broadcast programs from 7:00 to 8:00 each night. Refreshment stands were located near the entrances and exits at both ends of the Hall.

OPENING: The show was officially opened when Mayor John W. Smith threw the switch controlling the lights throughout the show.

Monday at the show was "Automotive Equipment Day," and Tuesday was "Manufacturers' Day." Thursday found the Michigan dealers in Detroit for their convention at the Book-Cadillac Hotel. Thursday was "Detroit Day" which usually proved to be the largest from an attendance standpoint. Friday the delegates to the SAE convention were guests at the show and in the evening held their annual frolic at the Oriole Terrace.

INSIDE THE SHOW: There were 33 makes of automobiles, with 300 different models. Of the 16 new cars shown for the first time, 11 were straight-eights. Nearly 70% of the 200,000 sq. ft. of floor space was taken up by the passenger cars. The remainder of the exhibit area was taken up by 13 makes of commercial

26TH ANNUAL DETROIT AUTO SHOW JAN 22-29 CONVENTION HALL WOODWARD at FOREST

cars, tractors, motor boats and equipment, a model service shop in operation, and accessories and equipment. Airplanes made by the Stinson Co. and the Hess Co. were exhibited in the Cass Street annex on the northwest side of the Hall, along with engines and equipment.

The passenger cars were displayed in the north and south Woodward halls and the south Cass hall, the three biggest units of Convention Hall. For the first time the DADA classified its passenger car exhibit according to price. In the north Woodward hall, in which the entrance was located, were all the popularly priced lines; in the south Woodward hall were the highest-priced lines, while in the south Cass hall were medium-priced lines.

On entering the north Woodward hall the show visitor found the Oakland and Pontiac, Star and Flint, Overland and Willys-Knight, Dodge Bros., Ford, Chevrolet, Oldsmobile, and the Hudson-Essex displays.

Passing into the south Woodward hall were the Cadillac, Packard, Pierce-Arrow, Marmon, Stutz, Lincoln, Franklin, Kissel, and Stearns-Knight. In the south Cass hall were displayed the REO, Chrysler, Rickenbacker, Buick, Jordan, Locomobile, Paige, Jewett, Studebaker, Erskine, Peerless, Nash, and Hupmobile.

A tour of the passenger cars left no doubt that the five-passenger touring car had passed away and was replaced by the closed style. Four-wheel brakes were almost universal except for the popularly priced lines, and balloon tires were becoming more prevalent. Very few of the cars had angles in the body line; practically everything was smoothed out to curves. In the interior of the body the harsh leather upholstery had practically disappeared and was replaced by softest mohairs, velvets, and cord upholstery, and this, like the shades of the body, came in many hues.

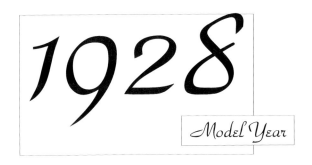

1928 *Model Year*

DATE: January 21-28, 1928

SPONSOR: DADA

BUILDING: Convention Hall

DECOR: An attempt was made to give an air of permanence and simplicity to the exhibit halls. The general scheme consisted of rich black and white tapestries on the walls with profuse silver cloth and ornaments. Such a setting was considered by the decorators to be the most effective background for the vari-colored cars. The pillars were wrapped in silver oak leaves. Overhead, there were variegated streamers and gilded banners with tassels concealing the iron beams. The scheme also provided splendid possibilities for special lighting effects. For the visitors' comfort, the walls were lined with white benches.

ENTERTAINMENT: Four orchestras gave concerts each afternoon and evening.

OPENING: Monday's theme was "Automotive Equipment Day," and Tuesday was "Manufacturers' Day." Wednesday was the convention and banquet at the Hotel Statler for the Detroit Dealers and Thursday was "Detroit Day." On Friday the SAE convention delegates attended the show and held their annual frolic at the Oriole Terrace, always one of the hot spots of the show week.

INSIDE THE SHOW: There were 300 models displayed with more than 200 different designs in motor car fashions. Compared to the early shows when everyone questioned the motor car mechanisms, cars had become mechanically sound and the visitors were becoming more interested in the beautiful looks of the cars.

There were 20,000,000 cars in the United States which went out of service annually. Accordingly, 40 manufacturers of shop equipment cooperated with the jobbers of servicing equipment to provide displays of a number of machines used in the construction of automotive products. The remainder of the displays were the commercial cars, accessories, and Stinson aircraft.

Among the features of the 1928 cars were: high compression ratios (they had typically been 3:1, and were increased to 5:1 and even 6:1); four-wheel brakes on all cars; oil, fuel, and air cleaners as well as crankcase ventilators; the absence of many of the clashing colors which featured the cars of 1927; and finally more pleasing and more comfortable bodies with improved accessibility and vision.

There were 150 models on display for the first time. The Chevrolet boasted a ball bearing worm and gear

steering mechanism for greater ease of steering. Among the many refinements was a fully enclosed instrument panel, oval in shape, with speedometer, ammeter, and oil gauge in full view. The new Hudson Super-Six was announced, featuring composite steel and wood bodies, with narrow front corner posts and piano-type door hinges. On Pontiac's second "birthday anniversary," new models were announced described as being "new from radiator to tail light."

While formally announced to the public on December 2, and already viewed and inspected by more people than ever before viewed a motor car, the Ford Model A continued to occupy a place in the sun of public interest. Upon its presentation, it was generally agreed that Henry Ford had produced a worthy successor to the Model T.

1928

Model Year

DATE: January 21-28, 1928

SPONSOR: DADA

BUILDING: Convention Hall

DECOR: An attempt was made to give an air of permanence and simplicity to the exhibit halls. The general scheme consisted of rich black and white tapestries on the walls with profuse silver cloth and ornaments. Such a setting was considered by the decorators to be the most effective background for the vari-colored cars. The pillars were wrapped in silver oak leaves. Overhead, there were variegated streamers and gilded banners with tassels concealing the iron beams. The scheme also provided splendid possibilities for special lighting effects. For the visitors' comfort, the walls were lined with white benches.

ENTERTAINMENT: Four orchestras gave concerts each afternoon and evening.

OPENING: Monday's theme was "Automotive Equipment Day," and Tuesday was "Manufacturers' Day." Wednesday was the convention and banquet at the Hotel Statler for the Detroit Dealers and Thursday was "Detroit Day." On Friday the SAE convention delegates attended the show and held their annual frolic at the Oriole Terrace, always one of the hot spots of the show week.

INSIDE THE SHOW: There were 300 models displayed with more than 200 different designs in motor car fashions. Compared to the early shows when everyone questioned the motor car mechanisms, cars had become mechanically sound and the visitors were becoming more interested in the beautiful looks of the cars.

There were 20,000,000 cars in the United States which went out of service annually. Accordingly, 40 manufacturers of shop equipment cooperated with the jobbers of servicing equipment to provide displays of a number of machines used in the construction of automotive products. The remainder of the displays were the commercial cars, accessories, and Stinson aircraft.

Among the features of the 1928 cars were: high compression ratios (they had typically been 3:1, and were increased to 5:1 and even 6:1); four-wheel brakes on all cars; oil, fuel, and air cleaners as well as crankcase ventilators; the absence of many of the clashing colors which featured the cars of 1927; and finally more pleasing and more comfortable bodies with improved accessibility and vision.

There were 150 models on display for the first time. The Chevrolet boasted a ball bearing worm and gear

DETROIT AUTOMOBILE SHOW

January 21 to 28

CONVENTION HALL

WOODWARD AT FOREST

steering mechanism for greater ease of steering. Among the many refinements was a fully enclosed instrument panel, oval in shape, with speedometer, ammeter, and oil gauge in full view. The new Hudson Super-Six was announced, featuring composite steel and wood bodies, with narrow front corner posts and piano-type door hinges. On Pontiac's second "birthday anniversary," new models were announced described as being "new from radiator to tail light."

While formally announced to the public on December 2, and already viewed and inspected by more people than ever before viewed a motor car, the Ford Model A continued to occupy a place in the sun of public interest. Upon its presentation, it was generally agreed that Henry Ford had produced a worthy successor to the Model T.

DATE: January 19-26, 1929

SPONSOR: DADA

BUILDING: Convention Hall

1929
Model Year

DECOR: In choosing the decorative setting, the
show committee worked out a plan to delight the visitor and give the hall an entirely new appearance. The exhibit area was surrounded above and on all sides by artistic draperies and decorative panels. The four main halls were transformed in such a way that, while each one had an individual setting, all blended together and the general effect gave the impression of one giant exhibition room. Various schemes included a Spanish court, a Venetian scene, and French-Italian gardens. An original scheme of lighting doubled the illumination and made it possible to show many vari-colored cars to better advantage than in former years.

ENTERTAINMENT: Four orchestras gave concerts afternoons and evenings.

OPENING: With the turning of a switch by Mayor John C. Lodge on Saturday evening, the lights of the huge exhibit hall blazed forth and the 28th Annual Detroit Automobile Show was ready for the eyes of its visitors.

The themes for each show day began with Monday as the "Automotive Equipment Day." Tuesday was "Manufacturers' Day," Wednesday was the Michigan Dealers convention and banquet at the Book-Cadillac, with speaker Capt. Eddie Rickenbacker, sales executive of Cadillac. Thursday was "Detroit Day," the best-selling night of the show.

INSIDE THE SHOW: The passenger car exhibits were generally concentrated in price groups. At least 150 of the 300 cars on display were entirely new to the majority of show visitors. Some of the cars were not recognized by the public without seeing the nameplates on the radiator, and even those makes which were not entirely redesigned presented new body styles and refinements which was believed to be what the public eagerly waited for.

The interiors of the closed cars were improved with better upholstery fabrics, and center folding arm rests in the back seat. Exterior improvements were chromium plating on the radiator shells, lamps, and other outside bright parts. Steering ratios were up to 15:1 on the large cars, not long before 9:1 was considered about right. Most cars had hydraulic brakes, and theft prevention received much attention.

Another interesting development was the gradual adoption by the cheaper cars of those luxuries and refinements once thought the exclusive property of the costly makes. An example of this trend was the adjustable driver's seat in several of the cheaper types of cars on display.

A large section of the building was devoted to commercial and delivery trucks, shop equipment, and motor boats. A new departure for the show was a custom body salon in which the country's foremost builders of high-grade special bodies participated. The salon occupied the north annex on the Cass Avenue side. While the salon occupied space in Convention Hall, it was really an individual show conducted by body manufacturers. In the velvet-carpeted salon, to which admission was granted by printed invitation only, the aristocrats of the show, great, sleek, luxurious greyhounds of the road, could be viewed. The most expensive car of the show, the keen-lined Deusenberg, had a price of $15,000.

NOTE: William Metzger, along with Hiram H. Walker of Walkerville, Ontario, was in the news again as president of the newly formed Cadillac Aircraft Company. Plans were made to manufacture one two-engine amphibian plane per week in the former Stinson factory in Northville, Michigan.

DATE: January 18-25, 1930

SPONSOR: DADA

BUILDING: Convention Hall

DECOR: One of the foremost decorating groups in the country was engaged to provide the setting for the exhibition. The decorations were futuristic in style and tone, riotous with color, with bizarre hangings and fantastic geometrical designs. "Miss 1930" of the automobile world made her debut under canopies of daffodil yellow and bright, light blue, suspended on artistic poles with modern spearheads. On entering the Hall an impressive avenue of palms offered an attractive vista for an unhurried promenade. The posts on each side of the center aisle were given an original, modern leaf effect, three lights being placed in each leaf. Daffodil yellow, trimmed with heavy blue cloth and with panels of fine mesh, containing colored butterflies, comprised the ceiling between the posts and a wall over the exhibit space.

OPENING: Detroit's 29th Annual Automobile Show sprang to life on Saturday night when Mayor Bowles threw the switch, which illuminated the great expanse of exhibits in Convention Hall.

The annual meeting of the Society of Automotive Engineers opened Monday morning and closed Friday evening. Tuesday was designated "Manufacturers' Day." The retail automotive trade of the state was in Detroit on Wednesday for "Michigan Day," as the Michigan Automotive Trade Association held its ninth annual convention at the Hotel Statler. Thursday was designated as "Detroit Day," when attendance always reached its peak.

INSIDE THE SHOW: There were 300 cars representing 41 different makes, departments for accessories, commercial cars, and a custom body salon. The entire south hall was used for passenger cars as well as the north Cass hall. The north Woodward hall was used for commercial cars and the two north wings were used for equipment and special exhibits. In place of the customary narrow aisles, which were generally found at exhibitions, two broad avenues were laid out running from Woodward to Cass Avenue, and on either side the car exhibitors were allotted spaces similar in size and shape to a well-arranged automobile salesroom. In these spaces the exhibitors found it possible to arrange the cars in such a manner that they could be examined without the visitor finding it necessary to stand in the aisles and be inconvenienced by the flow of traffic.

The show visitor found a number of outstanding style changes in the passenger cars. Curves entirely replaced the square line box-like effect. Curves resulted

General view of the show, looking down the main aisle at the statue of "Miss 1930." (Courtesy of the National Automotive History Collection, Detroit Public Library)

in greater beauty and permitted greater roominess. Open models had more protective fenders, and were more rakish. Closed models were lower hung.

Interiors of closed cars were improved generally. There was a noticeable trend towards more modernistic hardware. Upholstery fabrics were more attractive and color received more attention with more harmony.

The Graham featured safety plate glass for the windshield and all windows. REO cars were available with a radio made by American Bosch Magneto Corp. The arrangement of the parking lights on the Willys six was decidedly new. Instead of carrying the small lights on the fenders or on the cowl, they were mounted directly under the large headlamps.

The show management imported one of the new MG midget cars from England which was one of the lowest-priced cars in Europe, though it retailed for almost double the cost of America's lowest-priced roadster. It was hoped that it would give the show visitors an idea as to the wonderful values obtainable in America, where advanced manufacturing methods made it possible for practically everyone to enjoy motoring.

DATE: January 17-24, 1931

SPONSOR: DADA

BUILDING: Convention Hall

DECOR: The French idea was adopted, employing brilliant colors and thousands of subdued lights as a striking background for the more somber-hued motor debutantes. Many large wrought-iron scroll fixtures, containing hundreds of lights of a soft yellow shade, were placed throughout the great Hall, which embraced three-and-a-half acres.

In the center of the broad main aisles the silver vase motif, enhanced by electric flowers, was carried out, while the several hundred columns throughout the exhibit hall were attractively attired in green and yellow material, harmonizing with the ceiling and set off with silver electric-lighted prisms.

Large deep billows of sea green and daffodil yellow were festooned to form a ceiling over the main aisles while the color scheme of a very pale shade of blue, trimmed with daffodil yellow and coral, introduced a new note over the car displays.

The custom body salon was held in the north Cass Avenue wing. Crystal fixtures, walls which gave the impression they were covered with sheets of silver, black columns, and rich carpeting provided a fitting setting for the luxurious cars displayed.

OPENING: The show opened Saturday evening when Mayor Murphy threw the switch and flooded the three-and-a-half-acre Hall with light.

The annual convention of the SAE was held at the Book-Cadillac Hotel from Monday through Friday.

INSIDE THE SHOW: Thirty-one makes of passenger cars were represented, along with a full line of commercial vehicles, and the masterpiece of custom body makers, as well as accessories. An unusual feature of the show was an automotive historical exhibit contributed by Henry Ford. Located in the north Cass Avenue section of the hall were the milestones of the automotive industry in the previous quarter century, together with a reproduction of King Tut's state chariot of 30 centuries ago, a primitive Indian "drag," or travois, America's first known wagon, a crude ox cart, stagecoach, and a prairie schooner.

The four S's—style, speed, safety, and savings—characterized the offerings of the 1931 show. One of the surprises of the show was the number of cars that came out with "free wheeling," featured in no less than five makes. The show revealed that cars were not only getting better but also bigger. Linear dimensions of hoods were also increased. In many cases they led smoothly rearward into its new streamlined body that had borrowed much from the airplane: slanting windshields with little or no external visors, and fenders with a more graceful sweep.

No matter what the special interest of the onlooker was, he found something to please him at the show. If it was radiators, he found them in all shapes—shields to ovals, flat and crested, shuttered and grilled. He found dashboards that looked like the control room of a submarine, so studded with indicators, gauges, and thingamajigs. One of the interesting features, which was illustrated in different ways throughout the show, was the use of rustless steels.

Another eye catcher at the show was the little cars. There were two on the market: the American Austin announced in 1930 was not exhibited at the Detroit show; the American Mathis—pronounced "Matees"—sponsored by Durant, was on exhibit.

Important among the many safety features designed into Packard cars were the narrow windshield pillars. They were designed to give maximum vision to the driver of the car. Made of steel, the new pillars actually added strength to the body although they were only about half the size of the wood pillars normally used. Another important safety feature was the steel-cored, hard-rubber steering wheel. Tests indicated that under sufficient pressure they could be bent, but did not break.

On Friday, in the closing session of the Society of Automotive Engineers at the Book-Cadillac Hotel, Robbins B. Stoeckel, commissioner of motor vehicles of Connecticut, said that 80% of all automobile accidents are caused by failure or mistake on the part of the operator. The other 20% of accidents were due to accident, highway defect, actual criminality, or mechanical failure.

NOTE: For the first time in automotive history there were fewer cars registered during 1931 than during the previous year.

DATE: January 23-30, 1932

SPONSOR: DADA

BUILDING: Convention Hall

ADMISSION: Reduced to 50 cents

1932

Model Year

DECOR: Under striking Arabian canopies of red and yellow, the cars stood in clusters, in lines, in groups, or on revolving pedestals. Apart from the others, as befitted their distinguished lineage, the custom-built cars stood on deep carpets in a room hung richly in blue and silver and gold. Those were the aristocrats of the motor world.

ENTERTAINMENT: A special feature of the show was "Oldest Car in Michigan contest" which afforded the visitor an opportunity to study the development of the automobile from the one-

Preparing the GM exhibits for the show. (1978 GM Corp. Used with permission of GM Media Archives.)

The Chrysler exhibit. (Courtesy of the National Automotive History Collection, Detroit Public Library)

lung days up to the 1932 era. There were 55 cars on parade Saturday afternoon, from 33 cities in Michigan. Their owners were saying that they didn't build cars like that anymore.

Many new attractions were offered at the show. The evening's program included a visit to the "Little Theatre of the Auto"; motion pictures were prepared of different automobile plant operations. The visitor had the opportunity to note just what was under the hood of the car, how a motor car was built, and other interesting factory facts.

The world's most expensive toy—a $25,000 reproduction, in miniature, of the Desoto factory in Detroit—was displayed at the show. Like the plant it represented, the cameo factory built miniature automobiles at a rate of 14 vehicles every hour.

OPENING: The opening of the show was signaled by the throwing of the switch, flashing on a myriad of lights, by Mayor Murphy, H.K. Chambers, president of the DADA, and Joseph A. Schulte, chairman of the association's show committee.

INSIDE THE SHOW: Thirty-three different makes with more than 300 models were prepared for the exhibit along with 50 trucks and commercial cars, and a large representation by the accessory and shop equipment manufacturers. While under the sponsorship of the automobile dealers, the Detroit show was really "fathered" by the manufacturers themselves. Those carmakers whose plants were in the Detroit territory were showing new products to their "own people." Detroiters were considered by the trade as "motor-wise."

Bodies of many cars were all-steel except for a few trim stick and filler pieces, while the new Hudson and Essex had no wood at all. Never did automobile doors shut with a more satisfying "clug" than the new 1932 models. A visit to the show revealed the fact that door closing was still the thing that principally interested the public. There seemed to be a fascination about it since the days of the rear door tonneau at the turn of the century.

The art of selling. (Archives of Labor and Urban Affairs, Wayne State University)

Color combinations were becoming more daring and more pronounced in tone. Examples included canary and black, burnt orange and tan, black and sea green, green and gray, powder blue and red, and even some motors were painted blue.

The quickest to catch the eye among the car's innovations was the slanted windshield. Greatly lessened wind resistance made higher top speed possible with the same power, and there was a definite gasoline economy when the car was driven over 40 mph. Outside or cadet-type sun visors practically disappeared from the 1932 cars. The sun visor was moved to the inside of the car and could easily be reached for adjustment. At least one car had a visor that could be adjusted to shade the driver's eyes from the side as well as in front.

Radiator ornaments and filler caps were done away with and radiators were filled through openings under the hood. Spare wheels were carried in fender wells, making it possible to attach rear end trunk racks as standard equipment. Radio sets were improved and considerably reduced in price. Several makes of automobiles were furnished with built-in aerials. Instrument boards were more distinctive in appearance. Many were inlaid with scrolls and fine woods and more and more gauges, knobs, handles, and devices of all kinds. Many cars were equipped with a spring cord attachment to allow the driver to pull down the rear curtain and eliminate glare from headlights behind him.

DATE: January 21-28, 1933

SPONSOR: DADA

BUILDING: Convention Hall

ADMISSION: $1.00

DECOR: With colors very prominent in the new cars the show decorators went to considerable length to provide a suitable background. Under the direction of H.H. Shuart, show manager, the Hall was given probably its most striking treatment, with decorations in a coral shade, with billowy treatment over the aisles. A ceiling canopy of gold cloth with massive silver columns and cylinders of light of *moderne* design added a touch of dignity to the ensemble.

Cerise and silver decorations and rich carpeting were found in the salon where the custom-built models were on view.

OPENING: Members of the show committee made a final inspection of the Hall Saturday afternoon and pronounced the arrangements perfect. The lights were switched on at 7:00 p.m. Saturday by Mayor Murphy. It was the most brilliant spectacle of this character ever presented in Detroit, and was viewed by a throng of "first-nighters." Three famous race car drivers were present at the opening—Barney Oldfield, dean of speedways, Billy Arnold, an Indianapolis winner at 24, and Peter Paulo, holder of the speed record on the Indianapolis track.

The Society of Automotive Engineers held its 13th annual convention at the Detroit Auto Show, and the Michigan Automotive Trade Association held its meeting Wednesday night. Both groups met at the Book-Cadillac Hotel.

INSIDE THE SHOW: There were 26 lines of automobiles on display, along with commercial trucks and cars, accessories, and a collection of 1932 and 1933 license plates from other states. There were also trailers, buses, land yachts, a patrol wagon, and the only custom body salon in the country.

Streamlined bodies with futuristic cowls and fenders drew "oohs and ahs" from most of the visitors. Lincoln, REO, Murray Body Corp. of America, and many other coach builders used the U. of D. wind tunnel facilities, along with Stinson Aircraft Co., the Airplane Development Corp. of America, and the Ford Motor Co.'s aeronautical division.

There were cars, sleek and rakish, which pivoted on a platform. In the front seat were lovely girls gowned in evening clothes, just to demonstrate to the public exactly how the wife or daughter would look surrounded by several hundred or several thousand dollars worth of automobile. The girls were as up-to-the-minute

as the cars exhibited. They stood about explaining the automatic clutch, the no-draft ventilation, and other features. Hupmobile had a motion exhibit consisting of a car with young women at the wheel. Behind the car was an illuminated moving background which simulated a highway with the landscape gliding past. Featured in the Studebaker show was an illuminated closed car in which a pair of beauteous young women wearing evening costume enjoyed limousine luxury. The Rockne had a "mechanical man" that appeared from a cabinet every so often. The robot went through motions of exhibiting a series of placards under the guidance of a young woman.

Scarcely a car in the entire three-and-a-half acres of floor space was without its boast of bandit protection. "You see this small button," an attendant says. "All you do is press it and no bandit can get into your car as long as you're inside."

NOTE: Later in the year, William Metzger died in his home on April 11, 1933, after being ill for four years. Automobile history can never be written without using his name (see Appendix).

DATE: January 20-27, 1934

SPONSOR: DADA

BUILDING: Convention Hall

ADMISSION: Reduced to 40 cents

DECOR: A striking decorative treatment, embodying a setting of splendor hitherto unknown to motor car exhibitions, was arranged by H.H. Shuart, show manager. He accomplished an effect of a building within a building and provided a highly modernistic setting for the display. Billows of blue cloth transformed the ceiling of the vast Hall, while massive columns concealed with illuminated panels diffused a soft glow over the hundreds of glistening cars to carry out the alluring effect.

ENTERTAINMENT: Music at the show was performed by one of the country's leading bands, Eddie Griffith's "High Hats" ensemble; they had won favor at the "Century of Progress" World's Fair in Chicago during the summer of 1933.

OPENING: On Saturday evening Mayor Frank Couzens threw the switch and, as the big show burst into a blaze of light, the impatient public swarmed through the doors to inspect the offerings of 1934. The opening of the show was also the signal for the floodlighting of the General Motors building with 360 1000W lamps. The building was abloom with light for the first time in two years.

The master minds of motordom came together for the annual SAE meeting from Monday through Friday at the Book-Cadillac Hotel. A demonstration of television was a feature of the Monday evening program. The American Telephone and Telegraph Company's department of development and research explained in engineering language the means by which a moving image could be transmitted and received at a distant point by electrical means.

The Michigan Automotive Trade Association met on Wednesday evening at the Hotel Statler.

INSIDE THE SHOW: Three hundred cars representing 24 different makes were on display. So comprehensive in scope was the Detroit show that it really embraced five shows within the big show—passenger cars, commercial cars, equipment and accessories, the Little Theater of the Auto, and the Style Salon.

The Style Salon was off to one side, in a bower of palms, soft carpets, and subdued lights. There stood the aristocrats of the motor world, the final word in beauty and in luxury, and the newest spring and summer creations in women's apparel along with the latest modes in motor cars. Professional mannequins displayed the fashions from Paris and New York in a review three times daily.

In cooperation with President Roosevelt's recovery program, motor car manufacturers extended themselves to the utmost to present the ultimate in style, comfort, convenience, and mechanical perfection.

The driver of the 1934 car no longer had to worry about the heat control, idling speed, water cooling, lubrication, carbon removal, or the clutch. The new engines could be started and just about took care of themselves. An outstanding feature of the models on exhibit was the new streamlined bodies. Another feature holding the attention of the show visitor was the independent front-wheel suspension.

General view of the show. (Courtesy of the National Automotive History Collection, Detroit Public Library)

Complete insulation of the body against sound as well as fumes and noise was accomplished by new acoustic material applied to all flat surfaces in the Hupp bodies.

DATE: January 12-19, 1935

SPONSOR: DADA

BUILDING: Convention Hall

ADMISSION: 40 cents

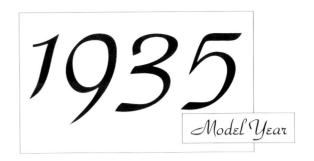

DECOR: Although 30 ft. of the Woodward Avenue frontage was taken off Convention Hall to modernize the building, it was split longitudinally down the middle and the front section was moved back to close the gap. The Hall was draped in thousands of yards of soft pastel-shaded cloth and every pillar in the place was shrouded beneath panels of veneer. The high ceiling in the center of the Hall was draped in three tones of green and silver. Permanent light fixtures in this area were "killed-off" and massive, specially built chandeliers, painted with scenes pertaining to the automobile and its development, furnished illumination.

In the north Woodward annex a highly modern note was struck in the decorations for the style and fine car salon. Dominant shades of gold and chromium were applied to the walls of the Style Salon with a telling effect. The ceiling was laid in panels of varying types to harmonize with the modern treatment of the walls. The lighting was indirect and a great number of lighting fixtures of modern design were employed.

ENTERTAINMENT: Buddy Field's Orchestra dispensed with syncopated rhythm each afternoon and evening.

OPENING: By throwing the switch in the presence of the show officials, Mayor Couzens officially opened the exhibition, and then broadcast over radio station WXYZ from the Custom Car Salon.

More than a score of conventions and special gatherings were held during the show. Most important of all was the National Automobile Dealers Association, which was held in Detroit for the first time. The railroads recognized the national interest manifested in the Detroit show for the first time by offering special low fares to Detroit from all parts of the country. Another leading convention was the annual meeting of the Society of Automotive Engineers.

INSIDE THE SHOW: More than 94% of the nations automobiles were produced within 100 miles of Detroit. There were 24 major automobile manufacturers with 300 cars on display. The designers went far beyond the engineering handbook and combined their skills with the physiologists and artists. All the women visitors to the show expressed admiration of the improved lighting systems, the roomier seats, and the new steel-roofed cars.

The show had a carnival splash of color and a carnival air, and to give it an extra fillip, the Style Salon featured beautiful girls displaying resort clothes that prompted the crowds, men and women alike, to go places quick—and in a new car.

Streamlining advanced another year along its road of development. Air roar, even while traveling at high speed, was practically eliminated by the aerodynamic design of the Hupmobiles. On the other hand, the Chrysler "potato bug" or "Which way am I going?" models which so startled the public in 1935 were largely modified and conventionalized. Their radical features were softened.

General view of the show. (Archives of Labor and Urban Affairs, Wayne State University)

Instrument boards looked less like the coning tower of a submarine. A tendency was to combine the multiplicity of gauges, indicators, and thingamajigs in one large instrument that tells the driver all he wants to know and leaves the rest of the board free to show off rich wood grains.

1936
Model Year

The National Automobile Dealers Association differed sharply with the Automobile Manufacturers Association as to the best time to hold the annual automobile show. Prior to 1935, the shows were held in January, but government economic advisors recommended advancing the dates by two months in an effort to stabilize employment in the industry over a longer period, particularly the winter months.

Some factory sales officials and most dealers claimed that the autumn introductory period would seriously interfere with what would otherwise be a good autumn market for current models and that the advantages of having new models to offer the Christmas trade was more than offset by their being forced to carry heavy stocks of trade-in cars through the winter, when there was a small demand for used vehicles until spring.

The 1936 models were the last to debut at the beginning of the year (there was no DADA show held); the 1937 models were introduced in the fall of 1936.

There were two other shows in March of 1936, which did display most of the 1936 models. The second Detroit and Michigan Exposition at Convention Hall included Ford and Chrysler with various manufacturing, styling, and testing exhibits. General Motors held its fourth annual spring showing of its products at the GM building.

(1978 GM Corp. Used with permission of GM Media Archives.)

129

General view of the show at the GM building. (1978 GM Corp. Used with permission of GM Media Archives.)

DATE: November 14-21, 1936

SPONSOR: DADA

BUILDING: Convention Hall

ADMISSION: 40 cents

DECOR: Decorators transformed the four big halls and two north annexes into an autumnal garden. The outdoors was virtually moved inside the building, dressing pillars, ceilings, and walls in warm tones of autumn and covering floors with 10,000 yds. of russet carpeting. In the center aisles, which extended more than 700 ft. from Woodward to Cass, the ceiling treatment consisted of horizontal planes running in shade from deep red to deep yellow, with splashes of orange intermingled. Columns bordering the aisles were tinted to match. As a centerpiece in the trailer department, a fountain was installed and surrounded with stone walls and flowerbeds.

ENTERTAINMENT: Another attraction outside the formal pageant of cars was a scientific battery of driver-testing equipment shown under the supervision of the American Automobile Association and the Automobile Club of Michigan. It enabled motorists to take tests, of their own volition, to learn their fitness for driving and their weaknesses. There was excitability, selective reaction, blood pressure, and strength tests.

OPENING: John W. Smith, council president, threw the single switch and turned on the dazzling lighting effects to set the 1936 show in motion at 2:00 p.m. on Saturday.

An invitation to the show was extended to Mrs. Franklin D. Roosevelt by the show committee. She was in Detroit to lecture at the Masonic Temple.

Members of the Detroit section of the Society of Automotive Engineers held their annual show dinner Monday night at the Hotel Statler.

The annual convention of the American Automobile Association was held at the Hotel Statler on Friday, and it was designated "AAA Night" at the show. Edward N. Hines, Wayne County Road Commissioner, who originated center-striping for highways and in 1909 put down the first mile of rural concrete roadway in the United States (on Woodward Avenue north of Six Mile Road), was honored at the AAA annual dinner.

INSIDE THE SHOW: There were 300 cars representing the products of 24 of the world's largest manufacturers, along with the usual bevy of commercial vehicles. Challenging passenger cars for public attention were 30 house trailers, the product of 12 manufacturers.

The mechanically inclined found hours of fun at the show. Cars were shown in all stages of undress, with the doors left off, and working parts exposed. There were stripped chassis and working demonstrations of oiling systems, cooling systems, and gear and brake operation.

Many of the cars had lower floors, and riding quality was improved with better shock absorbers. Windshield defrosters were standard or extra equipment on most models. In high-priced cars, electric clocks and radios were standard equipment. Many of the cars had batteries so regulated that the charging was controlled automatically. New visors and colored disc transparencies for softening bright headlight rays were offered. Some cars had seat cushions that moved forward and back and

The Pontiac display. The first Pontiacs were produced in 1926 as a "companion" car to the Oakland automobile. Pontiac sales began to exceed Oakland's, and in 1932 the Oakland Motor Car Co. became the Pontiac Motor Company. (Courtesy of the National Automotive History Collection, Detroit Public Library)

could be lowered, as well as varying the angle of back cushions. One company provided something new in a horn, a nickel ring nearly a foot in diameter, fastened to the steering wheel. It gave forth a raucous noise at the touch of any point on its perimeter.

Most cars had solid steel bodies, safety glass, hydraulic four-wheel brakes, no-draft ventilation, concealed spare tires, armrests, dual windshield wipers, electric gas gauge, electric temperature gauge, inside locks on the doors, glove locker, package shelf, rubber running boards, multi-beam headlights, and a headlight beam indicator.

The new Plymouth featured a "hushed" ride with complete soundproofing never before attained in any price class. Five kinds of insulation were used to block out rumble, hum, and drumming, and seal the interior against gas, heat, and cold.

A couple of advanced models at the show spelled the doom of the running board. One model was utterly without a running board. It was low slung and the riders could step directly into the body from the ground. Another car had only an elementary running board, not more than 3 in. wide.

Divided hoods captured the fancy of the designer for the 1937 models. They appeared on several makes with only the top section lifting. Some were hinged at the rear and when opened, reminded one of an alligator about to partake of a few tons of breakfast.

"A New World on Wheels"

1938

Model Year

DATE: November 6-13, 1937
(closed Sunday, November 7)

SPONSOR: DADA

BUILDING: Convention Hall

DECOR: On entering Convention Hall the visitor was impressed by the tremendous area of the place and the decorative treatment which more than ever before augmented the enormous proportions of the building. The aisles, which were 25 ft. wide, were treated in a manner which made them seem much higher than in previous years, and an indirect lighting effect left the gigantic expanses unbroken that generated a feeling of walking down a wide avenue covered with a canopy.

A peek at the decorations disclosed the fact that the color scheme was in various shades of coral and black, with a reproduction of a huge glass skylight giving the effect of an Italian loggia. More than 100,000 ft. of cloth, 78,000 ft. of lumber, and 54,000 ft. of masonite board were used. The settings of the show were planned very carefully for the convenience of the visitor even to the detail of carpeting which covered the entire exhibit area. More than 100,000 sq. ft. of carpet was used not only to provide a setting for the highly polished new models but also to add to the comfort of those who spent several hours walking around the exhibits.

ENTERTAINMENT: An orchestra and entertainers performed on a stage in the north Cass hall. In an annex adjoining the hall was a motion picture theater for 1,000 people which operated

The Pontiac display is on the left, followed by Cadillac. Notice the full carpeting. (Archives of Labor and Urban Affairs, Wayne State University)

The Oldsmobile exhibit. (1978 GM Corp. Used with permission of GM Media Archives.)

continuously from 1:30 p.m. to 10:30 p.m. showing sound films produced by various automobile manufacturers.

OPENING: A tiny, white-haired woman of 94, whose association with the automobile industry began in the late 1890s, formally opened the 37th Annual Detroit Automobile Show on Saturday. Mrs. H.J. Downey, affectionately known in Lansing as "Grandmother of the Automobile Industry," snipped a ribboned entrance at 11:00 a.m.

Her son, C.P. Downey, was proprietor of the famed Downey House in Lansing in the days when the budding industry existed largely by marks on tablecloths. Throughout the succeeding years her family was active in the formation of automobile companies. They were organizers and founders of Olds and REO, and were linked closely with General Motors. Downey and William C. Durant married sisters.

INSIDE THE SHOW: The 1937 show committee allotted space for 22 makes, with upwards of 200 cars for public inspection, along with eight makes of commercial cars. There were house trailers, automotive parts and accessory displays, the Automobile Club of Michigan, and the first

1938 Chevrolet Chassis. (1978 GM Corp. Used with permission of GM Media Archives.)

public presentation of Norman Bel Geddes "City of Tomorrow." This was a 40-ft. long, 10-ft. wide, and 10-ft. high portion of street traffic, with moving cars and pedestrians, showing traffic conditions of 1960 as predicted by Dr. Miller McClintock, Director of the Bureau for Street Traffic Research at Harvard University.

The general design theme for the 1938 models followed the themes of the previous two years with long, sweeping, horizontal lines, with horizontal radiator ribs in bright chromium and flaring fenders. A couple of makes introduced a new note, in which the lines leaned forward rather than backward. In such designs, the radiator leaned inward, giving the car an appearance almost marine in its trimness. Radiator openings increased and tended to slip around the side of the hood.

Upon entering from Woodward Avenue, one came immediately into the passenger car exhibits. The Nash and LaFayette cars were the first on the right and across the aisle was the Desoto exhibit. Other cars in the north Woodward hall included the Cadillac, LaSalle, Willys, and Hupmobile, the latter in the show again after an absence of one year.

Coming in the south Woodward hall, showgoers faced a highlight in an "Arrowbile" which was a newly created "flying automobile" shown by the Studebaker Corp., who supplied the powerplant and collaborated with the inventor of the novel machine. It was thought that perhaps it was a forerunner of what could be expected in the future.

"Sales Make Jobs"

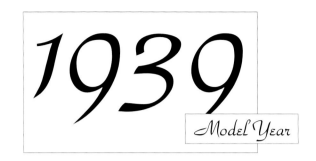

DATE: November 11-19, 1938
(closed Sunday, November 13)

SPONSOR: DADA

BUILDING: Convention Hall

ADMISSION: 40 cents

DECOR: The automobile show was a blaze of color for the hundreds of feet from Woodward Avenue to Cass Avenue in all the great halls of the huge structure. Yellow and black were the background colors, and intermingled in the general decorative scheme were the slogans and emblems of the "Sales Make Jobs" campaign.

Decorating the walls and ceiling were 124,000 ft. of cloth, 74,000 ft. of lumber, 54,000 ft. of masonite board, and 43,000 ft. of carpet.

OPENING: For the first time Detroit had the honor of firing the opening gun of the Automobile Show season. In past years, the New York Show was always held the week before the Detroit showing. The 1938 shows in Detroit, New York, and Pittsburgh were held simultaneously with Detroit beating the others to the starting gun by about four hours, opening at 11 a.m. on Friday, November 11, which was Armistice Day.

The fact that the Detroit Show was not open on Sunday, November 13, led the management to choose the holiday, Friday, as the opening instead of Saturday, which was the custom of the past. The opening was preceded by Armistice Day ceremonies on the part of various veterans organizations that were identified with the automotive industry.

INSIDE THE SHOW: There were 22 makes of cars, with 250 models on display, along with six truck manufacturers in the commercial exhibit. In addition to the cars, there were the usual entertainment features at the show.

There was great interest in the new Ford product—the Mercury. The Detroit Automobile Show was the first place that it was on display. All of the manufacturers showed complete lines of their products. All body styles were on display with Cadillac and LaSalle alone featuring 34 different styles of cars. They were exclusive among the 1939 models in that running boards were completely dropped, leaving no false step at the side of the car. Where running boards were eliminated, stainless-steel strips were substituted below the car doors.

Graham had five cars and Hupmobile had its new low-priced six and its senior six as well as several senior eights in the show. Otto Dykoff, director of the Volkswagen Werks of Germany, said that his firm had undertaken manufacture of a rear-engine, gasoline-driven motor car which would retail for $375. The new German car was a 25-hp machine.

Michigan viewed the annual automobile shows from a far different standpoint than the people of other states. The shows were, in truth, the state's annual industrial debuts, for upon their success depended the steady employment, creation of purchasing power, and general business prosperity of a large portion of the state.

The Studebaker display. Studebaker was the oldest automobile company, started in 1853 with horse-drawn wagons. In 1912, Studebaker took ownership of the Everitt-Metzger-Flanders Company and became the Studebaker Corporation. A Studebaker Commander is in the foreground on the right-hand side. (Archives of Labor and Urban Affairs, Wayne State University)

More than 15,000 parts were behind each of the new automobiles at the show. The average new car required, among other materials, the following: A little more than a ton of steel, 18 sq. ft. of safety glass, 33 lb. of copper and brass, 27 lb. of lead, 2 lb. of tin, 144 lb. of cast pig iron, 110 lb. of rubber including tires, 13 sq. yds. of upholstery fabric, and 2-1/2 gal. of paint.

Not only were the great car and truck manufacturing plants involved in this web of economic life, but likewise was the state's growing steel industry, the hundreds of parts and accessory manufacturers, and foundries and other industrial plants serving the auto industry.

1940 *Model Year*

DATE: October 21-28, 1939

SPONSOR: DADA

BUILDING: Convention Hall

DECOR: Showmanship touched a new high with each of the four main halls having its own color scheme with miles of blue, gold, rose, and green bunting and draperies to provide a harmonious blend with the particular products displayed there. These four colors were bound together by neutral shades appearing in the lower ceiling, the lighting, part of the upper ceiling, and in specially constructed conical columns which started at the floor to a height of 21 ft. These columns were constructed of ornamental plaster, which was new in temporary decoration and offered unique possibilities of design.

Like the foundry at the auto plant, ornamental pillars were cast to serve the dual function of concealing steel girders and providing a new decorative note. A total of 144 castings were required.

At both ends of each of the four halls were allegorical figures—eight in number, with illustrative backgrounds—representing different phases of the industry such as design, production, distribution, etc. While the aisles were indirectly illuminated by soft light emanating from the conical column caps, the lighting over the display area gave a more even distribution so that the visitors could have a clear view of each display.

Materials used in the decorations included enough cloth to make 10,000 house dresses or 30,000 aprons, and it would have furnished a handkerchief for every man in Detroit. There was nearly a half-million watts of light, fed by five miles of wiring, and underlying the entire exhibition was enough carpet to make a run up Woodward Avenue from the river to the Nine Mile Road.

ENTERTAINMENT: Every day during the show, an automobile was given away to the holder of a lucky ticket number. There was a stage presentation twice each afternoon and three times nightly except Sunday when the show was closed. The headline attraction was "The Iceolite Review," a great skating spectacle staged on synthetic ice installed by the newly formed Iceolite Corporation of Detroit. Dorothy Franey, of St. Paul, member of two olympic skating teams and a recent holder of 11 of a possible 14 women's skating titles, did specialty numbers, as did Laura and Harry Holmes, Detroit junior pair skating champions. The chorus was recruited from Detroit and Michigan girls who combined beauty and skating talent.

OPENING: Mayor Richard W. Reading of Detroit, with the assistance of "Miss America" (Patricia Mary Donnelly of Detroit), who was the official show hostess and appeared as a soloist for Del Delbridges orchestra,

Patricia Mary Donnelly of Detroit cuts the ribbon for the opening of the show while Mayor Richard W. Reading (right) watches. (Archives of Labor and Urban Affairs, Wayne State University)

opened the exhibit to the public at 11:00 a.m. Saturday in brief ceremonies. Miss Donnelly was on her first visit home since the Atlantic City contest.

Pre-show activities were scheduled on Friday. More than 1,500 dealers and salesmen of the Detroit district attended a luncheon at the Fountain ballroom of the Masonic Temple. Another special luncheon program was scheduled for the Adcraft Club in the Hotel Statler.

INSIDE THE SHOW: This show was scheduled three weeks earlier than ever before, and presented the new cars when they were really new. The passenger car displays included 21 different

Chevrolet convertible promotional picture. (1978 GM Corp. Used with permission of GM Media Archives.)

Notice the outdoor scenery behind the Chevrolet. (1978 GM Corp. Used with permission of GM Media Archives.)

American makes, each in a wide and attractive variety of models. In addition, there were a number of accessory displays, seven truck displays, and two Stinson airplanes. One hall featured a safety display, to which the Detroit Police Department, State Highway Department, Detroit Public Schools, Wayne County Sheriff's Office, and the Department of State all contributed, making the Detroit show truly an inclusive transportation exhibit.

A look at the 1940 model cars found streamlining more pronounced than ever. In many cases, the running boards became little more than a gesture—a mere token in deference to a useful past. Nearly all of the cars had the remote-control gearshift lever mounted on the steering wheel. Plastic was widely used, even to the binding element in the two sheets of "sandwich" glass introduced in 1940 for better vision.

Cars were generally wider and lower, with large glass areas. General Motors switched from sheet glass to plate glass for better depth perception. Weight distribution was improved for better riding. "Air conditioning" engaged the major attention of several manufacturers. Projections such as hinges, door handles, and controls were recessed or subdued for greater safety and convenience.

Safety warnings were on all vital instruments. New and specially designed upholstery for better "breathing" and easier cleaning was offered. There were glove compartments (for purses), steering wheels that were thin (to allow a women to wrap the little finger around it), mirrors on the back of sunvisors, adjustable front seats, and a lower step from the ground to the car.

NOTE: When the 1940 license plates were available, Henry Ford's secretary called the Detroit branch of the Secretary of State's office to get plate number 999. (It dated back to Henry Ford's famous race car "999" which veteran race driver Barney Oldfield made famous in 1903 when he became the first driver to go a mile in less than 60 seconds. The feat was accomplished on a circular track in New York City.) Ford's secretary was told it was impossible because the new plate numbering system started with 1001. It is not known if Ford perpetuated the famous number since 1903 but his secretary said it was at least 20 years.

"An Automotive House Party"

DATE: October 12-19, 1940

SPONSOR: DADA

BUILDING: Convention Hall

DECOR: The decorations were on an extensive scale. George Wittbold, a foremost designer, did the decoration work using gold, green, and yellow, and harmonizing tones. The decorative scheme was highlighted by murals mounted above the ends of the four major halls. The murals depicted men, methods, and machinery symbolic of the automobile industry.

ENTERTAINMENT: For entertainment, the show committee provided a full hour-and-a-half stage show, which gave three performances daily. It was presented on a 3,200-sq.-ft. elevated stage. The show highlighted styles in both motor cars and women's clothes, with the girls and the automobiles alternating in the spotlight.

Other entertainment features included Del Delbridge and his orchestra, a troupe of dancers, Mare Kuhlman with a troupe of twelve dancers, Pete Cusanelli and his donkey, and the California varsity eight, who sang vocal numbers, and other stellar acts.

OPENING: The 40th Annual Detroit Auto Show opened at 11:00 p.m. Saturday when Mayor Jeffries, in the presence of industry leaders, cut a ribbon across the Cass Avenue entrance to Convention Hall. At the opening, Mayor Jeffries made a brief address over Radio Station WXYZ and the Michigan network. This was the earliest opening the Detroit show ever had. It opened simultaneously with the New York show, in keeping with the long-standing belief of many Detroiters that the national show should belong to Detroit.

INSIDE THE SHOW: There were 17 makes of passenger cars and four makes of commercial cars displayed. The State Highway Department put in a replica of its roadside parks, complete in all details.

As the visitor entered the Hall, he observed sleek and colorful cars displayed in a setting of modern severity. Everything about them was stepped-up to enhance eye appeal. Models in slinky gowns sat behind the steering wheels while lecturers in uniform went into high-geared ballyhoo as to the attractions of the cars.

Car colors ran from dashing pastels with two-tone jobs in great profusion. One showed against a tropical background, with waving palms, warm sands, and a bright blue sea. Another make had a fiesta setting, complete with black-eyed senioritas and dashing gauchos.

143

Pontiac Deluxe Torpedo 6 convertible.
(1978 GM Corp. Used with permission of
GM Media Archives.)

Cars were better sprung, more comfortable to ride, and safer. Floors were lower and running boards were little more than a token. Plastics were more widely applied to instrument controls, steering wheels, and interior panels. Deep windows and wide one-piece "panorama" windshields provided maximum visibility for both driver and passengers in many of the 1941 cars. The "light piping" property of "lucite" methyl methacrylate was used on many models. On the instrument panel, light piping provided indicators that appeared to be self-luminous. One speedometer dial was fitted with a tiny lucite button as the pointer which glowed with a light as it swung around the scale. In all, 13 times as much lucite was used in the 1941 models as in the 1939 models.

General Motors began providing an electric window-regulating mechanism for the window separating the compartments for the driver and the passengers in their limousine models. Pontiac had the industry's first built-in oil filter that cleaned the oil before it passed through the pump. Rust-proof steel was used extensively on the 1941 cars. Belt and hood moldings, hubcap centers, headlamp rings, and much of the body hardware was made of the durable material.

NOTE: License plates for 1941 went on sale Monday during the auto show. These were the first plates in the U.S. to be designed according to the findings of science. The plates were maroon with white letters, with maroon letters for half-year plates. Visibility tests showed white figures on the maroon background was visible at 158.4 ft.—tested at the GM proving grounds near Milford, Michigan. More than 100 police chiefs, sheriffs, state police, prosecutors, and auto officials were used as test subjects.

DATE: October 11-18, 1941

SPONSOR: DADA

BUILDING: Open House at 300 dealers
in Metropolitan Detroit

DECOR: Huge banners were posted on the inside of each showroom heralding the week, surmounted—in the case of association members—by two large circular emblems identifying the store as a DADA member. Special door prizes were awarded during the "Open House." Patriotic bunting and streamers and window corner "fans" were on the outside of all participating dealerships to give them a distinctive and colorful appearance.

OPENING: "Open House" week was officially designated as such in a proclamation by Mayor Edward Jeffries, Jr. Dealers decided on an Open House to keep alive the spirit of the annual automobile show when manufacturers withdrew support from the exhibitions because of the WWII defense program. While all different makes were not in one building for easy comparison, dealerships were so concentrated in certain sections of the city that it was possible to see all makes in the space of a block or two.

Open House started officially on Saturday with a parade sponsored by the north-end dealers down Woodward Avenue and Seven Mile Road at 1 p.m. It traveled south on Woodward Avenue to Fort Street, west to Cass Avenue, north to Grand River Avenue, and out Grand River to Telegraph Road, where it disbanded. Several hundred gleaming new models were led by grim army trucks and "jeeps."

The east-side dealers held a parade down Gratiot Avenue on Monday, followed on Tuesday with the west-side dealers' parade down Michigan Avenue.

The Society of Automotive Engineers held an assembly at the General Motors proving ground on Monday. An inspection trip was followed by a national defense film and a dinner.

INSIDE THE SHOW: Fender and sheet metal treatment flows were more harmonious with body lines. Running boards were definitely on the way out. Cars were lower, wider, safer, and easier on the pocketbook for maintenance and operation. Improvements for the 1942 models included more standard equipment than the previous year's offerings as an offset to a higher price. The powerplants delivered greater economy in line with the national gasoline conservation program.

Plastics had wider use for utility and decoration. Chrome ornamentation was used only where a quick switch could be made for the war effort. Cars generally

had wider square-effect grills of massive design. Two-tones on the exterior and interior dipped down into the lower price field. Progress toward automatic transmissions was notable. With the war effort affecting white sidewall tires, various makes offered white wall wheel rings that gave the same pleasing effect without the same problem of dirt and fading.

NOTE: In 1942 all motorists received one set of plates, rather than 650,000 half-year plate owners receiving two sets, one in March, and one in September. The 1942 plate was a trifle smaller and had white numerals on a dark green background. This was the first year that the color was determined not only by the visibility test, but also by conferencing with the color stylists of the automobile manufacturers in order to secure a color that would harmonize with the colors of the cars.

1943-1952

On January 3, 1942, the United States government outlawed all sales or delivery of new passenger cars and trucks.

As a result of World War II and its effects on the industry, there were no auto shows during the years 1943-1952.

The Golden Jubilee of the U.S. automobile industry was celebrated in Detroit in 1946. A special gold paint was formulated to paint the streets for a parade. Many automotive legends attended the celebration at the Masonic Temple, including the founder of GM, Billy Durant. Barney Oldfield, the famous race driver, was talking with his former boss, Henry Ford. Henry said, "Barney, you made me what I am today." Barney replied, "Henry, you made me what I am today, only I did a better job than you." Pictured from left to right: Henry Ford, Barney Oldfield, Henry Ford II, and George Romney (the manager of the Golden Jubilee and later president of American Motors and Governor of Michigan).

The Ford Motor Company built B-24 bombers at a factory in Willow Run, Michigan, during WWII. The plant became the largest manufacturing site under one roof in the world, with 2,500,000 sq. ft. on 985 acres.

After the war, Henry J. Kaiser and Joe Frazier purchased the Willow Run factory from the U.S. government and started production of "Kaisers" and "Fraziers" in June 1946. Shown is a Frazier Manhattan, one of the first cars with blended-in fenders.

A Kaiser-Frazier dealership occupied a space on Cass Avenue in Convention Hall. The last show in Convention Hall was the Builders show in 1951.

148

The Michigan Motor Show

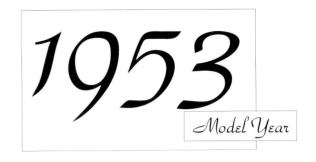

1953 Model Year

DATE: June 2-7, 1953

SPONSOR: The St. Clair Shores Lions Club

BUILDING: The State Fair Grounds Coliseum

INSIDE THE SHOW: More than 100 models, consisting of 50 sports cars, 12 hot rods, and special displays by the automotive companies were on exhibit. Foreign cars were present, having first appeared on any scale of consequence in the U.S. in 1948. Buyers imported them when they were unable to get American cars because of the great shortage after the war.

The most expensive car at the show was the Italian-built Abarth 1500. The aluminum-bodied sports car was the grand prize winner of the Turin, Italy, International Auto Show in 1952. Purchased by the Packard Motor Car Co. for research, the hand-built model was the only one of its kind.

Ten vintage models were displayed by the Ford Museum, including an electric racer that traveled 57.1 mph in 1901, along with Sir Malcolm Cambell's "Bluebird," the car that set the world's speed record in 1936 when it traveled 301 mph.

The Packard was always known as the car of "unchanging character." In 1952, a car named the "Abarth" was purchased at the Turin, Italy, auto show for $25,000 by Packard Vice-President of Engineering, William Graves. The vehicle was parked alongside the Packard factory where Packard's President, James Nance, viewed it. He said that Packard would stick to the lines that were architecturally correct and would forego the lunar asparagus.

Convention Hall was sold to the James Vernor Company in 1953. Vernor's was forced to move from its historic location at the foot of Woodward by the Civic Center development. Vernor's completely revamped the hall from 303,000 sq. ft. to 2,220,490 sq. ft. on 54 acres. The view is on the Woodward Avenue side of the building. (Reprinted with permission of the Burton Historical Collection of the Detroit Public Library.)

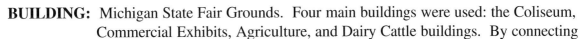

"The Latest and Greatest in Cars and Stars"

1954
Model Year

DATE: February 20-28, 1954

SPONSOR: DADA (its first Annual Auto Show since the 1941 model year)

BUILDING: Michigan State Fair Grounds. Four main buildings were used: the Coliseum, Commercial Exhibits, Agriculture, and Dairy Cattle buildings. By connecting them with protective canopies, the effect of the exhibition being all under one roof was created.

ADMISSION: $1.25 for adults
60 cents for children under 12

ENTERTAINMENT: A huge stage presentation was given twice daily in the Coliseum, with 7,000 permanent and 3,000 temporary seats. It featured name stars of radio and TV, including Joni James, one of the nation's top female singers, Don Cornell, Louis Jordan, The Harmonicats, The Step Brothers, The Beachcombers, Roy Tracy, master of ceremonies, and the 17-piece Herschel Leith Orchestra. The Nash exhibit featured a portable 24-by-24-ft. ice rink for a special skating show. Chevrolet featured a live stage review called "Musical Charades" which ran almost continuously. The review's setting was a huge television receiver.

OPENING: The 104th State Fair opened with a parade up Woodward from Jefferson and a ribbon-cutting ceremony at the main gate with Governor Williams as master of ceremonies. The governor delegated the actual ribbon cutting to Miss Betty Lou King, of Caro, who won the title of North American Bean Queen in 1953 by growing beans better than anyone else on the continent.

Mayor Cobo snipped a ribbon for the opening ceremonies for the auto exhibit with show officials and industry executives on Friday at 11:00 a.m.

A preview for press, radio, television, and trade representatives was held Friday night. The following were designated as special days: Saturday, "Detroit and Grand Opening Day"; Sunday, "Dearborn Day"; Monday, "Hamtramck Day"; Tuesday, "Highland Park Day"; Wednesday, "Down River Day"; Thursday, "Western Wayne County Day"; Friday, "Eastern Wayne County Day"; Saturday, "Oakland County Day"; Sunday, "Macomb County Day." Weekend crowds were so tremendous that the doors had to be closed seven times.

41st. Annual
Detroit Auto Show

FEBRUARY 20th thru 28th, 1954
MICHIGAN STATE FAIR GROUNDS

OFFICIAL PUBLICATION 50¢

Presented Under the Auspices of DETROIT AUTO DEALERS ASSOCIATION

Without Convention Hall, the Auto Show shifted to the Michigan State Fair Grounds Coliseum. This was the first DADA show since 1941. (Courtesy of the National Automotive History Collection, Detroit Public Library)

INSIDE THE SHOW: The aggregate floor space of the three buildings housing the car displays totaled 150,000 sq. ft. There were 18 makes of passenger cars and three lines of trucks totaling close to 150 models in all, including more than a dozen "dream" cars or special show models. There were scores of other engineering and special "try-it-yourself" exhibits.

Red, green, yellow, white, brown, blue, and gray cars were shown in every corner of the three buildings housing the show. Chrome gleamed like silver coins just out of the mint. White-clad attendants kept the shine and glitter fresh. On a great revolving platform half a dozen gleaming Packards, each in a different bright color or color combination, were displayed. A white Lincoln Mercury trimmed in gold was a crowd stopper. Production Lincoln, Mercury, and Ford cars were available with plastic transparent roofs.

The biggest eye catchers of the show were the several "dream" cars and specially built models. Cadillac presented a "dream" car in the form of a fiberglass model called the La Espada (the sword). Lincoln Mercury gave the visitors a glimpse into the future with its recently announced XM 800 car, combining a sports car with "dream" ideas. Hudson expected its Italia, the company's recent entry into the "dream" car field, to steal the show. The company said it was a practical car with production possibilities.

For the mechanically minded, cars were displayed cut lengthwise so the workings of the motor, the details of the frame, and the springs and padding of the upholstery could be studied. Chevrolet had such a car mounted on a revolving stand with a mirror underneath, so that all of the working detail could be seen.

Highlighting the Ford Division exhibit was the company's new Thunderbird sports car mounted on a turntable with a hotel scene in the background. It was the first public showing in America of the new car. The Kaiser-Willys display featured the fiberglass Kaiser-Darrin sports car. Other "action" displays were also part of the exhibit. The Chevrolet Corvette fiberglass sports car, which had

The Willys display is in the foreground. The Packard display is to the right, behind Willys. (Courtesy of the National Automotive History Collection, Detroit Public Library)

already captured the public's imagination, was a featured display, and Studebaker had a black, Commander Starliner sports car.

Chrysler had the La Comtesse (the countess), a New Yorker de Luxe coupe with a clear plastic top and a special six-passenger Ghia-designed experimental model in addition to its regular models. The Desoto exhibit included a car called the Coranada and the Adventurer, designed in America, but built in Turin, Italy. An extra feature was the showing of a Technicolor film demonstrating the new Desotos and a back projection which simulated color television.

Car tops in bright wallpaper patterns which could match the seat covers was suggested by Mrs. Claude T. Porlet to the automobile industry. She was a paint company executive in St. Louis, and tried the idea herself. Wallpaper with pink and red roses against a white background was applied to the top of her black hardtop convertible. A transparent plastic coating protected the wallpaper.

Engineers were working on a V-6 engine for the car of the future. The first attempts resulted in the conclusion that it did not promise enough savings of gasoline or manufacturing cost to warrant the heavy tooling costs involved in putting it into production. Some engineers said it would cost almost as much to produce a V-6 as a V-8.

NOTE: The United States had three-quarters of the world's passenger cars in 1954, and most were made in Detroit. Each year thousands of motorists came from all parts of the nation to accept delivery of their new cars at the factory. They could save enough on freight charges to pay for a vacation for the entire family. Many new car buyers wanted to tour the factory to see how their new car was made. In most cases they got a royal tour, complete with luncheon, and courtesy transportation from the hotel. Pacific coast residents made up the majority of new car buyers that came to Detroit. The factory delivery service reached its peak in 1954 before most companies put into effect freight equalization plans lowering freight charges to the distant parts of the country.

"The Latest and Greatest in Cars and Stars"

1955
Model Year

DATE: January 29 – February 6, 1955

SPONSOR: DADA

BUILDING: The Michigan State Fair Grounds: The Coliseum, Agriculture, Commercial Exhibits, and Dairy buildings

ADMISSION: $1.25 for adults at the door
60 cents for children 12 and under at the door
$1.00 for adults in advance at Cunningham drugstores
50 cents for children 12 and under in advance
(This was an effort to reduce the long lines waiting to buy tickets.)

DECOR: The walls were draped and ceilings covered. A huge 40-by-40-ft. stage was constructed in the Coliseum. Turntables and smaller display units were installed. Runways were constructed to tie the four buildings into a single display unit. The decorations and designs were under the supervision of George P. Johnson Co. of Detroit, designer of the Chicago Auto Show for 1955 and other national and international fairs in past years.

ENTERTAINMENT: The stage show, directed and produced by Don Ridler, included: Don Cornell, recording star; The Salt City Five, Dixieland band; The Fontaine Sisters; Detroit's own "Gaylords"; The Honey Brothers, dance and comedy team; and Hershel Leih's 18-piece orchestra. Detroit's leading disc jockeys acted as masters of ceremonies to introduce the various acts.

THE OPENING: Auto industry and civic officials attended opening-day ceremonies on Saturday at 11:00 a.m. Acting Mayor Louis C. Miriani and Hugh Gorey, show chairman, participated in the ribbon-cutting ceremonies at the entrance of the Agriculture Building.

The DADA was host to city and village officials on specific days as follows: Sunday, "Dearborn Day"; Monday, "Hamtramck Day"; Tuesday, "Highland Park Day"; Wednesday, "Down River Day"; Thursday, "Wayne County Day"; Friday, "Grosse Pointe Day"; Saturday, "Oakland County Day"; Sunday, "Macomb County Day."

OFFICIAL 50¢ PROGRAM

annual

DETROIT AUTO SHOW

JANUARY 29th thru FEBRUARY 6, 1955
MICHIGAN STATE FAIR GROUNDS

Presented Under the Auspices of DETROIT AUTO DEALERS ASSOCIATION

155

Packard was now part of the Studebaker-Packard Corporation. Packard's production in Detroit ceased in 1956 when it was transferred to South Bend, Indiana. It became a re-badged Studebaker and lasted only until 1958. Note that Packard retained its famous "yoke" grille treatment. (Courtesy of the National Automotive History Collection, Detroit Public Library)

INSIDE THE SHOW: Close to 150 of the latest passenger cars and sports models, representing 19 different makes, were scattered throughout the four buildings of the Fair Grounds. There were also three truck makers in addition to dozens of engineering exhibits showing how the vehicles ran. New phrases were used to describe high-torque, flair-fashioned, wrap-around windshield, ball joint suspension, and many others.

Several exhibits featured floral displays in the background for the female models, lecturers, and other attractions. Many of the dealers eliminated the expensive side shows because they did not want to compete with the stage extravaganza. Salesmen were instructed to make the show "the sellingest" auto show ever and were offered bonuses and other prizes for best accomplishments. Several dealers had "mystery buyers" circulating. If a mystery buyer was impressed by the sales effort of his contact, the salesman was awarded a bonus check varying from $10 to $25.

Buick featured a four-door hardtop without center pillars. The Dodge display featured Betty Skelton, holder of the women's world speed record for stock cars. The Dodge LaFemme, designed especially for the ladies, but not yet in production, was seen for the first time in Detroit. Also in the Dodge booth were six trucks, one of them gold-plated. Highlighting the Hudson exhibit was the four-door custom Hornet V-8 done in coral and snowberry white.

Kaiser-Willys, with a cutaway chassis as a feature, had a Kaiser Manhattan, Willys Bermuda, and a jeep two-wheel- and four-wheel-drive station wagon. The Nash Holiday series was shown in a country club hardtop, sedan, and station wagon. Animated air conditioning, which Nash pioneered, was shown along with a single-unit body construction, twin travel beds, and reclining seats. Packard

156

displayed five cars including the "400" Patrician, Clipper, Constellation, and Clipper Deluxe. Packard's new torsion level suspension was also part of the exhibit.

Chevrolet displayed a Corvette plastic-bodied sports car with a V-8 engine for the first time. The Chevrolet Nomad station wagon, a "dream" car at General Motors Motorama in 1954, was now in production. Studebaker had its proving ground diarama on a 14-by-18-ft. stage showing its South Bend test facilities in miniature with small cars in operation on hills and curves.

NOTE: In 1955, there were more than 61 million motor vehicles in America. The 46.5 billion gallons of gasoline they burned could have filled a canal 20 ft. wide and 18 ft. deep from Portland, Maine, to Portland, Oregon.

DATE: February 18-26, 1956

SPONSOR: DADA

BUILDING: The Michigan State Fair Grounds: the Coliseum, Dairy, Agriculture, and Agriculture Annex buildings

ADMISSION: Saturdays, Sundays, and all evenings, $1.25 for adults and 60 cents for children under 12
Matinee rates weekdays until 6 p.m., $1.00 for adults, 50 cents for children (included stage show)

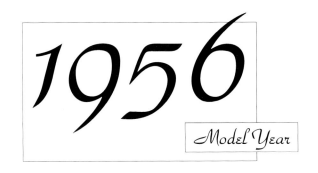

1956
Model Year

DECOR: Complementing the dazzling displays of standard make show cars, "dream" and experimental models, were special decorations with a "spring motif" of aqua green. All the buildings were decorated by George P. Johnson Co. of Detroit, under the direction of Ken Beer.

ENTERTAINMENT: Producer Haford Kerbawy was hired and dispatched to New York and Hollywood with $50,000 to spend on the entertainment portion of the show. Radio and television stars, including Gordon MacRae of "Oklahoma" fame, the Wiere Brothers, songstress Cathy Barr, and the dance team of Coles and Atkins, performed on stage in the Coliseum.

OPENING: More than 5,000 civic and business leaders and dealers' friends attended a preview showing Friday night, February 17th.

The show was officially opened on Saturday at 11:00 a.m. with Police Commissioner Piggins cutting a ribbon at the south entrance of the Agriculture building. Mayor Cobo originally was to cut the ribbon, but on his way back to Detroit his plane got stranded in a snowstorm.

INSIDE THE SHOW: The 1956 automobile look was one of safety. Chrysler and Ford advertised the safety of new door latches, seat belts, and dashboard padding. Chrysler's main contribution was a pushbutton gear selector on the left side of the steering wheel. Ford claimed a unique safety item in its deep-dish steering wheel to prevent the steering column from spearing the driver.

There were 18 makes of passenger cars, with over 100 cars on display, and three lines of trucks. The greatest array of "dream" and experimental cars ever displayed in Detroit, along with highly interesting and educational exhibits, helped create the most colorful show Detroit had ever seen. When the stage show

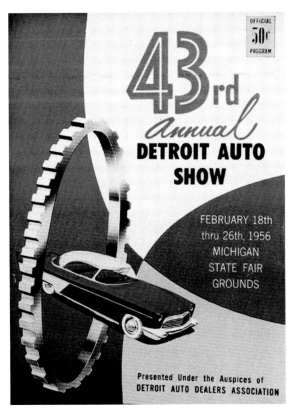

OFFICIAL 50¢ PROGRAM

43rd *annual*
DETROIT AUTO SHOW

FEBRUARY 18th thru 26th, 1956
MICHIGAN STATE FAIR GROUNDS

Presented Under the Auspices of
DETROIT AUTO DEALERS ASSOCIATION

Plymouth and Cadillac displays are on the left; Oldsmobile display is on the right. An Oldsmobile sign can be seen on the floor over the "Golden Rocket," a two-door sports coupe with a gold-colored fiberglass body. The front wheels were housed in twin torpedo pontoons that blended into a slim, aircraft-type nacelle. (Archives of Labor and Urban Affairs, Wayne State University)

started, Gordon MacRae began singing Cole Porter songs and everyone ran to the redesigned Coliseum to listen to him and other stars. After the floor show they went back to looking at carburetors.

The man who was painting the full-size clay model of a Ford Motor Co. future automobile had some trouble because the children said red and white was old-fashioned. "You want jet green and rocket gold?" he asked, and they said that might be attractive. They pushed the buttons on Dodge's pushbutton shift exhibit, and they pushed the buttons on the tilt-mounted Pontiac so fast it looked like a whirling dervish.

Chevrolet exhibits included air conditioning, the latest power and safety devices, and numerous engineering displays. Chrysler showed how its instant gasoline heater worked, and the Chrysler Imperial Southampton four-door hardtop was shown in Detroit for the first time. It had a rear side window, which opened and shut like a scissors. Most of the makes offered V-8 engines, and the most horsepower was available from Chrysler's model 300B, with 340 hp. Dual exhaust systems created a booming market in the muffler and tailpipe industry. The replacement market was helped further by an increase in city driving which cut muffler life by 25%.

Everyone knew that women were responsible for the rainbow of colors seen pouring down the nation's highways. Only 0.5% of American women were color blind compared to 7% of the male population (the colors changed with the weather, and matching some of those glamour shades when dented fenders were repaired was often as tricky as guessing which way a football would bounce).

Feminine influence in the car fashion was also seen in comfort and convenience. Car interiors were plotted around a pair of gauze-encased legs—door handles, ash trays, seat height, and door openings catered to 15-denier nylon hosiery. Practical, but ugly, black rubber floor mats gave way to fabric rugs. Automatic drive and power brakes were featured, along with record players and transistor radios available in the aftermarket from Motorola.

Suggestions from women called for a glove compartment that could hold a make-up kit, a man's electric razor, shaving lotion, and disposable towels. There was no reason why a small Pullman sink couldn't be added to the dashboard for freshening up while traveling. It could also provide cold drinking water. Other suggestions included a foot warmer, a hair dryer, electric heating unit for warming up a cup of coffee, a slot under the front seat to hold an umbrella, a space under the armrest to store a purse or portfolio, a massage machine to eliminate fatigue on the road, and a folding standup canvas bathhouse in the storage compartment, so a woman could change her clothes in privacy.

Ford Division's exhibit featured the Mystere "dream" car developed to study styling themes, particularly contours in steel. It had rear fins, a hinged bubble-type canopy, a steering wheel that could be positioned in front of either front-seat occupant and a rear engine compartment that could accommodate either a gas-turbine or conventional engine. Oldsmobile's Golden Rocket was a two-door sports coupe with a gold-colored fiberglass body. The front wheels were housed in twin torpedo pontoons and an aircraft-type nacelle that pointed out ahead of them and housed the engine. The Predictor, designed by the Packard Clipper division of Packard-Studebaker Corp., had roof doors which rolled up like the cover of a rolltop desk, and swivel-type front seats. What lies ahead? Charles T. (Boss) Kettering, who knew as well as anyone, said that it was utterly impossible to predict the future.

NOTE: In October 1956, the U.S. standardized with a 6-by-12-in. license plate, in which even the bolt holes were the same. The reasons given were to allow mounting the plate from inside the trunk, making them easier to install, easier to light, and harder to steal. With various sizes of plates, people tended to mount the brackets any old way and they were not protected from the mud either.

DATE: January 19-27, 1957

SPONSOR: DADA

BUILDING: Detroit Artillery Armory
(Eight Mile Road, east of
Greenfield)

ADMISSION: 90 cents for adults
45 cents for children under 12 (tax-free)

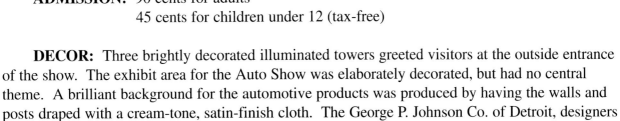

DECOR: Three brightly decorated illuminated towers greeted visitors at the outside entrance of the show. The exhibit area for the Auto Show was elaborately decorated, but had no central theme. A brilliant background for the automotive products was produced by having the walls and posts draped with a cream-tone, satin-finish cloth. The George P. Johnson Co. of Detroit, designers for the recent New York and Chicago shows, handled the decorations.

ENTERTAINMENT: In the quest for a new attendance mark, the usual stage show was eliminated to allow a reduction in the admission price. This led to a more evenly distributed attendance throughout the day, which helped reduce parking congestion since there were only 3,500 parking spaces.

OPENING: A special preview of the show was held Friday night for several thousand industry executives and their wives and guests.

Mrs. Henry B. Joy, 87-year-old widow of the Packard Motor Co. pioneer, arrived to the show in her 1915 Detroit Electric. She was greeted by Mayor Cobo and Harold C. Johns, show chairman, and cut the ribbons at 11:00 a.m. Saturday, officially opening the show.

INSIDE THE SHOW: The emphasis of the show was on the mechanics of the 1957 automobiles. With 262,000 sq. ft. under one roof, the displays consisted of 19 makes of passenger cars, four makes of trucks, and eleven makes of foreign cars. (There were ten foreign car dealers in the Detroit area, but only 800 cars, mostly German Volkswagens, were sold in 1956.) Seven Allied Industry companies displayed chemical, petroleum, and metallurgical exhibits, considered as an innovation for the show. Another highlight consisted of the Detroit Police Department, a special exhibit by Greenfield Village, and GM with its "Crossroads U.S.A." and "Preview of Progress" exhibits. The usual "Dream Car" displays were eliminated for the 1957 show.

The Auto Show had three times more space at the Armory than any previous exhibition. The photograph was taken with a new Japanese Panon wide-angle camera with a 140-degree angle. (Archives of Labor and Urban Affairs, Wayne State University)

The "safety packaging" trend, which started in the 1956 models of a few producers, became an industry-wide pattern. Instrument panels had recessed control knobs, crash cushions on the panels and sun visors, stronger safety door latches (which reduced door openings 60%), reinforced roofs and shockproof steering wheels (which reduced chest injuries by 50%). Seatbelts (which reduced injuries by 60%) were optional equipment with just about every 1957 line. Some models had the hood hinged at the front so the wind held them down in the event they opened accidentally on the highway (unfortunately, the hood could shear through the windshield and the front occupants, in the case of a head-on collision).

The garish colors of 1955 and 1956 were decreasing as more and more people chose softer colors for their 1957 cars. Black was returning, along with soft shades of blue, green, yellow, and off-white. The value of fins sparked a controversy among Chrysler engineers and stylists at General Motors. Fins could reduce steering effort in strong crosswinds by 20% according to Chrysler, but GM said it was only a styling feature.

Chevrolet's exhibit featured a 10-ft. water fountain on which colored lights played. The turntable technique was in widespread use to permit the prospective customer to inspect the car from all angles, along with its model. The Oldsmobile exhibit featured an automobile carousel called the "Merry Olds-Go-Round," with three of the company's nine models. The Chrysler Corp. featured the "forward look," including the Plymouth, said to be three years ahead of its time. The first Packards built in Studebaker's South Bend factories were shown as a four-door Clipper Sedan and a four-door hardtop station wagon. The top attraction at the show was the Ford exhibit of its retractable hardtop. This inspired a look at the European sliding roofs, and started a trend later called sunroofs.

NOTE: The first "National Show," sponsored by the Automobile Manufacturers Association (AMA), was held in New York in December 1956 after a lapse of 16 years. The Ford Motor Company joined the AMA as a full-fledged member in 1956, helping to spark dreams of a National Show in Detroit. George Romney, president of American Motors Corp., and the Automobile Manufacturers

Association, said Detroit should be the sight for the annual unveiling of new models. Detroit workers should be the first to see their products, and Detroit business and civic that put the world on wheels should reap the substantial benefits that go to the city that is the site of the big auto show.

The front license plate was abandoned in Michigan in 1945 and re-started in 1957. A scientific poll indicated that police used the front plate 85% and the rear 15% of the time while patrolling.

DATE: January 18-26, 1958

SPONSOR: DADA

BUILDING: Detroit Artillery Armory

ADMISSION: 90 cents for adults (tax-free)
45 cents for children (tax-free)
25 cents for students (tax-free)

1958

Model Year

OPENING: Dress rehearsal was held Friday night for civic leaders and press, radio, and TV representatives to preview the displays.

The show opened when a little Kelsey Motorette burst through a paper wall with the inscription "45th Annual Detroit Auto Show." Mayor Miriani rode with C.W. Kelsey at the tiller. The 77-year-old Kelsey was the car's inventor.

INSIDE THE SHOW: Luxury, fashions, and improved styling and engineering of the 1958 model passenger cars and trucks, mixed with a theme presented by foreign carmakers, were the keynotes of the 45th Annual Detroit Auto Show. (In August 1957 at the Statler Hotel, representatives from Ford, Chrysler, and GM said the foreign cars were an "eye catcher" and should be exhibited as a section apart from the American models. A vote was taken deciding in favor of the separate spaces.) George Walker, director of Ford styling, later made it clear that "although he did not think they were only a fad, American cars met the needs of the American public in a way that foreign cars were unable to."

There were 175 passenger cars, 30 trucks, and 60 foreign cars, consisting of 18 makes of American cars and 21 foreign makes, marking the first time foreign makes exceeded those of American makes. Also included in the show were the first public Detroit showing of the Army's Redstone missile, produced by Chrysler Corp., the Secretary of State's "telebinocular vision test," a display of 40 years of Michigan license plates, and a Junior Achievement display.

There were more than 400 accessories and optional equipment available that amounted to $500 to $1,000 per car. With air suspension, fuel injection, and a rear TV, the price of options could be as much or more than the car. Showing the largest gains on an industry-wide basis were power steering, automatic transmissions, power brakes, electric windshield wipers, and white sidewall tires, in that order. Declines were seen in tinted glass, dual exhausts, overdrive, windshield washers, and back-up lights.

How long could one auto plant keep producing without turning out two identical cars? Buick Division

FORTY FIFTH *Annual* DETROIT AUTO SHOW JANUARY 18 · 26 · 1958

DETROIT ARTILLERY ARMORY

OFFICIAL 50¢ PROGRAM

Presented under the auspices of the . . . **Detroit Auto Dealers Association**

The Detroit Artillery Armory, site of the 1958 show. (Courtesy of the National Automotive History Collection, Detroit Public Library)

of GM "guestimated" 1,830,196,293,120, or nearly two trillion cars. Parked end to end, 300 to the mile, that would have made a line nearly six billion miles long. At their rate of production, it would have taken more than 36 million years to make every possible combination of models, engines, color and trim, transmissions and other items that differed from car to car. Ford came up with 1,091,750,400 possibilities, and Plymouth ranged from 6,000,000 to almost infinite.

Oldsmobile displayed its television in the back seat and was one of the main eye catchers of the show. The new Edsel, ten years in the making, was the first volume production "name" car to be offered by the Big Three in 19 years and was closely inspected by the show visitors.

The Edsel display. The Edsel was named after Henry Ford's only child, Edsel Ford. The Edsel was introduced on Sept. 4, 1957, and lasted until 1961. The demise of this medium-priced car was mainly due to the post-Korean War recession. (Courtesy of the National Automotive History Collection, Detroit Public Library)

168

The foreign car displays. Note the Falvey Motor Sales sign on the curtains. Falvey was a pioneer of European car sales in the U.S.A. after WWII when U.S. cars were hard to get during the transition by automakers from war production back to automobiles. (Courtesy of the National Automotive History Collection, Detroit Public Library)

Lockheed Missile Systems announced that fuel cells, ten times more efficient than the car battery, might power future cars. Most automobile officials agreed that the flying automobile was a real possibility by the year 2000. Chrysler had an army contract to develop a flying Jeep. They imagined arriving at a beach club in an Aquacar, Autocopter, or just plane car.

DATE: November 22-30, 1958
(The show was moved up by two months, making it the first major exhibit of its kind in the United States.)

SPONSOR: DADA (the 50th anniversary)

BUILDING: Detroit Artillery Armory

ADMISSION: 90 cents for adults (tax-free)
45 cents for children under 12 (tax-free)
25 cents for students through high school (tax-free)

1959
Model Year

DECOR: Decorations for the exhibit were arranged by the Display and Exhibit Co., Detroit. For the first time in a Detroit show, the ceiling was completely draped to provide greater eye and sound appeal. Between 30 and 40 miles of fabric were sewn to fashion these decorations.

ENTERTAINMENT: More glamour and showmanship than ever before was put into the 1959 exhibition. While the crowds were interested in the cars, they also went for the stars of the show. Sometimes there were several musical productions underway at the same time. Emmet Kelly, world-famous clown, drew some of the largest crowds at the Desoto exhibit. Edsel arranged a large-sized swimming pool complete with bathing beauties and a tropical setting with live plants. Miss America, Mary Ann Mobley, reigned at the Oldsmobile exhibit.

OPENING: The show was opened at 11:00 a.m. Saturday, followed by Detroit Mayor Miriani and Windsor Mayor Michael J. Patrick driving a 1911 Stanley Steamer down the center aisle of the show and breaking the ribbon for the official opening at 2:00 p.m.

INSIDE THE SHOW: The exhibits included 17 American makes of passenger cars, and three makes of trucks. Because of the increased interest in foreign cars they were allotted 10% more space than the previous year, which accommodated the increase from 21 to 27 different makes. Together, the show was comprised of 170 American cars, 30 trucks, and 100 foreign cars. In addition to the 1959 lines of vehicles, there were several educational exhibits set up by the Secretary of State, Junior Achievement, and other sources.

Several American car producers reduced horsepower ratings to improve economy. Practically all of the 1959 cars were lower-priced than the previous year's models. The trend towards pushbutton operation for the transmission was continuing and new car finishes that required no waxing for two years were very popular.

Plymouth permitted visitors to take a safe driving test with up to 24 people participating at one time. Chevrolet presented a motion picture that made visitors hold on to their chairs as a five-minute film flashed across a portion of a 16-ft.-diameter sphere. Most of the exhibits had do-it-yourself displays that permitted visitors to learn for themselves how a certain part of a car worked. Women were especially intrigued with Chrysler's display of its new swivel seat. Mercury displayed its new "safety sweep" overlapping windshield wiper system that eliminated the old center blind spot of the windshield.

After WWII, people began to customize their cars and modify or replace engines to make them faster. Dragsters racing in quarter-mile "drag strips" were a result. The three-wheel dragster at the Auto Show was advertised as the world's lightest. (Archives of Labor and Urban Affairs, Wayne State University)

The new price labels on car windows—required by federal law—seemed to spur sales. People studied them and asked questions. Pound for pound, a car was considered a good buy. The average four-door, mid-sized sedan cost 72 cents per pound, compared to bicycles at 98 cents per pound, aluminum boats at $3.13 per pound, and a flannel suit or woman's hat at $17 per pound.

DATE: February 6-14, 1960

SPONSOR: DADA

BUILDING: Detroit Artillery Armory

ADMISSION: $1 for adults
                  50 cents for children under 12
                  25 cents students through high school

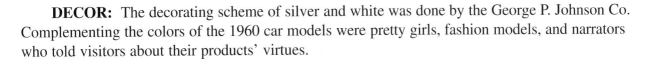

DECOR: The decorating scheme of silver and white was done by the George P. Johnson Co. Complementing the colors of the 1960 car models were pretty girls, fashion models, and narrators who told visitors about their products' virtues.

OPENING: A bicycle built for ten had the leading role for the opening of the 1960 show. The tandem bike, with members of the Wyandotte Oak Club in the saddles, drove through the ribbon to the waves and cheers of Mayor Miriani and officials of the DADA.

INSIDE THE SHOW: There were 25 makes of American passenger cars, three makes of trucks, and 28 makes of foreign cars. The Michigan Department of State had a special exhibit of eye-testing equipment. One of the more notable exhibits was Buick's fashion show where the latest in clothes as well as cars were shown. Another was Chrysler's Imperial exhibit where atomized perfume accented the French motif. Desoto's display featured an attractive model and French poodle with hair dyed the same shade of lavender.

Most of the new passenger cars were an average of 57 in. high, compared to 65-70 in. in 1953. Nobody was willing to say what the ultimate low would be, but the designers were limited by road clearance and the distance from the base of a man's spine to the top of his skull.

Compact cars became popular, following the lead of the Nash Rambler. The new Mercury Comet is shown here at the Auto Show. (Courtesy of the National Automotive History Collection, Detroit Public Library)

The 1960 Plymouth likely had the tallest fins ever on a production car. Chrysler engineers argued that the fins offered high-speed stability, while GM engineers said no. Strangely enough it was GM who started the fin craze with the 1948 Cadillac and its taillights that were designed to look like the tail fin of a WWII P-38 fighter aircraft. (Courtesy of the National Automotive History Collection, Detroit Public Library)

There was a revolution on as compact cars came into their own, with five companies producing them. Chrysler had the Valiant, Ford had the Falcon, GM had the Corvair, and Studebaker had its Lark. American Motors had the Rambler and boasted of pioneering the compact car. Some authorities believed the compact would have the biggest impact on the auto business since the 1908 Ford Model T.

The floor space for foreign cars was increased by 9,000 sq. ft. for a total of 42,000 sq. ft. to support the increasing interest in cars made outside the country. Models ranged from a two-seat Austen Healy Sprite to a Rolls Royce. Simca showed a futuristic car with functional fins that steered the car at high speeds when the front wheels lifted off the ground.

The term "low price three," referring to Chevrolet, Ford, and Plymouth, was no longer used since the compact cars destroyed the meaning. Also "medium-priced" was no longer used because the low-priced lines extended their lines into the medium luxury field, and the medium field extended their lines into the so-called "economy" field to achieve volume increases. There never was a "high-priced" field because of the negative connotation—they were always called "luxury cars."

"Wheels of Freedom"

1961

Model Year

DATE: October 15-23, 1960

SPONSOR: AMA (Automobile Manufacturers Association)

BUILDING: Cobo Hall

ADMISSION: 50 cents for adults
5 cents for children under 12

DECOR: A stage longer than a football field was used to display the passenger cars with a unique theme center measuring 350 by 90 ft. This stage was big enough to accommodate a 750-ft. continuous conveyor as well as space for the Auto Show's musical revue with its cast of 60 singers, dancers, and musicians. A dominant decorative feature was a 100-ft.-long structure symbolizing the show's theme of "Wheels of Freedom." Cars on the conveyor moved over pools of vari-colored water, with tires just skimming the surface.

OPENING: Nearly 84,000 people, by invitation only, jammed the Hall on Friday, prevue night. Attending was automotive, business, and government leaders, and a large audience of press, radio, and television representatives and their families. On Monday, October 17, the building's banquet hall was the scene of a black-tie dinner for automotive leaders and their guests, with President Eisenhower as honored guest and speaker. Top executives from the nation's automobile and truck companies, along with Mayor Miriani, turned the lights on at the show in a dramatic ceremony. They pulled levers on a large control panel on the giant stage, turning up the dimmed lights on the 6-1/2-acre floor, starting the 750-ft. carousel of cars.

An honored guest was Mrs. Ethel Cobo, widow of Mayor Albert E. Cobo, who was mentioned frequently as the driving force behind the imaginative plans for the tremendous building. Also present was Nancy Flemming, from western Michigan, crowned Miss America.

A one-hour television program of the show was carried on CBS on Sunday night. On Tuesday, government employees were given time off to see the show. Wednesday was "International Visitors' Day," and Thursday was "National Defense Day."

INSIDE THE SHOW: This was the 43rd National Automobile Show, the first to be presented outside New York city, sponsored by the AMA, and their first show since 1956. There were 13 passenger car and 12 truck producers with 300 displays. There were no foreign cars displayed at the show. In addition, a special World's-Fair-type exhibit called

NATIONAL AUTOMOBILE SHOW

OFFICIAL PROGRAM 50¢ · OCTOBER 15-23, 1960

Cobo Hall was dedicated at the opening of the National Automobile Show in October 1960. Although it was the 43rd show since the automobile manufacturers opened their first show in New York on November 3-10, 1900, it was the first one the manufacturers ever staged in Detroit.

"Auto Wonderland" (which alone was larger than most automobile shows of the past), was among the features of the show. This show-within-a-show was an integrated display, both entertaining and educational, showing what went into the making of automobiles and trucks. Altogether the vehicle suppliers, the petroleum industry, and 33 additional automotive supplier companies added up to 111 industry associations and company groups that exhibited.

President Eisenhower was the first U.S. President to attend a Detroit Auto Show. The President is in the center and AMA President "Tex" Colbert is to his left.

The American Motors "Rambler" display is in the foreground.

The first thing that became apparent for the 1961 models was that tail fins were becoming more subdued from an all-time high with the 1960 models, and compact cars were on the increase. Corvette stood alone as the only American sports car with a total volume of 43,000 from 1953 to the end of the 1960 model year. The other makers said they could not make a profit on such a low-volume car.

One driver in three was a woman and car styling was adapting to their needs. Efforts to please the woman went back to the glove compartment, "assist straps," inside lighting, carpeting, luggage space, the cigarette lighter, and the armrest. Women had much to do with the automatic transmission, power assists for steering and braking, adjusting seats, and operating windows, and cars which were lower and sleeker.

Door buttons were redesigned so they would not break a fingernail. Steering wheels were lowered and slanted and windows made larger to allow the smaller woman more vision. Instrument controls were moved closer together for the shorter feminine arm. The power brake was set at the same level as the accelerator. This enabled the high-heeled foot to pivot easily from one pedal to the other, reducing reaction time by 29%.

Other suggestions by women included wider doors for a more graceful entry and exit, decorative and easily cleaned upholstery, sun visors that were more adjustable with mirrors on the back, and glove drawers to replace the conventional compartment.

The experts forecast that by the end of the century, there would be a much wider variety of vehicles—some of them without wheels. Probably the greatest automotive changes in the 21st century would come in three fields: energy, materials, and controls.

This was the last year for Chrysler's Desoto.

NOTE: Plans for holding the show in 1961 (1962 model year) were dropped by the AMA due to the world's record crowd of the previous year of 1,403,000 visitors. They felt they should skip a year due to the high cost and to permit a better chance to prepare for such a huge event.

"*America Drives Ahead*"

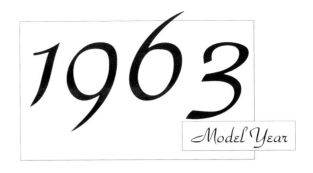

DATE: October 20-28, 1962

SPONSOR: AMA

BUILDING: Cobo Hall

ADMISSION: $1 for adults
35 cents for children under 12

DECOR: Dominating the center of the 300,000 sq.-ft. main display area was a 30-ft.-high, hourglass-shaped, white spectro-farm, with a revolving illuminated belt bearing the show's theme, "America Drives Ahead." There were reflecting pools and multi-color aluminum valences that bordered the theme center, along with carpeting and backgrounds for the various company exhibits.

General view of the show. The GMC display is in the foreground, followed by Dodge and Mercury.

The Studebaker display. Studebaker transferred production from Indiana to Canada from 1962 until 1966 when production stopped.

ENTERTAINMENT: A musical extravaganza, with the flair of a Broadway revue, was produced by John Wray, who for many years produced the Ed Sullivan television show. The revue featured original music, lyrics, and choreography, and was presented four times per day. Another invitational event was a special concert by the Detroit Symphonic Orchestra. Other sidelights of the show included a huge 50-car antique car rally on Sunday and a daily style show at Cobo Hall featuring some of the nation's best-known women's fashion designers. An Automotive Old-Timer's Dinner was held Friday before the show, featuring K.T. Keller as guest speaker.

OPENING: A nautical twist was added on Wednesday, prior to the show, when cars for the Chrysler-Plymouth Division were delivered to Cobo Hall on the steamship T.J. McCarthy. At noon, a 150-ft.-long Goodyear blimp arrived to advertise the show.

A national press luncheon and special preview was held on Friday, and a black-tie industry dinner was held Friday night where Henry Ford II, AMA president, presided at the opening and presented the city with flags from all 50 states to be permanently displayed in the main corridor at Cobo Hall. Ford called the cars at the show far better than those of five years before and added that they were materially increased in value per dollar. This was accomplished as a result of absorbing steadily rising costs of labor, materials, parts and services. But being a growth business, Ford said, it would involve for the future much more than giving better values. "It will also entail a constantly growing absorption with vast markets springing up all over the world. It will mean a growing exchange of skills and people and ideas throughout the free world."

Vice-President Lyndon Johnson was scheduled as principal speaker, but was forced to cancel due to the Cuban missile crisis, and Mayor Jerome P. Cavanagh, who was scheduled to give a brief speech prior to the Vice-President, took his place.

INSIDE THE SHOW: There were 34 lines of passenger cars and 11 lines of trucks totaling over 300 displays. There was a one-hour color telecast of the show on WWJ-TV from the NBC network.

One exhibit had cars arranged around a chalet surrounded by pools stocked with goldfish. Other settings included a country club entrance and a fraternity house. In another exhibit, the bodies of the cars rose 20 in. above their chassis, revealing all mechanical components in separation.

Oldsmobile had Jacquelyn Jeanne Mayer, Miss America for 1963, featuring special show cars called El Torero and a specially trimmed F-85 Cutlass convertible. Pontiac showed two dream cars, the Maharani and the Fleur-de-lis, and 23 production models. The theme of the Studebaker exhibit was "Outdoor Living is a Lark," with the Lark Daytona Wagonaire on display along with the revolutionary Avanti.

Flashy metallic car upholstery was dimming down to a discreet glimmer of Lurex threads in the 1963 models, due to feminine influence on interior stylists. Smooth upholstery replaced the tweeds—even truck drivers disliked nubby upholstery.

Because stiletto heels marked the carpeting and snagged in the area around the accelerator pedal, several companies provided vinyl floormats and nylon-strengthened carpets. Steering wheels swung away and adjusted up and down.

In the early days of the auto show, bathing suit contest winners were hired just to stand next to the cars and look alluring. In the late 1950s, the models wore gowns that matched the car's interior. For 1963, the upholstery fabrics were too stiff and didn't lend themselves to women's apparel, so the models were called narrators and they attended product sales training classes. They had to take care of the common questions such as "How much does this car cost?" "Are there other interiors available?" Are bucket seats available?"

NOTE: Wisconsin was the first of three states to require seat belts on new cars, followed by Rhode Island in 1964, and New York in 1965.

"Progress on Wheels"

1964

Model Year

DATE: January 18-26, 1964

SPONSOR: DADA

BUILDING: Detroit Artillery Armory

ADMISSION: $1 adults
50 cents for children under 12
25 cents for children through high-school age (11 a.m. to 5 p.m.)

ENTERTAINMENT: More than 5,000 people who crowded into an invitational preview Friday night were attracted by the action and animation that dominated the show. Visitors were entertained with balloon sculpturing, photo girls who took souvenir pictures, and a dialect comedian. There was also a free daily drawing for Kiddie Corvettes.

INSIDE THE SHOW: The show opened Saturday with all 30 American-built models and 18 foreign imports on display, along with three lines of trucks and several experimental "dream cars." The National Aeronautics and Space Administration displayed a Mercury space capsule with descriptive panels that explained the part played by the vehicle in launching men into outer space. There were also pretty girls galore; foremost of these was Miss America, Donna Axum, of Eldorado, Arkansas.

A Chrysler turbine car was under a spotlight on an elevated gold-carpeted platform. The Dodge Division featured a "sports truck" with bucket seats, a compact van, and a motor home with sleeping accommodations for eight people.

The opening ceremony. (Courtesy of the National Automotive History Collection, Detroit Public Library)

183

American Motors increased emphasis on their displays as seen with the Rambler in the foreground. (Courtesy of the National Automotive History Collection, Detroit Public Library)

Pontiac had two cars prepared exclusively for the Detroit show. There was the "Famme," a Tempest Lemans convertible with a brilliant red exterior, and a "Club de Mer," a Bonneville convertible.

Studebaker had a full line of cars on display, excluding the Avanti and Hawk which had been discontinued. There was a Canadian-built Cruiser and a two-door Commander Special with Daytona trim.

In a Lincoln-Mercury exhibit a team of six experts gave demonstrations of how a group of Comet cars were kept in condition to travel 100,000 miles in a durability run at Daytona Beach. In a matter of seconds, a team changed tires and fueled a car in a simulated pit stop. In other action, a Buick model exploded its front and rear panels to reveal the inner workings of the car, and Chevrolet had an exhibit that raised a Chevelle model, revealing the workings of the engine and other inner parts. Adding to the animation and action were bevies of glamour girls and male narrators, most of them on revolving turntables.

NOTE: Two-car families reached 8.7 million, double the number since 1954. The public had radios, heaters, whitewall tires, back-up lights, seat covers, and a side-view mirror on their list of "musts." Women drivers had increased 56% from 1956, while male drivers increased a mere 6%. The housewife was doing most of the family driving, and many spent more time driving than preparing food. Women had become a major influence on product design and automotive buying decisions. Items most frequently asked for by women were automatic transmission, power steering, and power brakes. Safety features such as seat belts, padded dashboards, and padded sun visors received enthusiastic support from women, largely for the extra protection they afforded their children.

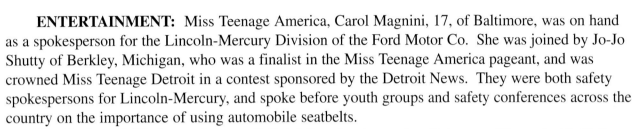

DATE: January 9-17, 1965

SPONSOR: DADA

BUILDING: Detroit Artillery Armory

ADMISSION: $1 for adults
50 cents for children under 12
25 cents for children through high school

ENTERTAINMENT: Miss Teenage America, Carol Magnini, 17, of Baltimore, was on hand as a spokesperson for the Lincoln-Mercury Division of the Ford Motor Co. She was joined by Jo-Jo Shutty of Berkley, Michigan, who was a finalist in the Miss Teenage America pageant, and was crowned Miss Teenage Detroit in a contest sponsored by the Detroit News. They were both safety spokespersons for Lincoln-Mercury, and spoke before youth groups and safety conferences across the country on the importance of using automobile seatbelts.

The Dodge exhibit featured pretty Gail del Corral, who made a living as a "live robot." Gail could stare for 15 minutes without blinking an eye and went through flawless mechanical movements that baffled the onlookers at the show. Chevrolet featured ventriloquist Jimmy Nelson, comedian and flip-flop tumble artist Mike Caldwell, and balloon sculptor Mel Snyder. Oldsmobile had 13 car models on display and on Tuesday and Wednesday presented Miss America, Vonda Kay Van Dyke, of Phoenix, a ventriloquist and singer.

OPENING: On Friday night, visitors braved a pouring rain to attend a preview of the show. Top automotive officials were enthusiastic over the exhibit, and said it was the most colorful ever held at the Armory. Among the general managers who attended the preview were Semon E. Knudsen of Chevrolet, Philip N. Buckminster of Chrysler-Plymouth, E.M. "Pete" Estes of Pontiac, and Paul F. Lorenz of Lincoln-Mercury.

The official opening was held Saturday morning when two young ladies rode a tandem bicycle through a ribbon stretched across the floor of the armory. The two young ladies were Donna Mae Mims, a national sports car driving champion, and Donna McKinley, who reigned as queen of the Indianapolis 500 in 1964.

INSIDE THE SHOW: The 49th Annual DADA Auto Show was sparked by more than 250 gleaming new cars and trucks, including foreign and experimental models, from 15 domestic makers, a dozen import makers, and three truck makers. Because the show was held earlier than in previous years, it was felt that many attendees would have otherwise missed it by going south on vacations.

Major styling changes included fastbacks with sloping roofs as well as those with the so-called "slab-styling," which had the sides of the cars flatter and more squared off with less sculpturing. There were more bucket seats and fold-down rear seats. Chrysler eliminated pushbutton transmission control and the industry accepted its curved window glass on the doors. Transistor ignition systems gained more prominence, and improvements in gas gauges and suspensions were made. Ford had an ignition key that could be inserted into the lock either side up. Chevrolet became the first company to introduce stereo into its radios.

The "Checker" was made in Kalamazoo, Michigan, until 1975. It was primarily used as a taxicab, but it found a market as a personal car also. (Courtesy of the National Automotive History Collection, Detroit Public Library)

Air conditioning was becoming regarded as a necessary item for all parts of the country. Some of the latest systems combined both cooling and heating in one unit. In addition to factory installation there was a growing market for "hang-on" units installed by the dealers or private businesses.

Six female narrators described the features of the special American Motors cars which were mounted on turntables. Pretty girls and male narrators explained the details of 17 different Dodge models, including a new "idea" car called the Charger II. It had a flowing fastback style with no visible bumpers, outside moldings, or sharp angles to interrupt what stylists called "flowing contours." An experimental Thunderbird at the Ford display had a unique "pistol grip" steering device, which permitted a driver to execute difficult hairpin turns or parking maneuvers merely by "twisting the wrist." Pontiac had a GTO Tempest convertible featuring seat panels of tiger skin and seat belts with tiger paw buckles; it was strictly a show car and not for production.

NOTE: Almost 15% of the cars on the road had faulty lights, faulty brakes, a leaky exhaust system, or unsafe tires.

DATE: November 27 – December 5, 1965
(The show date was changed to be
closer to the new model announcement
period when the public was most
interested in seeing and comparing the
new models. Also, the weather was
typically better at the end of November
than January, which made visiting the
show more pleasant.)

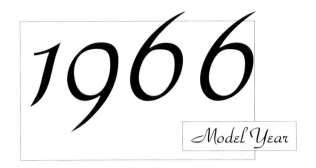

SPONSOR: DADA

BUILDING: Cobo Hall

ADMISSION: $1 adults
50 cents for children under 12
25 cents for students through high school on weekdays

DECOR: The 50th anniversary of the DADA Auto Show was emphasized by a number of old-time cars from the Henry Ford Museum. These included 50-year-old cars and some even older. Highlighted were the Stanley Steamer, Detroit Electric, the eight-cylinder Cadillac, and more than a dozen others.

ENTERTAINMENT: One of the exhibit stoppers was Gail del Corral, a famed "mechanical model" who could stand rigidly for eight hours like a store manikin or move mechanically like a robot. Miss America, Deborah Bryant, of Overland Park, Kansas, was at the Oldsmobile exhibit for four days.

The 1966 show was determined to be the 50th Annual Detroit Auto Show on the following basis: The shows started in 1902; there were no shows between 1942 and 1954; and the 1961 and 1963 shows were really national shows sponsored by the AMA. (Courtesy of the National Automotive History Collection, Detroit Public Library)

The Chevrolet display in the foreground is followed by Pontiac to the left and Plymouth to the right. (Archives of Labor and Urban Affairs, Wayne State University)

OPENING: An invitational preview was held Friday night. Mayor Cavanagh helped open the show, riding in a 1911 Chalmers "Pony" tonneau which broke through a ribbon stretched across a Cobo Hall aisle. Also riding in the vehicle was Patrice Gaunder, America Junior Miss of 1965. One of the features of the preview was the appearance of Countess Sybille Von Krockow, who was acting as women's consultant for the BMW line of cars.

An auto industry dinner was held on Wednesday attended by top officials of the American car companies, Detroit civic leaders, and presidents of the foreign car sales concerns in the United States. Honored at the dinner was Walter Bemb, old-time Hudson dealer and later Buick dealer of the late 1920s, who was the only living honorary member of the Detroit Auto Show committee.

INSIDE THE SHOW: The show contained 375 vehicles displayed across the 300,000 sq. ft. of space making up the main floor. They included 260 domestic models, 30 trucks, and 85 imported models.

American Motors had one show car called the St. Moritz, a classic station wagon with a specially designed observation roof in the rear, and glass that was tinted to reduce the sun's rays. Another show car, the Tahiti, was a luxury version of the fastback Marlin. An unusual feature was the appearance of several pedigreed dogs in the American Motors exhibit. Dog lovers, instead of looking at the cars, were busy seeking information about the animals.

The principal attraction at the Oldsmobile exhibit was the Toronado, the first full-size U.S. car with front-wheel drive since the 1937 Cord. Buick had a moving "spectacular" with a Wildcat body that exploded away body panels, trunk lid, fenders, and other components to permit the visitors to see its inner workings.

Among the scores of safety features predicted for future automobiles were soft padded interiors, contoured seats with lap and shoulder belts, recessed instruments and switches, and increased road stability. Further into the future, cars with computer guidance systems were predicted; insert pre-punched cards into a slot and the car would take you to a destination without the need to touch the steering system.

NOTE: When 1966 license plates were purchased, an extra dollar was included for those who had automobile insurance, but $35 was added for those without insurance. An extra $15 million was estimated to be added to the claims fund for the protection of "innocent" victims of accidents with negligent, uninsured drivers. The new law's philosophy was simply that the more drivers who were insured, the better off the public would be.

DATE: November 26 – December 4, 1966

SPONSOR: DADA

BUILDING: Cobo Hall

ADMISSION: 75 cents for adults in advance
$1.50 for adults at the door
35 cents for children under 12 in advance
50 cents for children under 12 at the door
50 cents for students through high school on weekdays

1967

Model Year

ENTERTAINMENT: For the first time in 10 years the Auto Show featured professional entertainment. Such stars as Margaret Whiting, Vikki Carr, the Four Lads, and Si Zentner entertained twice daily.

OPENING: The 51st show actually got started Friday night with an invitational preview for auto industry executives and public officials and their families. Among those present were Robert Anderson, general manager of the Chrysler-Plymouth Division, which included its new Barracuda, and John Z. DeLorean, general manager of the Pontiac Motor Division. Anderson quipped that "DeLorean and I toured the whole hall and decided we like our cars best."

The official opening took place Saturday when a golf cart-type vehicle driven by the show manager, Boyce Tope, with four pretty girls riding behind him in the cart, pulled a tent camper trailer down an aisle between rows of cars. Mayor Cavanagh was sitting in the trailer and was given the assignment to cut the ceremonial ribbon at noon.

INSIDE THE SHOW: It was the nation's largest auto show with 400,000 sq. ft. of exhibit space containing 250 domestic and 100 imported cars, plus more than 150 recreational vehicles. The

One of the many radio booths at the Auto Show. (Courtesy of the National Automotive History Collection, Detroit Public Library)

The import displays. Note to the left is a sign reading "Datsun." They were one of the top-selling imports but then changed their name to "Nissan." Perhaps not taking brand recognition into account, they have never fully recovered. (Courtesy of the National Automotive History Collection, Detroit Public Library)

campers, trailers, motor homes, and other recreational vehicles took the place of the big trucks displayed at prior auto shows. A new addition was Hall C, reserved for manufacturers of automobile accessories; exhibitors showed radios, air conditioners, batteries, luggage carriers, and related items.

Since 1956 the number of women drivers increased by 53% while the number of males had gone up by only 8%. "We estimate that women cast the final vote in three out of four car purchases in the United States," said William L. Mitchell, VP of the GM styling staff.

The Dodge exhibit had a mixture of the Old West where "Fort Rebellion" was staffed by a bevy of beautiful models. The Mercury exhibit had a caged display of live cougars. Oldsmobile had Miss America, Jane Ann Jayroe, and America's Junior Miss, Diane Wilkins, was at the Chevrolet display. Pontiac displayed two new customized show cars, the St. Moritz and the Surfrider. The St. Moritz was a Grand Prix convertible finished in a high pearlescent ice blue, with interior trimmed in ice blue leather. The Surfrider was a GTO trimmed in "surf blue" pearl leather with Hawaiian floral print insert on the seats. Also on display were old and rare automobile emblems. Plymouth had a simulated raceway and dragstrip in a special "performance corner."

There were many advances in the 1967 models, including efforts to improve ride and reduce noise and vibration. A number of changes were made to transmissions to provide smoother automatic shifts, and greater economy. There was a move toward low-profile tires to help improve performance for the high-horsepower cars.

A plastic "wire" that transmitted light like copper wire transmitted electricity was being used on some General Motors cars and GMC trucks. It could transmit light to places where instrument panel bulbs weren't practical. Batteries had improved inter-cell connections that improved cranking power in cold weather by 16%. The new batteries were improved so much that failures were almost a thing of the past.

There was a warranty war taking place that stirred up buyer confusion. In 1959 the new car warranty was 90 days or 4,000 miles. In 1960 Ford ended that 50-year tradition by instituting the first 12-month, 12,000-mile warranty. Other makers followed the Ford 12-12 pattern. But it lasted only 2 years, when in the summer of 1962, Chrysler announced a five-year, 50,000-mile power train warranty on its 1963 models. GM and Ford countered with a 24-24 warranty. Chrysler followed by guaranteeing the engine and driveline for five years, and the rest of the car for one year. In August of 1966 GM announced a 5-50 power train warranty and kept the 24-24 on the rest of the car. Ford and AMC followed suit. Chrysler upped the ante in September of 1966 by matching the 24-24 general warranty along with the 5-50 power train warranty, and that's where it stood at the time of the show.

DATE: November 18-26, 1967

SPONSOR: DADA

BUILDING: Cobo Hall

ADMISSION: $1.50 for adults
50 cents for children under 12

ENTERTAINMENT: Woody Herman, Bobby Vinton, Della Reese, the Detroit Wheels, the Debutantes, and the Tidal Waves were featured entertainers.

OPENING: Governor Romney cut the ribbon Saturday morning to open the show. He was greeted by three pixie-like girls in pink and orange miniskirts who looked to him "like characters from Shakespeare."

1968

Model Year

Chevrolet is in the foreground, followed by Plymouth. (Archives of Labor and Urban Affairs, Wayne State University)

INSIDE THE SHOW: There were 450 vehicles, including well-represented foreign cars. They ranged from VW to Rolls Royce with a velvet rope discreetly barring visitors from doing anything but looking from a distance. Recreational vehicles, campers, trailers, and motor homes were also represented at the 52nd Detroit Auto Show.

Entering the vast Hall, the spectators were greeted by a glittering display of cars and cuties, all color-coordinated and coached to the peak of sales appeal. Charlene wore a microskirt at Ford's display, looking like Robin Hood with hip boots and net hose. Her job was to stand next to a copper XL Fiera and smile. Pontiac's wide-track girl was dressed in James Bond black tights, tempting prospective buyers to be "pampered" in a bright yellow Firebird. A bevy of go-go girls in silver minis demonstrated Oldsmobile's "mod-rod" 4-4-2, and sang the praises of a fully synchronized 3 "on the floor" transmission.

American Motors had five art students painting a pink, blue, and yellow psychedelic Javelin. Chrysler had a driving game for "future drivers." The kids ran down a simulated pedestrian crossing and crashed into a school bus to learn valuable lessons in reaction time. Joe Kaliff drew caricatures of Dodge exhibitors.

Teenagers headed for the sporty cars, housewives loved the sub-compacts, and families tried out big four-door models or station wagons. Rising young executives looked at expensive sports cars, while the established executives climbed into the biggest limousines.

Tire kicking was out; visitors patted the fenders, rubbed the chrome, and slammed the doors. Next, they sat in the cars and ran through the gears, turned the steering wheel, twisted all the dials and pushed all the buttons on the dash, and uttered "oohs and aahs."

"Cars and Stars"

DATE: November 30 – December 8, 1968

SPONSOR: DADA
(There was some speculation that
the industry might resume
sponsoring a national auto show in
Detroit. But the Detroit dealers felt their show had become so popular that the
manufacturers would let things stand the way they were.)

BUILDING: Cobo Hall

ADMISSION: $1 for adults in advance
$1.50 for adults at the door
50 cents for children under 12
free for servicemen in uniform
free for senior citizens Monday, Tuesday, and Wednesday

DECOR: 400 workers laid 275,000 sq. ft. of carpeting and 20 miles of electrical cable.

ENTERTAINMENT: The formula for the entertainment consisted of lots of pretty models and
sports celebrities. Hall D on the lower level was turned into a 2,500-seat theater for a twice-daily
show featuring, among others, Tigers stars Mickey Lolich singing and Denny McLain on the organ,

(Courtesy of the National Automotive History Collection, Detroit Public Library)

The import displays. (Courtesy of the National Automotive History Collection, Detroit Public Library)

although he missed the first three days because of an appendectomy. Bob Durant and his orchestra, singer-comedian Paul Lennon, and ventriloquist Jimmy Nelson were also featured.

Other celebrities such as Bobby Unser and Dan Gurney, golfers Arnold Palmer and Byron Nelson, Miss America, Judith Ann Ford, and members of the Detroit Tigers and Lions also made show appearances.

OPENING: The traditional Friday night invitational preview was cancelled. The show opened at noon Saturday when "The Milk Truck," a customized hot rod, broke the ribbon for the 53rd Detroit Auto Show. Aboard the showpiece were Fran Garten, Miss Teenage America; Harry Tennyson, chairman of the show; Judith Anne Ford, Miss America, and Linda East, Miss Detroit Auto Show.

A special auto industry dinner was held Tuesday night, attended by all the top executives, with Senator Philip A. Hart as guest speaker. An award of honor presentation was made to automobile pioneer Charles S. Mott for his outstanding contributions to the industry.

INSIDE THE SHOW: There were 230 American cars and 50 imported cars on display. Several experimental or show cars like the hot rod "Milk Truck" and the "Bathtub Car," made largely of bathroom fixtures, and sport and recreational vehicles were also featured.

Many of the so-called standard models had a longer wheelbase, or a greater overhang length, or both. The extra length coupled with a rounder appearance gave many cars a "torpedo look." Hidden windshield wipers was growing in popularity.

The safety race was on! Ford Motor Co. offered anti-skid braking on the Continental Mark III as an option, and a collapsible frame on all of its full-size cars. General Motors' full-size cars all had a hidden bumper built into the doors and side panels. Many of the GM cars had a metal bulkhead between the trunk and the rear seat. For better interior occupant protection, instrument panels and door interiors were made with padding. The instruments were clustered directly in front of the driver, with the rest of the panel a broad expanse of padding. This "cockpit" approach, best executed on the big Ford and the Pontiac Grand Prix, was attractive and was expected to be copied by other cars. Front headrests were required after the first of the year, with many of the 1969 models already equipped with them. Shoulder and lap belts continued to be required.

Sales of the imports was reaching the one million mark and was not going unnoticed in Detroit. The Dodge exhibit had nearly 30 gorgeous models and Karrel Fox, known to Detroiters as Milky the Clown, entertained visitors with his magic shows. The Chevrolet display included a "doubleheader" Camaro, billed as one of the most complicated animated exhibits ever built. Using three turntables, a Camaro changed front ends: One had a six-cylinder engine and a standard grille; the other had an SS 350 V-8 front end with a Rally Sport grille.

DATE: November 15-23, 1969

SPONSOR: DADA

BUILDING: Cobo Hall

ADMISSION: $1.75 for adults
50 cents for children under 12
Free for servicemen in uniform
Free for senior citizens on Monday, Tuesday, and Wednesday

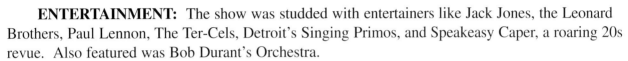

ENTERTAINMENT: The show was studded with entertainers like Jack Jones, the Leonard Brothers, Paul Lennon, The Ter-Cels, Detroit's Singing Primos, and Speakeasy Caper, a roaring 20s revue. Also featured was Bob Durant's Orchestra.

Personalities on hand included Detroit's Pam Eldred, Miss America, at the Oldsmobile display; world champion skier Jean-Claude Killy at the Chevrolet display; and golfer Lee Travino at the Dodge display. The Lincoln-Mercury display featured racer Cale Yarborough, Jesse Owens, Gordie Howe, Mel Farr, Mike Lucci, Wayne Walker, and Al Kaline.

OPENING: A VIP preview was held Friday night, attended by some of the top brass of the auto industry. Among the guests were GM Chairman James M. Roche and Chrysler Chairman Lynn A. Townsend and their wives. All the car division general managers attended the preview. They took some close looks at competitors' exhibits and didn't seem to mind being photographed there. The black-tie preview was for the benefit of the Old Newsboys Goodfellow Fund, which still pledges "No Kiddie without a Christmas."

INSIDE THE SHOW: The 54th Detroit Auto Show featured 300 vehicles on display, which included the leading domestic and imported models, totaling 30 separate exhibits. All of the U.S.

Miss America for 1970 was Detroit's Pam Eldred, and she served as Miss Detroit Auto Show. To her right is the show manager, Boyce Tope. (Courtesy of the National Automotive History Collection, Detroit Public Library)

carmakers had displays along with 14 foreign car manufacturers. There were also recreational vehicles, trucks, and far-out show cars.

Many cars wore sparkling new color combinations, which looked like the show cars in the previous year's show. Wing-like spoilers on the trunk and air scoops on the hood were popular. There were new engines that were bigger and more powerful than the 1969 models, such as Cadillac's 500-cu.-in., 400-hp engine, which was the largest production engine in the world. Also new were hidden radio antennas fitted between the layers of windshield. The trend toward longer hoods and shorter rear decks continued. Some of the Pontiac models had plastic gas tanks which could be molded into many different shapes and were lighter than conventional metal tanks. Side windows were discontinued on several car lines, much to the chagrin of smokers. Some of the cars were easier to service with clocks and other electrical equipment that could be removed from the front of the instrument panel.

All of the firms made changes to meet the evaporative emission control standards in California. To comply with U.S. safety standards, all cars were required to have a device to lock the steering column and the transmission. Ford made anti-skid braking standard on the Continental Mark III, and almost all of the cars had the longer-wearing, bias-belted tires.

The fastest-growing accessory on the new models was air conditioning. Factory air conditioning was installed on 29% of the 1966 models, 35% of the 1967 models, 41% of the 1968 models, and 55% of the 1969 models. There were also several hundred thousand aftermarket installations, particularly on the smaller cars.

"Dream cars" were a featured attraction, although they were on the decline. A Dodge show car, named the Mink Challenger, was trimmed with Natural Ranch Mink, Autumn Mink, and White Mink, with floor carpeting made of a specially dyed Icelandic sheep pelt. The Plymouth Beep Beep X-1 was described as a royal roadrunner-inspired idea car featuring dual racing fuel fillers in both rear quarter panels, and a functional roll bar containing adjustable airflow spoilers which the driver could use to increase or decrease the downward forces exerted on the vehicle. Other show cars included the Pink Panther from California and the Outhouse car with design to match.

NOTE: In January 1970, Ted's, a landmark at Woodward and Square Lake Road, closed its drive-in. For more than four decades, Ted's was a magnet for hot cars and cool teenagers. The drive-in was the terminus for a drag strip along Woodward, extending from Royal Oak. The general feeling among the police was that it would cut down on drag racing.

DATE: November 21-29, 1970

SPONSOR: DADA

BUILDING: Cobo Hall

ADMISSION: $1.00 in advance
$1.75 for adults at the door
50 cents for children under 12

1971

Model Year

ENTERTAINMENT: Instead of a live stage show, there were drawings for nine free trips to Hawaii and one trip around the world. There was also a chance to win a new motor home. Showgoers used part of their tickets to enter the contest. The object was to guess how many plastic balls were placed in the motor home. After the count was made, J.P. McCarthy, radio personality, Federal Judge Damon Keith, and Circuit Judge George Bowles examined the entries to determine who was closest. In addition, each night, radios, televisions, and cars were auctioned off.

OPENING: The show was given a formal preview Friday night by members of Detroit's Society for the Benefit of Children's Hospital. The official opening took place Saturday morning when Detroit's Mayor Gribbs drove Dennis Gilbo, a quadriplegic and an honor student at Wayne State University, across the ribbon. The new Maverick driven by the Mayor was later equipped with a special control and presented to Dennis Gilbo on behalf of the Detroit auto dealers. The annual auto show dinner was held Tuesday night with featured speaker Douglas Toms, director of the National Highway Safety Bureau.

INSIDE THE SHOW: The show featured 330 American cars, 20 imported cars, and recreational vehicles. The expression "look at those beautiful models" had a double meaning with 150 striking feminine attractions at the show.

(Courtesy of the National Automotive History Collection, Detroit Public Library)

203

The automobile industry had almost given up those "Gee, golly, look at that" dreamboat show cars. The show car had become a practical market probe which could be brought into production within a couple of years. They had become known as "pushmobiles" formed with fiberglass or sheet metal with an eye-catching high finish. The carmakers "floated" them around to the big shows to test public reaction.

The Ford exhibit included two new dream cars. One called the Tridon was based on the Thunderbird. Broad, low and rakish, it featured a long sleek hood and forward-thrusting fenders with a fastback roofline. It was finished with 20 coats of lacquer called "Moongold Mist." The biggest attention grabber at the Ford exhibit was the new Pinto.

Cars were not designed specifically for men anymore, but rather for all drivers. The industry began to realize drivers came in all sizes and the petite woman who had to struggle to reach the pedal could be a hazard on the road. Women's smaller hands, often with long fingernails, were taken into account. They wanted knobs and handles that were easy to operate. They wore high-heeled shoes, so padded areas that prevented heels from tearing the carpet were added, as well as upholstery that would not damage fur coats or snag stockings. Tilt steering wheels allowed easy entry and exit without awkward movements, and interior fabrics had color stability and soil resistance.

Some of the not-so-obvious changes for the 1971 models included polyurethane foam for seat construction to provide more comfort. The hood release was located inside the passenger compartment for added protection from theft. Stereo cassette tape players and recorders were featured in the Dodge, Chrysler, and Plymouth cars. Chrysler wagons had "auto-lock" for the tailgate door. Standard-size GM cars had instrument panels designed so repairs could be made quickly from the front instead of underneath. The top could be removed from the Cadillac instrument panel for easy access of the various parts inside. GM station wagons featured an all-new "disappearing" tailgate, and Chrysler had headlamp washers. VW introduced a space-age one-plug diagnostic system and Ford's new AM-FM radio featured integrated circuitry (IC) to give better performance.

NOTE: Amidst all of the technology of the automobile, an experienced blacksmith could make $30,000 per year shoeing horses, far in excess of the autoworker.

"Wheels & Winners '72"

1972
Model Year

DATE: November 20-28, 1971

SPONSOR: DADA

BUILDING: Cobo Hall

ADMISSION: $1.00 in advance
$2.00 at the door (The 25-cent price increase had to be approved by the Office of Emergency Preparedness. The decision to raise the price was made in May, well in advance of President Nixon's wage-price freeze. The extra quarter was added on to cover the higher rental rates at Cobo Hall.)

ENTERTAINMENT: The twice-a-day professional stage show again was omitted in favor of daily drawings for expense-paid trips to Acapulco and a drawing on the final night for a trip to the Fiji Islands. Visitors to the motor home exhibit, in addition, had an opportunity to win one of four recreational vehicles by guessing the number of nuts and bolts contained in a plastic dome. Also, veteran auto auction circuit rider Joe Tate of Warren auctioned off a car each of the nine nights of the show.

OPENING: A black-tie charity preview of the show was held Friday night. The $25-a-couple affair raised $40,000 for the benefit of Children's Hospital.

INSIDE THE SHOW: The 56th Auto Show hosted more than 300 vehicles, including 18 imported makes, and 85 recreational and specialty vehicles as part of the motor home exhibit. A special show area was set aside for a half-dozen championship racing cars.

There were several experimental vehicles in the show. The foremost was General Motors' Experimental Safety Vehicle, a prototype built for the U.S. Department of Transportation under a $1 contract. Buick featured a Silver Arrow III model of a Riviera which incorporated an experimental headlight system.

The dream car was dead but the automotive stylist was very much alive, testing his talents as never before on problems thrown at the auto industry by Ralph Nader-style critics and the federal government. There were fewer beautiful women than in previous years describing the cars on display. With the emphasis on safety and engineering—so-called nuts and bolts rather than styling—men seemed to be more believable.

There were few styling changes for the 1972 models—a trend expected to continue industry-wide. The big Chevrolet featured a stronger, heavier bumper designed to withstand a 5-mph crash. The Vega minicar got a glovebox and a new three-speed transmission. Cadillac offered an anti-skid braking system. The Chrysler Imperial had an electronic ignition system as standard.

The American cars included a number of new comfort features. The buyer wanted his auto to ride quietly, without vibration. He wanted to get in and out without banging his head or knees. People wanted stereo radios and tape players and air conditioning. Some cars were equipped with automatic headlight dimmers, electric door locks, hood and trunk locks, and electrically adjustable seats. American cars were going soft. Ford Motor Co. offered a reclining passenger seat on its top line LTD and Thunderbird cars.

The import displays. (Courtesy of the National Automotive History Collection, Detroit Public Library)

"*1973 Auto Circus*"

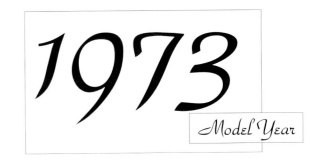

DATE: November 18-26, 1972

SPONSOR: DADA

BUILDING: Cobo Hall

ADMISSION: $2.00 for adults
50 cents for children
$5.00 for large families

ENTERTAINMENT: A circus motif was featured with 20 clowns providing almost constant entertainment. There were contortionists, puppeteers, jugglers, and magicians who worked balloons into fascinating animals. In addition, there was a 640-sq.-ft. model circus, built on a miniature scale by a former Ringling Bros. clown. Why clowns at the auto show? The show chairman, Jerry Bielfield, said: "If this gets the kids after their parents we may get another 50,000 people at the show."

In the adjoining Cobo Hall Arena, showgoers were able to view the full-length motion picture "Grand Prix." A highlight of the show was the nightly auction of a new car, snowmobile, and trail bike to the highest bidders.

OPENING: There was a black-tie preview of the show on Friday night at $25 a couple to benefit Children's Hospital.

INSIDE THE SHOW: On view at the 57th Detroit Auto Show was more than 250 of the 1973 model cars and trucks of all U.S. manufacturers and most manufacturers from abroad. The entire

A 640-sq.-ft. model circus, built on a miniature scale by a former Ringling Bros. clown, is in the background. (Courtesy of the National Automotive History Collection, Detroit Public Library)

207

area of Hall D was given over to an exhibit of 100 recreational vehicles, including motor homes, pickup campers, folding camp trailers, and travel trailers.

There were displays of futuristic safety cars by Ford and Toyota as well as many special exhibits featuring the safety equipment being installed in the 1973 cars. Some of the car exhibits featured entertaining "side shows"—demonstrations by sports stars and live family entertainment.

Low-speed-impact bumpers were the major highlight of the new cars—front bumpers protected for a 5-mph impact and rear bumpers for 2.5-mph impact. Some models had bumpers 5 in. away from the grille, while the Oldsmobile had a grille designed to move with the bumper in a crash. Openings in the hood allowed both the bumper and grille to move backward together. Other makes used the rubber ball approach, with a unique soft nose design to absorb energy.

It was clear that 1973 was the "year of the bumper" for the auto industry; however, there were other changes such as thick side pillars. The conventional hardtop and convertible disappeared from these lines. Aside from bumpers, only Ford had any major styling changes.

NOTE: Everyone knew that Detroit was the automobile capital of the world, but only 11% of America's cars were assembled there—including 4% which was actually done in Hamtramck. Chrysler's headquarters was in Highland Park, and Ford's in Dearborn. Although General Motors and American Motors had their headquarters in Detroit, they didn't build a single car there. Although the final assembly of cars was scattered around the country, the bulk of the basic parts manufacture and administration still lay in Michigan, where more than 300,000 people were employed in the vehicle and parts manufacturing business. The next most-involved state was Ohio with 120,000 people working in automotive manufacturing.

"A Ride Down Memory Lane"

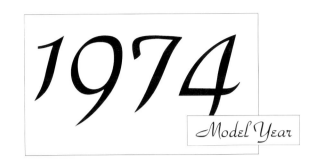

DATE: November 17-25, 1973

SPONSOR: DADA

BUILDING: Cobo Hall

ADMISSION: $2 for adults
$1 for teenagers
50 cents for children under 12

ENTERTAINMENT: The top attraction of the show was the dance competitions, when local radio and television personalities such as Dick Purtan, Jimmy Launce, Sonny Eliot, and Bob Hines played recorded music of the 30s on Tuesday, 40s on Thursday, and 50s on Saturday.

W.C. Fields was impersonated by nationally known Karrel Fox at the Dodge exhibit. Another attraction was the selection of Miss Detroit Auto Show, chosen by a panel of judges, from entrants by each of the U.S. auto companies' divisions.

OPENING: A black-tie charity preview of the cars was held Friday night before the official show opening, attracting some of the big names of the auto industry, and benefiting Children's Hospital. The 58th Detroit Auto Show opened officially on Saturday morning after a parade of more than 100 antique cars through downtown Detroit. The parade was in keeping with the "nostalgia" theme of the show. Walter J. Bemb, one of the foremost auto pioneers, rode in the car that broke the ribbon to open the show. He began his career in 1902 as a mechanic for Detroit's first dealership, The William L. Metzger Co. At 88, he still worked daily as a manufacturer's representative in the Fisher Building.

INSIDE THE SHOW: The show was held at a time when the industry was beset with problems caused by the nation's energy crisis. The firms tried to continue selling full-size cars but were

(Courtesy of the National Automotive History Collection, Detroit Public Library)

Publicity tour with Boyce Tope standing in the passenger seat. The GM building is in the background. (Courtesy of the National Automotive History Collection, Detroit Public Library)

converting some of their plants to increase production of smaller, more economical cars. In addition to 300 cars and trucks by domestic and foreign carmakers, the show featured nine antique cars. More than 100 recreation and camping vehicles, whose sales were being hurt by the energy crisis, were downstairs in Hall D.

A trend toward personalization and nonconformity helped people turn to trucks as a means of transportation. There was much less of a need to keep up with the Joneses, and trucks accounted for 33% of domestic vehicle sales. Pickups were used as a car, recreational vehicle, farm truck, off-road vehicle, delivery van, service truck, wrecker, and even highway tractor. This was a pretty good indication that trucks were close to becoming the best-selling product.

The 1974 cars offered a better view due to increased usage of glass. You could watch the pitter-patter of raindrops through a silver- or gold-tinted glass moonroof, available on Lincoln-Mercury's Mark IV and Ford's Thunderbird. Oldsmobile had "Vista Vent" of tinted plastic glass over the front seat area. Chrysler increased glass by more than 25% over the amount in 1973. The hottest thing going was the "porthole" window in the rear side pillar. It was a return to the so-called "opera windows" that came in during the horse and buggy.

General Motors had a convertible top on six of its lines but Chrysler and Ford felt it phased itself out and died a natural death. The design people said the convertible leaked and rattled, the tops needed frequent replacement, and the back windows were difficult to see through; it also let in engine and road dirt, and produced an aerodynamic effect that blew hair forward from the back of the neck, producing both disarray and discomfort. The introduction of air conditioning, the hardtop body, and the vinyl roof were the biggest factors in the decline of the convertible.

New safety items were featured such as the fail-safe accelerator that was required so that if a failure in the gas pedal system occurred, the engine returned to idle speed. The cars had stronger roofs for rollover protection. In addition the cars had a controversial starter ignition interlock system. The driver and the front seat passenger had to buckle their combined lap-shoulder belts before they could drive away. Federal law also made it illegal to change the odometer to make a car appear less traveled than it really was.

The new mid-size American Motors Corp. Matador had all-new sheetmetal for 1974 along with new frames, door glass, sloping hood, and rear deck. After having interior styling created by Gucci,

Pierre Cardin, and Levis in prior model years, American Motors selected Oleg Cassini to take the concept further and play a large role in exterior styling as well as the interior.

A unique option on full-size Pontiacs was adjustable brake and accelerator pedals. They could be moved forward or backward 4 in. to offer more driving comfort especially for shorter people. Officials said it could be the forerunner of cars with fixed seats, integral with the body for additional strength and safety, and fully adjustable pedals and steering wheels.

Oldsmobile featured a "message center" design instrument panel with warning indicator lights in one centrally located area directly in front of the driver. Chrysler had an electronic instrument panel system using light-emitting diodes (LEDs). Officials said the LED, a solid-state device that glowed when a voltage was applied, was superior to a light bulb. They were used as warning lights on fuel and temperature gauges. Cadillac had an automatic antenna that rose when the AM-FM radio was turned on. Ford Motor Co. had a new solid-state ignition system standard on the large V-8s. They promised elimination of the point and condenser replacement and more precise ignition over extended mileage.

NOTE: The Automobile Club of Michigan predicted that 84% of gas stations would be closed on Sundays due to the energy crisis. There were long lines at the gas stations to keep cars filled up. Probably the ultimate answer to the energy crisis was a gasoline-powered pogo stick that was shown at the Chicago Auto Show. It was called a "Hop Rod" and cost $70. It had a small engine enclosed in its frame and was supposed to get 565,000 hops per gallon. The stick went "ker-pop, ker-pop," at every hop, with the engine driving the frame upwards, traveling at a full speed of 2.1 mph.

DATE: January 11-19, 1975

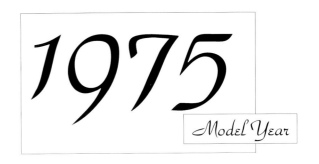

(There was no auto show in 1974, with the previous one held in November 1973. Jerry Bielfield, the chairman of the show, said the DADA had been waiting for some time to change the date to January but the time slot was held by the Society of Automotive Engineers for its annual conference and exposition. However, the SAE moved its show to late February and gave the DADA the opportunity to get the January period. Bielfield thought it was a good idea to have the show later because it gave the dealers a chance to shake things out, so the manufacturers, dealers, and public all knew where they were going. The November period came too soon after public introduction and the dealers felt they weren't getting the mileage out of the show that they should have been getting. The show had to compete with football season, the hunting season, Thanksgiving holiday, and so on.)

SPONSOR: DADA

BUILDING: Cobo Hall

ADMISSION: $2 for adults
50 cents for children under 12
Free to senior citizens (65 and over)
Free to laid-off autoworkers and their families on weekday afternoons

OPENING: The traditional charity show was held Friday night, preceding the official opening Saturday morning. Board Chairman and presidents of three of the four largest U.S. auto companies, along with their wives, roamed about Cobo Hall inspecting the new car exhibits. They headed to their own exhibits first, and then set off to competitors' displays. Funds from the $25-per-couple preview went to Children's Hospital.

INSIDE THE SHOW: The show featured 250 domestic and imported cars and motor homes in exhibit areas prepared by the auto manufacturers and manned by Detroit area auto dealers. Another crowd pleaser was a collection of old cars that once belonged to movie stars Charlie Chaplin, Jimmy Dean, Rita Hayworth, and gangsters Bugs Moran and Al Capone.

A new era of practicality set in and caused the demise of the so-called "dream cars." The emphasis was changing from styling to safety and practicality. The auto companies could ill-afford the huge costs for dream cars at the same time of meeting federally required pollution and safety controls along with slumping auto sales. Futuristic cars had become "feelers" to see if the public had an interest in them—they were used for market research.

The big American car accounted for only half of all U.S. sales. All the auto executives believed the long-term future was in small cars, and expected 80% of sales by 1980. The star attraction of the show was the new AMC Pacer, which was expected to be a trend-setter. It was a small car, but wide with 50% more glass than any car in its size. It was available in one body style—a two-door, with a

Cars were auctioned at this year's show. (Courtesy of the National Automotive History Collection, Detroit Public Library)

larger curbside door to ease entry and exit of rear-seat passengers. The car was designed from the inside out "with people considerations being paramount."

Chevrolet introduced its new Chevelle Laguna Type S3 as a mid-year 1975 model. It featured a new front-end design that was color-keyed to exterior and interior trim and paint treatments, including optional roof and body striping. Also shown for the first time in Detroit was the 1975 model Dodge Colt, Chrysler Corporation's subcompact import.

Imported cars featured new styling including Opel, British Leyland, Fiat, Saab, Volvo, Subaru, Capri, and Colt. Volvo, noted for its emphasis on safety, redesigned the front end of its new 240 series for even more crash protection. It also featured new "see-through" headrests, which improved rear vision.

Every year, more optional equipment was ordered regardless if it was a bad year or good year for car sales. Conventional items like sunroofs as well as new options such as a lighted outside thermometer were in demand. There was a trend toward standardization of the popular options because it simplified production; but pricing competition was a factor working against it.

"The Great Cars...Today's Hits, Yesterday's Dreams"

1976
Model Year

DATE: January 10-18, 1976

SPONSOR: DADA

BUILDING: Cobo Hall

ADMISSION: $2.50 for adults
50 cents for children under 12
Free for senior citizens Monday through Friday

OPENING: A charity preview on Friday night drew a record crowd, attended by about 1,000 auto dealers and the top executives of the four auto companies, and Detroit's business, financial, and civic leaders. Absent from the charity event and the topic of much conversation was Henry Ford II.

The show opened Saturday morning with traditional ceremonies and the unveiling of a 5-by-12-ft. painting depicting the history of the American automobile industry, by former Detroiter Robert Thom, an internationally known artist. Following the exhibition, the painting was donated by the DADA to the National Automotive History Collection of the Detroit Library.

INSIDE THE SHOW: There were 250 domestic and foreign cars, including experimental models, as well as the latest recreational vehicles. Featured at the show were a number of cars from the famous Harras collection in Reno. A 1908 Bugatti was billed as the first one ever made, and was surrounded by a 1937 Airmobile Sedan with front-wheel drive, a 1938 Phantom Corsair, and a 1925 Julian Sport Coupe.

(Courtesy of the National Automotive History Collection, Detroit Public Library)

A 5-by-12-ft. epic painting depicting the history of the American automobile was on display at the Auto Show. The painting was done by world-renowned artist Robert Thom. Following the show, the painting was donated to the National Automotive History Collection at Detroit's main library. It is seen here as it appeared in 1999.

In the 1976 model year the name of the game was fuel economy. The results could be seen in the new economy models: the Plymouth Arrow, Buick Opel by Isuzu, Chevette, and Ford "MPG" models. The rising price of gas, the threat of gas shortages, and new fuel economy legislation put the premium on cars with better mileage. Virtually all of the 1976 cars offered improved economy over the 1975 models. The firms also held their price increase well below the levels of the prior two years when cars were hiked by $500 annually.

The number-one scene stealer at the 60th Detroit Auto Show was the Dodge exhibit with a quartet of professional athletes demonstrating the art of free-style skiing, which combined downhill skiing with acrobatic maneuvers.

One dream car on display was an experimental model called the Monza Super Spyder II by Chevrolet. It was described as "a design and engineering concept for small, personalized vehicles of the future." It featured an aerodynamic front-end housing and a unique strip-lighting system. It also had a special gold-flake custom exterior paint, a low-profile hood with fresh air intake, exterior-mounted digital readout speedometer, and a functional rear-end spoiler mounted across the rear deck.

The imports were well represented at the show. One of the larger exhibits was by Datsun, the leading foreign manufacturer in the U.S. market when car and truck sales were combined. Fiat of Italy was another popular import line on display.

NOTE: The internal-combustion engine celebrated its 100th year. It was patented in 1876 by German inventor Nikolaus A. Otto. The industry's heritage to the Otto engine was recognized at the Society of Automotive Engineers annual convention in Detroit later that February. A special exhibit included early versions of the engine from the U.S. and Europe.

"Design and the Future"

1977

Model Year

DATE: January 15-23, 1977

SPONSOR: DADA

BUILDING: Cobo Hall

ADMISSION: $2.50 for adults
50 cents for children under 12
Free for senior citizens and all uniformed police officers and their families

OPENING: A charity preview was held for the 61st Detroit Auto Show Friday night in Cobo Hall. Proceeds went to the Boys Clubs of Metro Detroit, the Northeast Guidance Center, and the Wayne, Oakland, and Macomb County Easter Seals Units. Most of the industry's big wheels were missing except Elliot M. "Pete" Estes of General Motors Corp., the lone president of autodom's Big Four to show up at the black-tie gala. Estes and his wife, Connie, toured the exhibits before heading to the London Chop House with William L. Mitchell, GM Vice-President, and his wife, Marion.

Cloak room attendants declined to check fur wraps, causing many previewers to mutter about the inconvenience of having to carry them around. Chevrolet's General Manager Robert D. Lund stuffed his wife Emmy's white mink in the trunk of one of the cars in his display.

(Courtesy of the National Automotive History Collection, Detroit Public Library)

217

INSIDE THE SHOW: There were some 250 models of cars, plus over 30 trucks and vans. Each automaker had a complement of stars, athletes, and attractions in its exhibit area, in addition to the usual bevy of pretty narrators. There were ski teams, table tennis champs, magicians, and give-aways. As in previous years, the show featured auctions of new cars. The media center at the show gave visitors a chance to meet radio, TV, and newspaper personalities on an informal basis.

At a time when few cars in the auto showrooms were sold by women, they were out in front at the auto show. If the new cars played second fiddle at the auto shows, it was to the winsome women selling them. There was a belief that glamour, not car know-how, sold cars. It was, after all, a show. Auto show talent hunters looked for looks, composure, speaking ability, and charm. Knowledge of the product, or salesmanship, wasn't even mentioned. A spokesman for an automaker said: "Let's face it, next to a car, women just look more, well, elegant."

"You get a completely different type of person for foreign cars," said a pretty brunette, a mother of five. "People interested in American cars might ask about gas mileage or how much it costs. But the car buffs asked every kind of question—about wheelbase, gear ratio, gas tank capacity." She said that on the stage some men came to flirt and she heard the line "Do you come with the car?" at least a hundred times. Each guy thought he was clever.

Round headlights seemed to be going the route of the crank starter on American cars. Pontiac used the show for the surprise unveiling of the first American car with new large, rectangular headlights; they were on the compact Phoenix.

Volkswagen unveiled its diesel-version Rabbit, and Datsun, Toyota, British Leyland, and Saab also showed their new models. Ford showed new mid-year models of the Limited Edition versions of the Granada, Mustang II, Pinto, and light truck "Explorer." The highlight of the Cadillac exhibit was the Eldorado custom Biarritz coupe with pillow-style seating. The big three all had truck displays at the show. The Ford display included one of the Pinto wagons turned into a mini-van, a new model offered for 1977.

NOTE: General Motors became the first automaker to agree to take part in a massive federal program aimed at demonstrating the feasibility of the conventional air bag. GM sold 10,000 air bags as an option on some 1974, 1975, and 1976 full-size models and took a loss because of low volume production.

"Something for Everyone"

DATE: January 14-22, 1978

SPONSOR: DADA

BUILDING: Cobo Hall

ADMISSION: $2.75 for adults
50 cents for children under 12
Free for senior citizens

ENTERTAINMENT: Cameras were welcomed by the show promoters. The auto makers were happy to have visitors taking pictures of their cars and the live models who were delighted to pose with the vehicles. Local celebrities—sports figures, television, radio and newspaper personalities—and even comic strip characters like Spiderman made appearances at the show.

Skating star Peggy Fleming joined the Lincoln-Mercury sports panel with hockey great Gordie Howe, the Tiger's Al Kaline, and track star Jesse Owens.

The guy with fire coming out of his hands was Karrel Fox, who also could read your mind and perform other neat tricks. Jackie Panaretos of Wayne and Marge Philpot of Dearborn were there with him. Mr. Whoodini, the magician, and Sir Graves Ghastly were there with Bozo the Clown, who gave away balloons to the kids. Monday night was scheduled as "Kids' Night."

It was a fun, carnival-type atmosphere with most of the manufacturers having some kind of free game people could play to win prizes. Ten vehicles including a Cadillac Coupe de Ville were auctioned and sold to the highest bidders on Thursday and Friday.

OPENING: A charity preview was held Friday evening with a number of industry VIPs in attendance. Upon entering the show, one of the first attention-getters was "2001: A Space Odyssey," booming out over a loudspeaker system at the Ford Motor Co. display. A little further along the Hall, silver-suited robots pranced around the Chrysler Corp. exhibit, showing off the Omni, the newest car in the Dodge line. Chrysler board chairman John J. Riccardo and Chrysler president Eugene Cafiero draped themselves across the hood of the Omni and shook hands while photographers snapped away.

A number of the VIPs stalked the aisles carrying yardsticks. They were given away at the Oldsmobile exhibit. Mrs. Thomas A. Murphy, wife of the General Motors Corp. board chairman, went home with two. She said she could never find one around the house when she needed one. Mrs. Murphy toured the show wearing a white mink coat. There were lots of young couples at the preview, including Mr. and Mrs. Lee Wulfmeir III. Mrs. Wulfmeir was the former Barbara Posselius Ford, and was dressed in a vested white satin trouser suit.

Proceeds from the preview went to the Boys Club of Metropolitan Detroit, Northeast Guidance Center for Emotionally Disturbed Children, and the Easter Seal Society for Crippled Children and Adults of Wayne, Oakland, and Macomb counties.

INSIDE THE SHOW: The three exhibit halls were made into a single area to provide room for 255 cars and trucks, representing ten domestic and eight import manufacturers. "Vanning" had

An AMC Pacer can be seen beyond the AMC sign to the right. The Pacer was originally designed to incorporate GM's rotary engine but it never went into production. The Pacer had a larger door on the right side to allow passengers to more easily get into the back seat. Its "bubble" design inspired the shape of the Ford Taurus. (Courtesy of the National Automotive History Collection, Detroit Public Library)

become a sub-culture in the United States, and the automakers moved to meet the market. Ford had their Econoline Super Wagon, Plymouth had the Voyager with a new instrument panel, and Chevrolet had a new grille.

Two things could be counted on at the Detroit Auto Show—cars and women. The female models were originally added like a bunch of fresh-cut flowers to liven up the show. Over the years the models' role evolved and they became involved in stage productions, shows, and narrating the same kind of spiel you would expect from a showroom salesman. Their duties ranged from wearing hot pants and passing out yardsticks at the Oldsmobile exhibit to explaining a new on-board computer by Cadillac, which calculated certain functions on the cars while they were driven.

For fear of theft, General Motors products used to be tied down to make them look as they would with a full load of passengers and cargo, but they stopped doing this because there was no bounce when people got into the cars. Pontiac glued shift levers and radio controls to dashboards to prevent theft, but people stole them anyway, damaging the interior in the process. At later shows, they simply replaced knobs that were stolen from the cars.

Car sellers tried to match buyers' personalities by making something for everyone (the theme of the show). A buyer could find a whole lot more in the dealer's showroom than basic transportation. The Ford Motor Co. retained Bill Blass, Hubert de Givenchy, Emilio Pucci, and Ralph Destino of

Cartier to coordinate new interior and exterior color-and-trim combinations for the 1978 Continental Mark V Designer series.

For the less financially able, there were many new options like spoke wheel hubcaps. A trip odometer, which could be set at zero, would measure the mileage of a particular trip. There was a CB radio built into an AM-FM radio, rear window defogger, a power sunroof, an electronic digital clock, and a luggage rack.

The auto companies were offering a variety of sound systems as optional equipment, including cassette tape players, but stores specializing in sound equipment were boasting larger lines of items for installation in cars after the vehicle was purchased. The real sound buffs preferred to install their own system. They started out by adding an FM converter to an existing AM radio, but could also get an in-dash AM-FM with cassette tape players with co-axial speakers and power amplifiers that sounded better than their home system.

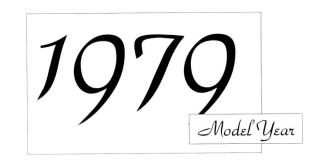

DATE: January 13-21, 1979

SPONSOR: DADA

BUILDING: Cobo Hall

ADMISSION: $3.00 for adults
                 50 cents for children under 12
                 Free for senior citizens

ENTERTAINMENT: "Kids' Days" on Monday and Tuesday featured children's favorite characters and entertainers who visited with the young showgoers and autographed photos. A senior citizens' party was held Wednesday, which included entertainment and refreshments. "Celebrity Night" was held Wednesday evening with well-known Detroiters including sports figures and radio and television personalities. Traditional auto auctions were held Thursday and Friday with a professional auctioneer.

INSIDE THE SHOW: More than 300 domestic and imported motor vehicles, including cars, trucks, special show cars, and other exhibits were displayed at the 63rd Detroit Auto Show.

The display of the full range of Chrysler-Plymouth vehicles was the largest exhibit at the show. The Chrysler Newport had a newly designed, gauge-filled instrument panel, a compact spare tire as standard equipment, and increased corrosion protection. A copy of Tattoo's Wagon, the red and white miniature customized Volare with a striped canopy (just like the one on *Fantasy Island*) was given away to a lucky visitor.

The "Amazing Kildon" performed his breathtaking escape act in mid-air from a broom, an illusionist levitated a Chevrolet LUV truck, and professional disco dancers whirled and twirled at the Chevrolet exhibit. At the Lincoln-Mercury exhibit, the spotlight was on Rick-o-Shay the bobcat and a panel of sports celebrities including Gordie Howe, Peggy Fleming, Al Kaline, Byron Nelson, Jesse

The VW Rabbit was made in the U.S.A. (Courtesy of the National Automotive History Collection, Detroit Public Library)

The French Renault "Le Car" was too underpowered for the U.S.A., but it was popular. (Courtesy of the National Automotive History Collection, Detroit Public Library)

Owens, and Tony Trabert. AMC featured the Concord DL sedan, Pacer limited wagon, and the luxury Jeep Wagon Limited on turntables, with model narrators telling the visitors about the cars. Freddie Ford, a 9-ft.-tall talking robot, attracted visitors and answered questions about the 40 Ford cars and trucks on display. The Volkswagen display centered around a live scientific demonstration unit. It featured the "Volkswagen Engineer" explaining scientific principles as they related to automobile construction and driveability.

The Lincoln Continental was one of the hottest cars at the show. It was the very last big "standard-size" American car. Station wagons were the poorest-selling cars and used to improve around hunting season, but that wasn't happening this year: the pickups and vans were taking their place.

Foreign cars drowned in unwanted currency-related price increases in 1978, and America's automakers threw them a life preserver by raising their own prices. They missed a big opportunity to wage a killing price battle by boosting their profits instead, and the importers were able to hold on to their 18% share of the U.S. car market into the 1979 model year.

"The Exciting 80s"

1980

Model Year

DATE: January 12-20, 1980

SPONSOR: DADA

BUILDING: Cobo Hall

ADMISSION: $3.50 for adults
50 cents for children
Free for senior citizens

ENTERTAINMENT: Among the entertainment attractions were comedian Jim Teter, who performed at the GMC truck display, the Pat Derby Cougars and Bobcats at the Lincoln-Mercury display, and world figure skating champions Ray Chappatta and Karen Mejia, who performed at the Chevrolet turntable.

Special events followed the traditional pattern with "Kids' Nights" on Monday and Tuesday, featuring personalities such as Graves Ghastly, Mona and Yolanda of the Hot Fudge Show, Mr. Whoodini, Oopsy the Clown, and others. There was a senior citizens' party on Wednesday, and one of the most popular segments were the auctions on Thursday and Friday of vehicles from GM, Chrysler, and Ford, Europe and Japan.

OPENING: Detroit's top auto executives mingled at a black-tie charity preview of the 64th Annual Detroit Auto Show on Friday night. The nearly 3,000 VIP guests paid $30 a couple to admire the new cars and enjoy roller-skating, Las Vegas-style showgirls, and bagpipe and guitar bands. The queen of the show was Jane Meneely of Farmington Hills, a graduate of Michigan State University.

At noon on Saturday, a helicopter lowered an American Motors Eagle, the first domestically produced automobile with four-wheel drive. The arrival was greeted by a rousing march played by the Athens High School band from Troy. The band led show dignitaries into the Hall to officially open the show, followed by thousands of people.

INSIDE THE SHOW: Ford Motor Co. president Philip A. Caldwell called the array of 250 U.S. and imported cars and trucks "colorful, attractive and glittering." The show's theme, "The Exciting 80s," was chosen because at no time in automotive history had the entire industry produced a new car lineup with more pleasing styling, comfort, and sophistication, while at the same time being more responsive to the demands of the fuel-conscious environment.

Japanese car sales soared to more than 20% of the U.S. market and layoffs of U.S. workers were mounting. A picket line was thrown up briefly around Toyota, Datsun, and other Japanese exhibits.

A walk through the auto show made it clear that the "far out" cars were being replaced by "feasible" concepts—vehicles with features that could be produced in the near future. In fact, they were not even built for auto shows, but rather for management to show new ideas, materials, paints, and new ways of putting them together. Using them at the auto show was just an added bonus. For instance, Chrysler had a 1978 LeBaron with 20 lightweight parts applications including plastics for wheels, oil and transmission pans, side windows, leaf springs, and pushrods. These parts were

Chrysler Corporation had a partnership with Mitsubishi, and the Dodge "Colt" was formulated for the U.S.A. (Courtesy of the National Automotive History Collection, Detroit Public Library)

composites of materials, a plastic matrix with reinforcing fibers. The public was wary of cars using plastics because it had an image of being used only in cheap toys.

Throughout the show there were 150 female models, either as narrators or "floor girls," and almost 75 salespeople, but you could not buy a car there. There were a lot of deals on new cars made at the show, but the final paperwork and delivery had to be made at the showrooms. The salesmen came from dealerships throughout the city and it was too complicated to have facilities at the show for financing new car deals. Some of the cars could be ordered off the auto show floor if a buyer insisted it was the only car he wanted.

"Excitement '81"

1981
Model Year

DATE: January 9-18, 1981

SPONSOR: DADA

BUILDING: Cobo Hall

ADMISSION: $3.50 for adults
50 cents for children under 12
Free for senior citizens

ENTERTAINMENT: Monday and Tuesday were "Kids' Nights," featuring Willie T. Clown, Mr. Whoodini, Sir Graves Ghastly, characters from the Hot Fudge Show, and lots of clowns. Tuesday evening was the industry dinner with E.M. "Pete" Estes as the featured speaker at the gathering of auto executives, dealers, and others. Wednesday was a senior citizens' party, including refreshments, mystery song and car contests. Wednesday was also "Celebrity Night" with media personalities and professional athletes greeting visitors and signing autographs. Thursday and Friday evening featured new car auctions.

OPENING: There were more than 300 persons who attended the black-tie premiere held Friday night to get the auto show rolling. Lee Iacocca, Chrysler Corp. Chairman, and retiring GM Chairman Pete Estes and his wife Connie were among the visitors.

INSIDE THE SHOW: On display were more than 260 cars and trucks, including all of Detroit's new models and the current offerings from Detroit's foreign competition. Attractive young women stood at most of the exhibits presenting technical information. There were cutaways of cars and other exhibits to bring people up to date on the new technology.

At the 65th Annual Detroit Auto Show the dozens of salesmen and saleswomen were not allowed to cut any deals, but they could hand out their business cards.

Upon entering the show, you were greeted first by the Ford Division display, which included the new subcompact Escort. Chrysler had its K-cars—Plymouth Reliant and Dodge Aries—the key to the automaker's plan to stave off bankruptcy. A big "K" decorated the nameplate of each Reliant and Aries, lest the public forgot these were the miracle cars Chrysler told Washington would save its life. Chrysler gimmicks included a cleverly built robot named K481. It was remotely controlled and traveled through the Chrysler exhibit to attract a following. The rolling robot approached women with comments such as "Kissy Kissy." If you wanted to know how the robot talked, you had to look in the crowd and you could see a guy who appeared to be scratching his nose a lot. He had a microphone up his sleeve and spoke remotely through the K481 speaker.

None of the volume automakers had an electric car prototype at the show, but one production model was on display. The Computa-Car, turned out in Florida by Commuter Vehicles Inc., a subsidiary of General Engines Co., could hit a top speed of 45 mph.

The vinyl roof was on its way out and was being replaced by two-toned paint jobs. Perhaps one reason was that some buyers were aware that the vinyl roof added weight to a car and increased its fuel usage. Americans were adjusting to riding in shorter, less roomy cars, but were getting them

The K-car at Chrysler was basically an "appliance" but it saved the company from bankruptcy. The first one rolled off the assembly line on August 8, 1980. (Courtesy of the National Automotive History Collection, Detroit Public Library)

outfitted in big-car luxury style. Power steering, cruise control, and electronic gadgets were being ordered more than ever before. "People want smaller cars, but they still want to ride around in a living room," said Robert English, programming manager for Ford Division.

The Olds Omega Sport Coupe was displayed with fenders made of soft, flexible plastic using reinforced injection molding or RIM. These fenders saved 5 lb. and did not rust. Only 2,500 vehicles with the plastic fenders were built in 1981. This was a trial to eventually produce a car with doors, a rear deck lid, and other none-structural parts with plastic. The color match required the use of a special urethane plastic paint. Assembly lines could not accept plastic parts like the metal ones because the body and panels went through the paint shop and ovens together for color matching. The plastic panels had to be painted separately, and then mated to the car on the assembly line.

DATE: January 16-24, 1982

SPONSOR: DADA

BUILDING: Cobo Hall

ADMISSION: $4.00 for adults
50 cents for children under 12
Free for children under 12
   accompanied by an adult
Free for senior citizens

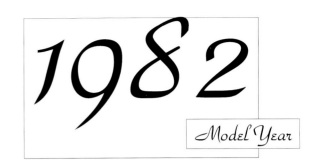

1982

Model Year

ENTERTAINMENT: There was plenty more to do at the show than just ogle cars. Soap opera stars signed autographs and, at the same time, the first of four area drawings for Super Bowl tickets started on Wednesday. The winners were driven to the game in a limousine and accompanied to the game and dinner by TV personalities John Kelly and Marilyn Turner.

OPENING: Frank Sinatra cancelled his appearance for Chrysler at the black-tie charity review Friday night due to rough weather in Palm Springs. According to one Chrysler spokesman: "You can never tell with the weather." Bill Hart, a comic from Detroit, and his dummy Harry carried on the Chrysler show without Frank. One show attendee said: "It doesn't bother me a bit about Frank. I came to see the new Buehrig car." The Ford promoters had positive feelings about Frank's absence. They were dazzling their audience with J.R. the lynx and Christopher the cougar. A Ford spokesman said: "I would have hated to make a woman choose between Frank Sinatra and the cats."

INSIDE THE SHOW: The 66th Annual Detroit Auto Show featured 250 cars and trucks—both foreign and domestic—in exhibits covering about 300,000 sq. ft. Almost every conceivable model from a DeLorean to an American Motors Jeep was on display. For the first time in the auto show's 83-year history cars valued at more than $100,000 were on display.

In previous years the show was a pleasant diversion from Detroit's cold winter days. The 1982 show was stacked in the middle of the National Football League's biggest week of the year, with the Super Bowl played in the Pontiac, Michigan, Silverdome. With concerts, tennis matches, and big parties scheduled all week, auto show officials hoped to attract many of the 70,000 out-of-state visitors during the show's final weekend.

Visitors got a chance to reach out and touch someone at Ford's Lincoln Continental Communications Concept Car. Visitors were invited to fill out a card to become one of four winners at an hourly drawing to make a long-distance call. A pushbutton dial was built into the dashboard and a microphone was located in the sunvisor above the driver's seat. Each winner got to make a three-minute call that was amplified outside the car so others could listen.

A variety of small cars and trucks were introduced at the show. American Motors had the sporty Fuego, imported from Renault, that debuted in March. Cadillac already made its new Cimarron available to its 1,600-plus dealers prior to the show. Nissan replaced the Datsun 210 later in the spring; it was the first Datsun to carry the Nissan name. Ford showed its new Ranger, a small pickup truck, in March, and Subaru had a new small pickup truck called the Brat.

The 1982 Auto Show was held during Super Bowl week but still attracted a sizeable crowd. The DeLorean Motor Company (DMC) display is shown. A sports car with gull-wing doors and a stainless-steel exterior, left unpainted, was a big hit. (Courtesy of the National Automotive History Collection, Detroit Public Library)

The big-car era wasn't over yet: there was a strong surge in sales and backlog inventories were much lower than for the compacts and subcompacts. One theory was that only the affluent could buy cars at that time during many plant closings and so many people out of work. Another factor was that the prices for the compacts and subcompacts went up more than traditional larger models. Part of the increase was due to expensive new technology developed for smaller cars. A Chevrolet full-size Caprice sold for about the same price as the subcompact Cavalier.

230

"We're All Revved Up"

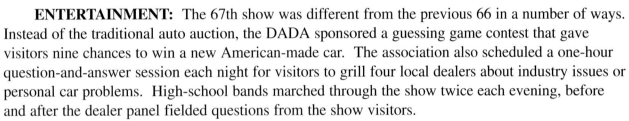

DATE: January 15-23, 1983

SPONSOR: DADA

BUILDING: Cobo Hall

ADMISSION: $4.00 for adults
$1.00 for children 12 and under
Free for children 12 and under accompanied by an adult
Free for senior citizens

ENTERTAINMENT: The 67th show was different from the previous 66 in a number of ways. Instead of the traditional auto auction, the DADA sponsored a guessing game contest that gave visitors nine chances to win a new American-made car. The association also scheduled a one-hour question-and-answer session each night for visitors to grill four local dealers about industry issues or personal car problems. High-school bands marched through the show twice each evening, before and after the dealer panel fielded questions from the show visitors.

"This year we're putting the emphasis on cars and getting away from the superficial things the show depended on in the past to bring people downtown," said Jim Grossman of Yaffe Berline, Inc., the advertising and public relations company handling the show. Gone were the usual show trappings, including the usual array of autograph-signing guest stars. However, there were still some superficial things. An assortment of magicians, dancers, singers, robots, and professional models provided a colorful backdrop to the vehicle displays.

OPENING: People, not cars, were the attraction at Friday's charity preview of the Detroit Auto Show. For $30 per couple, anyone could mingle with Detroit's elite as they strolled through the gleaming displays. "Mr. Jenner, there are two girls here who want to touch you," said one man in a tuxedo. Bruce Jenner—tall, tan, and the biggest attraction at Ford Motor Co.'s exhibit on Charity Preview Night—turned and extended his hand. The girls—formally attired women in their mid-40s—shook hands and smiled. Jenner, was a 1976 Olympic decathlon gold medal winner and an amateur race car driver.

Showgoers wandered around the exhibits listening to silver robots beeping sales pitches and gawking at glamorous models dressed in skin-tight gowns and jumpsuits. They filled plastic shopping sacks with brochures they probably never read. Many stopped to kick a tire or slide under the wheel and adjust the rearview mirror. Some even looked under the hood.

INSIDE THE SHOW: The show featured 407 cars, trucks, vans, and specialty vehicles, including a new super-aerodynamic car from Ford Motor Co. and Richard Petty's NASCAR Pontiac Grand Prix.

U.S. automakers were picking up on small trucks. Until 1982, the small truck market was almost exclusively Japanese. U.S. automakers unveiled some competition for the 1982 model year, and for 1983, GM and Ford added optional four-wheel drive, as well as new compact utility vehicles derived from the trucks. Chrysler did not have a pick-up truck of its own, and elected instead to build pick-up versions of the subcompact Dodge Charger (called the Rampage) and Plymouth Turismo (called the Scamp).

Show officials assembled unique and luxurious cars with prices up to $165,000. Two Avantis were shown with a moon roof and wire wheels. Only 200 were built annually. The Bitter SC was a sleek, swift, handmade sports sedan developed by Erich Bitter. A 3L aluminum engine with 180 hp could power it up to 135 mph. The longest car in the exhibit was a Cadillac Limousine stretched 46 ft. A Duesenberg was handmade in Elroy, Wisconsin, with scheduled production sold through 1984. The Rolls Royce Corniche convertible was priced at $165,000. For those who remembered the Rolls Royce ad which declared that at 60 mph the loudest sound inside the car was the clock, the new Rolls had a noiseless electronic digital clock.

The 1970s' Federal anti-pollution regulations led to on-board computers. Many auto executives were willing to admit that the Federal emissions rules accelerated the modernization of American cars by launching computers in cars. Ford and Chrysler offered "talking cars." These were computer voice-alert systems that warned of such things as open doors, unbuckled seatbelts, and keys left in the ignition. Ford also offered on-board travel computers on luxury models. But GM did not introduce "talking cars" for fear of negative consumer response. Ironically, the Japanese automakers, who packed the cars they built for their home market with the latest electronics, were slow to introduce such systems in the U.S. Toyota said the American drivers were not as gadget-oriented as their Japanese counterparts. Among the European car companies, Mercedes-Benz did away with gadgetry. "We have a fundamental philosophy about the attention span of the driver," said A.N. Shuman, a Mercedes spokesman. "The interior is subdued with nothing to draw the driver's attention from the road."

DATE: January 14-22, 1984

SPONSOR: DADA

BUILDING: Cobo Hall

ADMISSION: $4 for adults
$1 for children 12 and under
Free for children 12 and under accompanied by an adult
Free for senior citizens

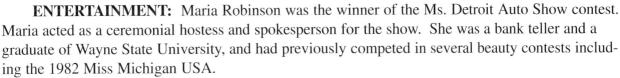

ENTERTAINMENT: Maria Robinson was the winner of the Ms. Detroit Auto Show contest. Maria acted as a ceremonial hostess and spokesperson for the show. She was a bank teller and a graduate of Wayne State University, and had previously competed in several beauty contests including the 1982 Miss Michigan USA.

The Association persuaded nine local radio stations to broadcast nightly from "radio row." In addition, they revived the traditional auto show program, which was discontinued in 1969.

Some of 1983's successful events were repeated. Twice each night there were high-school bands from southeastern Michigan marching through the show. A panel of local dealers fielded questions from showgoers each evening, and any question was fair game. In addition, the DADA repeated the "Most Incredible Contest" in which visitors could win one of 13 new vehicles by guessing how many objects—spark plugs, oil cans, tennis balls—were in the passenger area, glove box, or trunk of a car.

The Chrysler Corp. hired a mime company with a magician, and the Pontiac Division of General Motors Corp. exhibit featured a set of identical triplets assembling a Fiero to music and theater lighting. Before attaching body panels to the chassis, the Westland, Michigan, triplets explained the unique mill and drill process Pontiac developed to ensure precise fit and finish on the plastic body car.

OPENING: A few thousand of Detroit's elite put on black-tie and furs to attend the Charity Preview Night on Friday night. Everyone was whispering about the recently announced GM reorganization. The proceeds of the show went to the Boys and Girls Clubs of Metropolitan Detroit, the Children's Center, the Easter Seal Society, and the Assistance League of the Northeast Guidance Center.

INSIDE THE SHOW: Twenty-three foreign and domestic vehicle manufacturers showcased 422 new cars, trucks, and vans, plus there was a special van conversion exhibit at the 68th Annual Detroit Auto Show. In the late 70s, American-built cars were either econo-boxes or gas-guzzlers; few seemed worthy to be judged for their aesthetic value. But style was making a comeback in Detroit. Whether designs emphasized soft, aerodynamic curves that improved fuel efficiency or hard, high-tech lines, the 1984 models were arguably better looking.

"Isn't that the new Alliance?" a young woman was asked. "How do you like it?" "It's really comfortable and I get great gas mileage," the young woman replied. "AMC really did a good job on that car, didn't they?" "AMC? It's a Renault!" the young woman responded. Eventually, buyers got the message that it was designed by Renault and built by AMC. Buyers purchased enough Alliance models in 1984 to give AMC its best sales year since 1976.

Renault needed a high-quality, dependable car to overcome the poor image of its U.S. models. AMC, who was partnered with Renault, had an image of slow, heavy, low-mileage cars. Buyers purchased enough Alliance models to give AMC its best sales year since 1976. It was Motor Trend *magazine's "Car of the Year." (Courtesy of the National Automotive History Collection, Detroit Public Library)*

American Motors Corp. wasn't the only auto company to bring out an "image" vehicle—cars that either boosted public perception of a specific division or attracted showroom traffic even though sales might be relatively low. Ford had its Thunderbird, Chrysler had the Laser and Dodge Daytona, Chevrolet had its Corvette, Pontiac had the Fiero, and VW had its GTI.

Chrysler Corp. said it was the first of the domestic automakers to crack the minivan market with its Dodge Caravan and Plymouth Voyager. These were front-wheel-drive units using a passenger car chassis. Ford and GM also were coming out with minivans which were scaled down versions of their conventional rear-drive vans.

The most sophisticated devices on production cars were multi-function trip computers to monitor average fuel economy, elapsed time, and distance to destination. Chrysler was the first U.S. automaker to follow Japan's lead in developing the talking car. Ford and GM spokesmen said it was just a gadget and expressed more interest in voice-command, so that you could lock your doors, start your car, and turn on the wipers and lights. Jerome Rivard, chief engineer of Ford's Electrical and Electronics Division, predicted new developments in powertrain and vehicle controls, instrumentation, and convenience and entertainment systems.

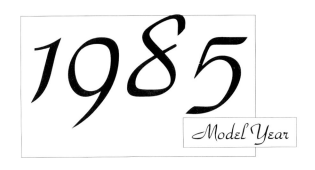

DATE: January 12-20, 1985

SPONSOR: DADA

BUILDING: Cobo Hall

ADMISSION: $4 for adults
Free for children 12 and under
accompanied by an adult
Free for senior citizens

ENTERTAINMENT: The "Most Incredible Contest" consisted of cars packed with basketballs, pop cans, or oil filters for visitors to guess how many to win a prize. There was also a short-story contest that offered prizes of $250, $500, and $1,000. There were twelve radio stations broadcasting live from the show.

OPENING: The traditional charity preview was held Friday night, which showcased the work of 40 Michigan artists. The affair was a benefit for the Boys and Girls Clubs of Metropolitan Detroit, the Easter Seal Society for Crippled Children, and the Northeast Adults Guidance Center.

INSIDE THE SHOW: The 69th show staged over 500 domestic and foreign-made cars and trucks. Visitors could view offerings from the four major U.S. automakers as well as imports from Honda, Nissan, Peugeot, Porsche, Jaguar, Maserati, and a number of other firms.

At the show, there were dozens of women draped over cars, like human hood ornaments, dressed in sequins and winning smiles, earnestly reciting vehicle specifications to everyone. There was a talking, animated piece of assembly-line machinery, and four break-dancers jiving and lip-syncing to a rock ditty about trucks. A car on steel pinions rotated in the air, like a four-passenger Ferris wheel.

There were few 1985 talking cars. "Voice commands were a novel idea, but people did not like their cars talking back to them on a regular basis," said Susanne Gatchell, assistant chief engineer of vehicle design and engineering for General Motors Corp.'s new small car division. "Some people said they got nagged from their husbands and wives, and the last thing they wanted was for their car to do the same."

The Ford display had a banner that read "RACING INTO THE FUTURE," which spotlighted Motorcrafts return with a display of race cars and component performance parts. Oldsmobile pulled a stunner by showing two of its dragster models. American Motors displayed its Formula Renault, which ran in the Detroit Grand Prix later that year in June.

NOTE: U.S. automakers called 1985 the "Year of the Yuppie." That meant the newest cars were targeted at America's young, ambitious, and affluent professionals, i.e., the cream of the baby-boom generation. They were 25 to 40 years old, earned more than $40,000 a year, and bought cars to befit their affluence.

The yuppies were also interested in imports. Foreign autos captured 40% of the yuppie market in 1984, in contrast to less than 24% of the total U.S. market. "We've seen enough," said Ford Motor Co.'s North American marketing chief Joseph Kordick. As a result, sleek, new, option-laden,

Jennifer Hook, an 18-year-old actress, is shown with Automation robot Ralph (left) and industrial robot "T-3" to the right. (Courtesy of the National Automotive History Collection, Detroit Public Library)

high-profit domestic cars with European lines were offered that looked and performed much differently from the kinds of cars they remembered viewing the last time they looked.

General Motors made headlines when it announced that it was creating a new company, the Saturn Corp., to compete with the Japanese import market.

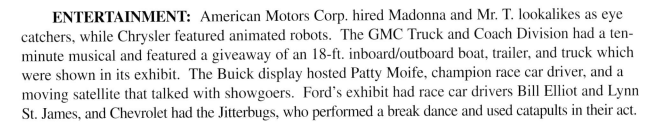

"Talk of the Town"

DATE: January 11-19, 1986

SPONSOR: DADA

BUILDING: Cobo Hall

ADMISSION: $4.00 for adults
Free for children under 12 accompanied by an adult
Free for senior citizens

ENTERTAINMENT: American Motors Corp. hired Madonna and Mr. T. lookalikes as eye catchers, while Chrysler featured animated robots. The GMC Truck and Coach Division had a ten-minute musical and featured a giveaway of an 18-ft. inboard/outboard boat, trailer, and truck which were shown in its exhibit. The Buick display hosted Patty Moife, champion race car driver, and a moving satellite that talked with showgoers. Ford's exhibit had race car drivers Bill Elliot and Lynn St. James, and Chevrolet had the Jitterbugs, who performed a break dance and used catapults in their act.

OPENING: A charity benefit was held Friday night with 3,000 black-tie partygoers. Sequined models extolled the virtues of the 1986 displays. Dry-ice fog drifted around the feet of hired disco dancers. And, depending on where you stood, you could hear anything from country music to classical string quartets.

Lee Iacocca and his fiancée, Peggy Johnson, were in attendance with Chrysler Corp. Vice-Chairman Robert Miller and Chrysler Motors President Harold Sperlich. Ford Motor Co. President Harold Poling was asked whether Ford would be forming an Alpha Corp. similar to GM's Saturn. "We haven't decided yet," was his reply. General Motors Chairman Roger Smith was asked what it would take to recoup the three percentage points it lost in 1985, and he responded: "Just look at our cars here and you know we're going to do it in '86."

INSIDE THE SHOW: The 70th Annual Detroit Auto Show stretched over 440,000 sq. ft. showcasing 49 exhibits with 500 cars and trucks. The show's theme, "Talk of the Town," was chosen because during its nine-day run, the Auto Show truly was the talk of the town, according to the show's chairman, Nathan Conyors.

Trucks were becoming more prevalent—three of every ten motor vehicles purchased in the U.S. were trucks and 32% of American households owned at least one truck. Trucks were becoming more car-like with the addition of air conditioning, carpeting, and power windows.

Many of the automakers were betting that technology, not styling, would give them the edge in future car sales. If they were right, there would be many more four-wheel-drive vehicles in the future. The move to four-wheel drive had been underway since the 1970s when Subaru of Japan brought out a four-wheel-drive station wagon and American Motors Corp. brought out its Eagle and Concord four-wheel cars.

Trip computers were being offered on medium-priced cars for the first time. The Buick Riviera had a touch-screen video terminal that displayed information about the sound system, climate control system, and trip computer. There were predictions that cars of the future would have navigational

General view of the show. (Courtesy of the National Automotive History Collection, Detroit Public Library)

systems with a video display. Some would use weather and military satellites, and others would use gyroscopes with a preprogrammed map.

During the previous 30 years, the leader in low-priced cars had shifted from Germany to Japan. Now it was Yugoslavia's turn with its "YUGO GV." Toyota was the overall undisputed import champ with a wide range of models. Chrysler Corp.'s minivan sales continued to increase in spite of new competition from Ford's Aerostar and GM's Safari.

DATE: January 10-18, 1987

SPONSOR: DADA

BUILDING: Cobo Hall

ADMISSION: $4.75 for adults
$1 for children 12 and under
Free for children 12 and under accompanied by an adult
Free for senior citizens

1987
Model Year

ENTERTAINMENT: The show offered blondes sheathed in sequins, an array of exotic autos, glitzy high-tech and laser displays, singing and dancing, magic shows, and car-oriented music videos.

Buick had B.T., a talking satellite. Lincoln-Mercury featured Robot Sico. Dodge upstaged them with a Dakota pick-up truck called Dakota Dave that talked and sang. Candi and Randi Brugh, the Doublemint Twins, and the Heartbeat of America dancers performed at the Chevrolet exhibit.

OPENING: Nearly 5,000 auto buffs in tuxedos and evening gowns attended a charity preview Friday night. The showgoers included top executives from the Big Three automakers, along with dealers, suppliers, and local celebrities. Ford Motor Co. Chairman Donald Peterson came to the preview after being named its Man of the Year by *Motor Trend* magazine, for leading the development of the Thunderbird and Taurus models.

The show offered the Detroit area a first look at several models that went on sale shortly after the show ended. The new models included the Renault Medallion and Alpine, Lincoln Mark VII and Town Car, and shown for the first time were the Dodge Daytona concept car and the Plymouth Grand Voyager concept mini-wagon, as well as Pontiac's new concept vehicle, the Pursuit. One woman leaving the preview called out to her friend: "I don't care about the cars—I came to see the clothes."

After years of marketing to "yuppies," carmakers began to redirect their energies to more traditional audiences, the same ones who created the Big Three. The new buzzword in marketing was "tradition," to re-establish corporate identities that started to dissipate when the divisions attempted to branch out. (Courtesy of the National Automotive History Collection, Detroit Public Library)

Proceeds from the annual show went to Boys and Girls Clubs of Metropolitan Detroit, Easter Seal Society, Northeast Guidance Center, and the Children's Center.

INSIDE THE SHOW: Detroit's 71st Auto Show featured 500 cars, trucks, and conversion vans from the Big Three U.S. automakers and American Motors Corp., six Japanese automakers, and eight European automakers, including Yugo.

After years of pursuing yuppies, possibly the most overrated demographic group ever, the carmakers tried to appeal to the more traditional audiences, the same ones who helped form the Big Three. Each car division had its own image and cars. Whereas the 1986 show featured more male narrators in acknowledgement of the increased number of female car buyers, the 1987 show returned to women in sequined evening gowns poised on turntables, with only a few men.

Toyota offered free plastic shopping bags—"Who could ask for anything more?"

NOTE: The 1988 model year Chevrolet Corsica and Beretta coupe, Pontiac's Korean-built LeMans subcompact, and Cadillac's new Allante were scheduled to debut in the spring. Ford's Korean affiliate Kia would begin shipping the mini-compact Festiva, and the made-in-Mexico Mercury Tracer and made-in-Germany Scorpio were also scheduled to debut in the spring. The Chrysler TC, built by Maserati in Italy, was scheduled for a fall debut.

DATE: January 16-24, 1988

SPONSOR: DADA

BUILDING: Cobo Hall

ADMISSION: $4.75 for adults and teens
Free for children under 12
   accompanied by an adult
Free for senior citizens

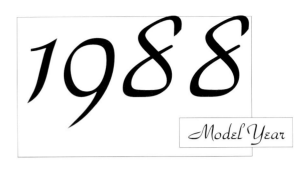

ENTERTAINMENT: The auto dealers featured: a visit from Miss America; drawings for pedal trucks, gas-powered miniature Corvettes, and skis; a variety of displays of off-road racing; racing videos; and displays of seemingly everything automotive.

OPENING: A gala charity party was held Friday night to kick off the Auto Show. There were 3000 party-goers having fun sipping wine and strolling around millions of dollars worth of automotive hardware. Ricardo Montalban, actor and television star of "Fantasy Island," was a paid spokesman for the Chrysler LeBaron luxury cars, and was there talking with guests.

Among the most impressed was Miss America, Kaye Lani Rae Ratko, who was from Monroe but never had been to an auto show before. "The moment I walked in here I fell in love with the place," Ratko said at the Chevrolet display where she was being photographed at the wheel of a red Corvette.

An automotive safety show for children, narrated by robotic versions of the Muppet characters Miss Piggy, Kermit, and a dozen small singing frogs was incomplete when the party started. A costume of the Sweetums character, which was to be worn by John Henson, was lost following a Northwest Airlines flight from New York. However, Sweetums was found, dispatched to Cobo, and Henson was roaming the display areas and shaking hands only an hour into the party.

To blaring music, GM Chairman Roger Smith pushed a button opening a silk canopy, designed to look like a giant clamshell, and revealed the new Buick Reatta two-seat touring car. Joining him in the glitzy display were tuxedo members of the United Auto Workers.

The event raised money for the Boys and Girls Clubs of Southeastern Michigan, the Easter Seal Society, the Assistance League to the Northeast Guidance Center, and the Children's Center.

INSIDE THE SHOW: The 72nd Annual Show comprised 52 exhibits, with over 500 cars and trucks, on about 400,000 sq. ft. of floor space. The show had little show-biz activity and the car had become the star. Sales staffers from Metro Detroit auto dealerships were on-hand at each exhibit, but they were not allowed to sell on the spot. They were instructed to answer questions and pass out business cards to potential customers.

A harbinger of the Chevrolet Blazer and GMC "Jimmy."

Setting up the auto show was a fussy business. Display designers agonized over the speed and the height of the turntables. The typical height was 18 in. to allow enough room for turntable motors and mechanisms and that perched the car high enough for the crowd to see it. The turntables rotated fully every 30 to 90 seconds, depending on how long it took to absorb the looks of a given car. The cars parked on the floor were frequently reparked to display their most flattering profiles. Factors taken into account included the direction most people took to go to the exhibit and features of cars that were most striking, such as redesigned front or rear ends. The colors had to be pleasing and have continuity. Certain colors did not work well in Cobo Hall; its profusion of small spotlights could result in bad reflections. The light favored the dark colors—blacks, reds, and other shades that absorbed light. The Pontiac Division of General Motors tried a different strategy and displayed one car in every color they marketed. They did not want to exhibit too many cars; generally each car was allowed 500 sq. ft. of space—enough room for a visitor to open doors and walk comfortably around it.

There were concept cars from General Motors, Ford's Lincoln-Mercury Division, Chrysler, and Nissan. One thing that differentiated the concept cars from many shows in the past was that they were driveable. Designers insisted that every feature, however strange it seemed, either worked on the cars or would be made to do so. Among the most popular features of the concept cars was a rearview television system instead of mirrors. That, the designers said, helped eliminate drag caused by external mirrors.

North American International Auto Show

1989

Model Year

DATE: January 7-15, 1989

SPONSOR: DADA

BUILDING: Cobo Hall

ADMISSION: $5 for adults
$1 for children under 12
Free for children under 12 accompanied by an adult
Free for senior citizens

OPENING: The annual black-tie charity opening, which benefited six different children's welfare agencies, drew all the big names as expected.

On Friday night, the newly renamed "North American International Auto Show" featured the new, improved Cobo Hall. About 100 national convention planners from across the country were impressed by the vehicle displays but reserved their biggest raves for the Hall's $220 million expansion and renovation. Virtually all of the out-of-town visitors gave Cobo Hall high marks for everything from color scheme to the more open, airy feel of the facility, 35 additional meeting rooms, and 25 extra loading docks.

"A world-class show and a world-class convention center in which to hold it," were Mayor Coleman Young's words as he cut the ribbon to open the show. The Mayor declared: "As I look at this sea of faces wall to wall, in the new expanded Cobo Hall . . . I feel this opening marks a new era for Detroit . . . We lay claim once again to the title of Auto Capital of the World. This show is in the right place." Then, an estimated 6,000 people surged in waves through the exhibits.

Visitors included: Soviet Ambassador Yuri Dubinin, escorted by Ford Automotive Group President Phil Benton and wife, Mary Ann; General Motors Chairman Roger Smith and wife, Barbara; Lee Iacocca with his girlfriend, California restaurant owner Darrien Earle; and actors Richard Crenna and Ricardo Montalban. Conspicuous in their absence were executives and visitors from Japan: Word of Emperor Hirohito's death came close to the gala opening time.

A couple from Flat Rock sighed with relief after working their way out of a crush around the Chevrolet concept truck display with two hula hoops in their hand: "We were there just looking at the truck and watching the demonstration, and all of a sudden they gave away these hula hoops, and there were 80,000 people on top of us. It just goes to show, no matter how dressed up people get, they still go crazy for something free."

INSIDE THE SHOW: To be significant internationally the auto show had to offer an abundance of new vehicles available for purchase, plus concept cars which illustrated an automaker's vision for the future. The show had to attract national and foreign journalists to tell the world about the event and draw high-ranking executives to make news.

The 73rd Annual Detroit Auto Show featured 41 car and 10 van conversion companies. The key to the show's momentum was a pair of foreign-model introductions: Toyota's new Lexus

Detroit had coach makers and design studios, and wanted to attract famous international car designers. A working studio like the one pictured was one of the biggest attractions at the auto show. It was located above the Buick and Cadillac displays. (Courtesy of the National Automotive History Collection, Detroit Public Library)

sports-luxury cars and Nissan's Infiniti series. Two Japanese reporters with the car-styling magazine *In Tokyo Today* smiled when asked if an apple-red GM Sierra Sport truck would be popular in Japan: "The roads are narrow, Japanese garages are very small. American cars are practical here, not in Japan."

The concept cars were close to real models. The GM Syclone was based on an S15 compact pick-up, featuring a racy trim package including lower-body ground effects and a rear spoiler. The Oldsmobile Aerotech III was touted as a touring sedan of the future. The Plymouth Speedster was designed to appeal to 18- to 25-year-olds, intended to mate high performance motorcycles and open sports cars. A molded plastic tub formed a fixed seating surface with seating pads that could be removed so the car could be hosed out for cleaning. The Dodge Viper featured a V-10 engine, 17-in. wheels, and an open cockpit. A possible future vehicle by Ford was designed by the Center for Creative Studies in Detroit. It was not a car or a truck, but it carried four passengers, had removable windows, roof panels and hatch, and could be used as a ski vehicle, surfing vehicle, sports car, or a mountain rescue vehicle.

The show put an improved Cobo Hall on center stage, brought suburbanites to the city, and gave many people outside the city good things to say about Detroit. The added space appealed to the exhibitors. "With the expansion, we went from 2,500 sq. ft. to about 6,000," said a spokesman from Audi of America Inc. The public liked it, too. "I love all the glass, and the carpet on the wall," said a visitor from Royal Oak. "It's great for the acoustics."

DATE: January 6-14, 1990

SPONSOR: DADA

BUILDING: Cobo Hall

ADMISSION: $5 for adults
Free for children under 12
accompanied by an adult

OPENING: Hundreds of people in tuxedos and cocktail dresses waited in the foyer of Cobo Hall on Friday night for their first glimpse of the auto show. There was an apparent upbeat mood among the crowd that prevailed throughout the annual charity-night show opening. Even Mayor Young, after months of tough sledding with the press, was jovial. He called the show a smash hit and said: "Detroit has moved into the number 3 spot in terms of auto shows world-wide, and I predict that in two years, we'll be number 1."

Governor James Blanchard and his wife, Janet, toured the show with two other couples. GM Chairman Roger Smith, there with his wife, Barbara, and daughter, Tory Chichester of Rochester, took some good-natured ribbing about the name of GM's new electric concept car, the Impact. Ford Chairman Don Peterson, with his wife, Jody, walked through his last auto show as top man at Ford as he retired that March: "When I look back over 40 years with the company, it's pleasing to see how this show has gotten bigger and better." The flu knocked out an appearance by Chrysler Chairman Lee Iacocca.

A big draw of the show was two joint UAW-company management displays that were experiments at the show. A UAW-Ford exhibit showed different components of the new Escort with lots of UAW and Ford representatives there to explain the quality control and manufacturing process. A neighboring UAW-GM display showed actual partial assembly of a Buick Reatta.

Each guest paid $75 and the total collection was about $600,000 which went to a conglomerate of seven children's charities.

Before the show opened Saturday, *Automobile* magazine hosted a brunch at the Detroit Institute of Arts, drawing 200 automotive and advertising executives. They were serenaded by a Mexican mariachi band as they ate breakfast beneath the museum's Diego Rivera murals. Guests included John Grettenberger, VP of GM's Cadillac Division, and Michael Losh, who headed GM's Oldsmobile unit.

INSIDE THE SHOW: The show consisted of 70 displays and 45 exhibitors showing 750 vehicles. New for the 1990 show was the "concept center" with 50,000 sq. ft. of displays by Ford, GM, Pininfarina, ASC Inc., C&C Inc., and the Center for Creative Studies. The number of radio stations had grown to 24, playing everything from rock to classical music and producing live remotes from the show. More than 70 international journalists representing 22 countries, and more than 1,000 local and national journalists attended the show.

At the car exhibits, spokespersons were more knowledgeable and better-versed about their product and product literature than in prior shows. Exhibit managers no longer considered cleavage and long legs as essential for attracting buyers to an automaker's display.

Mary Ellen Sweet-Andrews of Bloomfield Hills had been assigned to talk up the Mazda 323 subcompact for the 1989 show, and ended up buying one herself: "I spent so much time studying the car and memorizing facts that I really got to like it. So I just bought one."

Most of the auto companies offered between eight and twelve colors instead of 18 as in past years. Chrysler was the only American carmaker at the show that offered airbags as standard on all of its domestically produced cars. The CERV III concept car showcased GM's latest electronic devices. CERV was a Corporate Experimental Research Vehicle that featured an electronic roadmap for navigation, a head-up instrument display, active suspension, and four-wheel steering.

NOTE: A U. of M. study indicated that auto leasing was expected to become increasingly popular, climbing from 15% of new car sales in 1990 to 36% in 2000.

DATE: January 12-20, 1991

SPONSOR: DADA

BUILDING: Cobo Hall

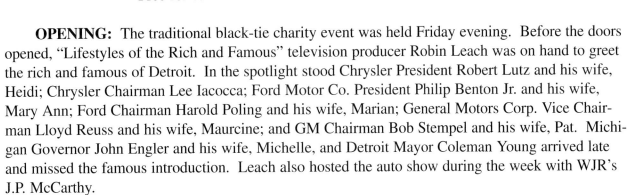

ADMISSION: $5 for adults
$1 for children under 12
Free for children accompanied by an adult
Free for senior citizens

OPENING: The traditional black-tie charity event was held Friday evening. Before the doors opened, "Lifestyles of the Rich and Famous" television producer Robin Leach was on hand to greet the rich and famous of Detroit. In the spotlight stood Chrysler President Robert Lutz and his wife, Heidi; Chrysler Chairman Lee Iacocca; Ford Motor Co. President Philip Benton Jr. and his wife, Mary Ann; Ford Chairman Harold Poling and his wife, Marian; General Motors Corp. Vice Chairman Lloyd Reuss and his wife, Maurcine; and GM Chairman Bob Stempel and his wife, Pat. Michigan Governor John Engler and his wife, Michelle, and Detroit Mayor Coleman Young arrived late and missed the famous introduction. Leach also hosted the auto show during the week with WJR's J.P. McCarthy.

It was hard to tell if the new automobile models or the glamorously gowned women in sequins drew the most attention. Cynthia Ford, Pat Stempel, and Barb Fisher wore black with gold braid. Heidi Lutz was stunning in a form-fitting red cotton dress with black trim.

Proceeds from the fundraiser went to Barat Human Services, Boys and Girls Clubs of Southeastern Michigan, Children's Center, Children's Services of Northeast Guidance Center, Detroit Institute for Children, Easter Seal Society, and the March of Dimes Birth Defects Foundation.

INSIDE THE SHOW: There were more than 40 auto manufacturers and coach builders with 750 cars and trucks on display. The show also included prototypes and concept cars.

The first electronic transmissions ever to go into GM's light-duty trucks debuted in 1991. GM got into the car phone business by allowing its dealers to offer cellular telephones as a $700 option. A Dodge concept car, called the Neon, was shown with Liz Claiborne confetti print seats set against cobalt-blue tubular frames. To hype Chrysler's concern for the environment, it even came with a trash compactor.

General Motors corporate exhibit featured three solar-powered cars that had recently raced across Australia, including the Sunrunner, built by U. of M. students. BMW had a two-story display featuring safety and technology. An electric-powered 320i, which was being driven in Germany, was also on display. A Mercedes concept vehicle, which looked like a minivan but wasn't called one, had a steering wheel in the middle of the front seat.

A woman from Bloomfield Hills braved an hour-and-a-quarter wait in line to experience the thrill of piloting a Jeep Cherokee through the Rocky Mountains, using a video screen. "I loved it. It was fun," she said after the ride. It was made complete by a simulated rock slide and mountain animals pouncing on the hood.

Automotive technology was changing: the way cars were built, the materials, and new engines. Technology displays were aimed at engineers. The vibration test, shown here at GM's Milford proving ground, was taken to Cobo Hall for the show. It required a great deal of logistical support and equipment to run it. (Courtesy of the National Automotive History Collection, Detroit Public Library)

The Volvo and Canadian-built Avanti display. (Courtesy of Exhibit Enterprises)

NOTE: The Japanese automakers gained a record 32% of the new car market in 1990, which included Japanese-built products that the Big Three sold. According to the National Auto Dealers Association, the 1991 model year was the first year in history in which American retailers sold more used cars than new ones.

DATE: January 11-19, 1992

SPONSOR: DADA

BUILDING: Cobo Hall

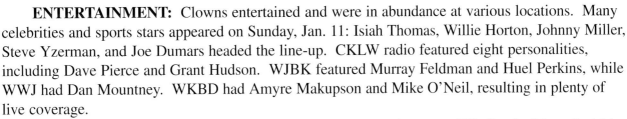

ADMISSION: $6.00 for adults
$3.00 for children under 12
Free for children under 12 accompanied by an adult
$3.00 for senior citizens

ENTERTAINMENT: Clowns entertained and were in abundance at various locations. Many celebrities and sports stars appeared on Sunday, Jan. 11: Isiah Thomas, Willie Horton, Johnny Miller, Steve Yzerman, and Joe Dumars headed the line-up. CKLW radio featured eight personalities, including Dave Pierce and Grant Hudson. WJBK featured Murray Feldman and Huel Perkins, while WWJ had Dan Mountney. WKBD had Amyre Makupson and Mike O'Neil, resulting in plenty of live coverage.

Show officials planned to have Cobo Hall equipped with big-screen TVs for the Lions-Redskins matchup on Sunday, Jan. 19, but the NFL disapproved of the plan because of the $6.00 auto show ticket price, saying they would not allow anyone to profit from the broadcast.

OPENING: A charity preview with 10,000 guests was held Friday night with visitors wearing lots of sequins and smashing colors. Eight charities benefited from the event. With the economy in a slump, liquor was restricted to wine. The Big Three chairmen were just back from Tokyo. They appeared drained after long hours of discussing "unfair trade."

INSIDE THE SHOW: The show featured 40 auto manufacturers with 750 cars and trucks, including concept vehicles. The lower level contained a display of 35 van conversions. The biggest news at the show was Chrysler's eagerly awaited LH full-size sedans, although they didn't go on sale until the fall.

The automakers displayed several cars with environmental features. BMW had the world's "first thoroughbred electric car." A Chrysler concept vehicle had a two-stroke engine that could operate on gasoline or alcohol. Ford featured an electric-powered family taxi called the Connecta. General Motors had an ultralite 1,400 lb. car that could get 100 mpg on the highway. Honda had a two-seater ultralite that could get 100 mpg, and Volkswagen had a commuter car with a gasoline engine and an electric motor drive to increase fuel economy and extend the range.

The auto show featured another environmental theme—recycling. Germany had passed laws requiring automakers to recycle all the materials in junked cars. Both Mercedes and BMW included descriptions of their recycling programs in their exhibits. An average 1991 car weighed 2,896 lb. and had 50 sq. ft. of glass, 217 lb. of plastic, 7 sq. yds. of floor and truck carpeting, 11 sq. yds. of seat covering, 100 lb. of aluminum, 700 lb. of steel, 3,300 ft. of electrical wiring, and 2.75 gals. of paint.

NOTE: For the first time in nine years, white was the most preferred car color, followed by red.

GM's ultralite concept car was a four-seater capable of 100 miles per gallon on the highway. (Courtesy of the National Automotive History Collection, Detroit Public Library)

DATE: January 9-17, 1993

SPONSOR: DADA

BUILDING: Cobo Hall

ADMISSION: $7.00 for adults
$3.00 for children under 12
Free for children under 12 accompanied by an adult
$3.00 for senior citizens

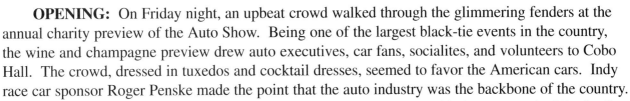

OPENING: On Friday night, an upbeat crowd walked through the glimmering fenders at the annual charity preview of the Auto Show. Being one of the largest black-tie events in the country, the wine and champagne preview drew auto executives, car fans, socialites, and volunteers to Cobo Hall. The crowd, dressed in tuxedos and cocktail dresses, seemed to favor the American cars. Indy race car sponsor Roger Penske made the point that the auto industry was the backbone of the country.

Charities benefiting from the event included the Detroit Police Athletic League, the March of Dimes, Easter Seal Society, Boys and Girls Clubs of Southeastern Michigan, Barat Human Services, and the Judson Center.

INSIDE THE SHOW: There were 40 automobile manufacturers displaying 750 production and show cars, and trucks. Highlights of the displays included the AM General "Hummer," the civilian version of the HUMMVEE which was aimed at the more serious off-roader. Buick celebrated its 90th year with a 1905 Model C. Hyundai showed its HCD-II prototype, two-door, front-wheel-drive sports coupe. It was powered by a 150-hp engine and featured a collision-avoidance system. Rolls Royce showed its "entry level" sedan Bentley Brooklands, priced at only $135,500.

Some of the more interesting cars included a model of the new Cadillac Fleetwood Brougham presidential limousine that president-elect Bill Clinton was to use during his inauguration. A Porsche concept car called the Boxter drew the crowd's attention. The comparison of the 1941 and 1993 Chrysler Thunderbolt coupes was a popular exhibit, and so was Chrysler's hands-on environmental exhibit, with fourth-graders' concept designs.

Dealers were trying to attract and accommodate the female car buyer. Women accounted for 47% of the total car-buying market and had a say in 80% of all vehicle purchases. There was a difference between women's and men's tastes. Many of the sales personnel said a man's style was more ego-based, while a woman's style was much more detail-oriented; a woman is interested in what the car would do and how it would perform. In the late 70s, General Motors Corp., Ford Motor Co., and Chrysler Corp. created women's advisory committees whose main objective was to review advertising and make sure it was not offensive to women. In 1993, the advertising review continued but the emphasis on the committees shifted to product design. Women advised the designers and engineers on everything from the car's exterior to the knobs on the radio.

NOTE: "If the color isn't right; there is no deal," said a salesman. Psychologists said color choice was often influenced by personality traits. Color could reflect who you are or who you wanted to be: You could choose red to protect you from being seen as a nerd, or it could be the person that you are. So red could mean opposite things. Green, which connotes nature, was a

A Chrysler LH with sheet metal cut away to allow visitors to see the inside. (Courtesy of the National Automotive History Collection, Detroit Public Library)

popular color since the environment was a big concern. White, red, and black were consistently the most popular colors among car buyers. Women don't usually buy black cars because they were not into the "power thing." Women like white because it is a clean color and blue because it is maternal, like the ocean and the color of the sky. A consistent psychological factor in the choice of colors is the need to appear unconventional.

DATE: January 8-16, 1994

SPONSOR: DADA

BUILDING: Cobo Hall

ADMISSION: $7.00 for adults
$3.00 for children 12 and under
Free for children 12 and under
accompanied by an adult
$3.00 for senior citizens (65 and over)

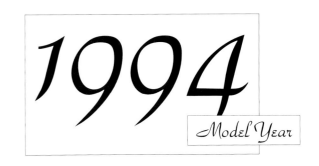

OPENING: Detroit's new mayor, Dennis Archer, confided that he was on the other side of the dignitaries' podium at the 1993 show, and prayed for a chance to be onstage someday. His wish came true Friday, as he and his wife, Trudy, were honorary co-chairs for the 1994 North American International Auto Show (NAIAS) charity preview.

For the first time, executives from international auto companies such as Nissan, Volkswagen, Jaguar, and Saab joined Detroit auto executives for the ceremonial gesture. The preview was held to benefit ten Detroit-area children's charities.

INSIDE THE SHOW: More than 40 of the world's auto manufacturers displayed more than 700 cars and trucks. Production and concept car introductions, both North American and worldwide, were featured. A van conversion show was also held in the lower level. Critics argued that the NAIAS was still largely a provincialistic showcase for the Big Three. Although it didn't draw the same number of overseas executives as the shows in Tokyo, Frankfurt, Paris, or Geneva, there was an ever-growing influx of foreign journalists each year. This suggested an intense interest not only in the American market, but also in the American products that could someday be in their local showrooms.

Accessibility for visitors, including the disabled, was the hot option in the show's exhibits. At the Mercedes-Benz exhibit, the disabled could reach displays over a gradual slope, easily maneuvered in a wheelchair. Pontiac became the first exhibitor to have its presentations offered in sign language. The goal of the Detroit show was to be free of barriers to any disabled person.

There were several 1995 vehicles that were premiered at the show: the '95 Dodge/Plymouth Neon, Oldsmobile Aurora, Buick Riviera, Ford Windstar, and the Dodge/Chrysler Cirrus.

Volkswagen showed its Concept I, an updated Beetle, cleaner and safer, but as cuddly as the old one. Mercedes Vision A93 had the engine and transmission under the floor of the passenger compartment; as a result, it was 3 ft. shorter than Mercedes' smallest sedans, but still easily seated four people. The Cadillac LSE was a small, sporty, luxury sedan meant to appeal to younger buyers.

Experts named anti-lock brakes, airbags, traction control, power locks and windows, hands-free phone, power mirrors, and four-wheel drive as the features that were really necessary. Armor could have been added to the list as several security firms were offering protection for "smash-and-grab" thugs and even shooters. The side windows were most vulnerable, so a set of replacement glass was sold for $3,000.

NOTE: After capturing one-fourth of the U.S. car market, Japanese automakers were late in realizing that a big percentage of the American market would soon belong to trucks. About four out of ten vehicles sold in the U.S. were trucks, mostly sold by the Big Three. The U.S. carmakers were more attuned to what buyers wanted.

DATE: January 7-15, 1995

SPONSOR: DADA

BUILDING: Cobo Hall

ADMISSION: $8.00 for adults
$4.00 for senior citizens
$4.00 for children 12 and under
Free for children 12 and under accompanied by an adult

1995

Model Year

OPENING: A record crowd streamed from a light snowfall into Cobo Hall Friday night to attend a black-tie charity preview of the NAIAS. Attendants with buffing cloths kept a high gloss on the chrome stars of the show, while other attendants stood by with powder puffs taking the shine off the noses of the Big Three executives who took turns appearing on live telecasts.

As guests reviewed the concept cars, "Taxi" star Marilu Henner co-hosted a live telecast from the Buick display with WJR morning man J.P. McCarthy. CNN talk show host Larry King did a live broadcast of his show from the Pontiac display.

General view of the show. (Courtesy of the National Automotive History Collection, Detroit Public Library)

Chrysler Chairman Robert Eaton wasn't worried about the plans of millionaire investor Kirk Kerkorian, who raised his share of Chrysler stock to over 10%. "I have no concern about it at all," Eaton said. "He has been an excellent shareholder."

The proceeds from the preview were distributed to ten children's charities.

INSIDE THE SHOW: More than 40 of the world's automakers displayed 700 cars and trucks and concept cars. A van conversion show was held in the lower level. The biggest element in Ford's display was an 18,500-lb. AeroMax truck so huge it had to come in through Cobo's so-called elephant door.

Showmanship was on the rise. At the Ford display, the house lights darkened. A backlit globe 75-ft. in diameter rose behind a custom-built hill. Strobe lights activated and then two circles of fast moving flame scored the hand-painted globe. Next, two fiery lines ignited on the hill itself and burned slowly. Four pots of explosives at the base of the hill detonated. Fog pumped in over a stage and a trap door opened, revealing headlights from a 1996 Sable through the smoke, followed by a Taurus. Chrysler made a huge splash in self-promotion when its new version of the Dodge Caravan sprang through the air and landed in a frog pond.

A jury of 49 auto journalists voted the Chrysler Cirrus as the North American Car of the Year, and the Chevrolet Blazer was chosen Truck of the Year.

DATE: January 6-15, 1996

SPONSOR: DADA

BUILDING: Cobo Hall

ADMISSION: $8.00 for adults
$4.00 for children under 12
Free for children under 12 accompanied by an adult
$4.00 for senior citizens

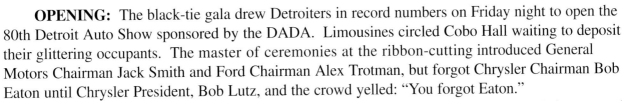

OPENING: The black-tie gala drew Detroiters in record numbers on Friday night to open the 80th Detroit Auto Show sponsored by the DADA. Limousines circled Cobo Hall waiting to deposit their glittering occupants. The master of ceremonies at the ribbon-cutting introduced General Motors Chairman Jack Smith and Ford Chairman Alex Trotman, but forgot Chrysler Chairman Bob Eaton until Chrysler President, Bob Lutz, and the crowd yelled: "You forgot Eaton."

After the ceremony, the crowd herded through the doors of the main hall and ogled the cars and sipped champagne set out on 30-yd.-long tables throughout the exhibit. Broadcast personality Sonny Eliot waved and blew kisses to the crowd through plexiglass walls of the WWJ-AM radio remote booth. The party was a sellout with 15,000 guests providing over $2 million for ten charities benefiting Michigan children.

INSIDE THE SHOW: This was Detroit's 80th annual automobile exhibition and its eighth international show. It was the only North American auto show fully sanctioned by OICA, the international organization of motor vehicle manufacturers. In one room with 600,000 sq. ft. of floor space, there were more than 700 cars and trucks, including concept and future models from 40 different manufacturers. There was also a van conversion exhibition in the 100,000-sq.-ft. Michigan Hall in the lower level.

As the auto industry changed, the car-show model, or product specialist, also changed. Included in the group of product specialists were graying men and women and a disabled man in a wheelchair. The product specialists were trained on the car and dressed more corporately. They had less glitz, less glamour, and more information and realism. The auto show was no longer a male domain with half of the new cars purchased by women. With more women working in the auto industry, the show had become a family attraction.

In the final month before the show, Ford's vice-president of product development agreed to spend a half-million dollars for a new display to show off their flashiest concept car, the Indigo. The reason for the expensive late change was the increasingly competitive car market, which put a premium on creating strong brand images. Automakers no longer could simply plunk down cars on turntables and hang signs. The Indigo had to be exhibited at its most appealing level, which was lower than its original display. There were two ways to view new vehicles at the show: Either look at them from ground level or walk up a ramp to an elevated platform for a closer look. The new Indigo display was a walkup. The display required 20 gals. of glue, 3,500 screws and bolts, 445 sq. yds. of carpet, and enough 2 x 4s to build three 2,000-sq.-ft. homes. It also used enough aluminum tubing to make 440 baseball bats, its plywood could cover almost the entire surface of the Joe Louis Arena one and a half times, and it had enough plastic laminate to cover 500 kitchen countertops.

Chrysler's "Prowler" was a big hit at the show. (Courtesy of the National Automotive History Collection, Detroit Public Library)

Likewise, other products were shown in eye-catching scenes such as the GMC trucks, which were exhibited in an art-gallery setting, a Jeep Wrangler atop man-made rocks, and German cooks working in kitchens above Volkswagen Jettas. The BMW exhibit featured an enormous video screen featuring scenes from the new BMW Z3 in the James Bond movie "Goldeneye."

NOTE: 1996 marked the 100th anniversary of the automotive industry in the U.S. Celebrations were held throughout the industry but were primarily focused in Detroit. There were 36 states with motor vehicle manufacturing facilities, led by Michigan with 139, Ohio with 48, and California with 28. A celebration was held in the summer at the Michigan State Fair Grounds where DADA auto shows were previously held.

DATE: January 11-20, 1997

SPONSOR: DADA

BUILDING: Cobo Hall

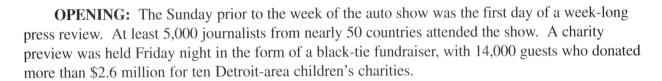

ADMISSION: $8.00 for adults
$4.00 for children 12 and under
Free for children 12 and under accompanied by an adult
$4.00 for senior citizens

OPENING: The Sunday prior to the week of the auto show was the first day of a week-long press review. At least 5,000 journalists from nearly 50 countries attended the show. A charity preview was held Friday night in the form of a black-tie fundraiser, with 14,000 guests who donated more than $2.6 million for ten Detroit-area children's charities.

INSIDE THE SHOW: There were more than 700 cars, trucks, and concept vehicles from more than 40 automotive manufacturers on display. There were 37 new vehicles displayed that went on sale within the following year. In addition, new exhibits in auto racing and two of Detroit's classic car shows—eyes on the Classic Design and Concours d'Elegance—were on the lower level,

(Courtesy of the National Automotive History Collection, Detroit Public Library)

replacing the conversion van show. There was special access for people with disabilities one hour earlier than the public opening each day.

Despite hostile weather conditions, attendance was excellent and show visitors were treated to a spectacle of glimmering chrome, pulsating disco music, and flashing strobe lights. The spectators seemed genuinely appreciative of the multi-million dollars invested in the presentations and the whole slew of concept cars from the Big Three. Mercedes insisted on repainting backdrops to its stand every 24 hours in a different shade just to keep things exciting and fresh.

The new Corvette, redesigned from the ground up for the first time in 13 years, was a top attention-getter. Two million dollars was spent for overall display expenses. There were 250 coordinators, actors, and stage hands, and 15 trucks with equipment, including 250 light fixtures and 50 TV monitors.

NOTE: Until the late 1980s, the unspoken credo of the American carmakers was "ship 'em now and fix 'em later." Shoddy quality had a price as fed-up customers turned to cars they thought they could trust, and those often had Japanese nameplates. American cars had 2.5 things wrong for every one thing wrong with the Japanese cars. Finally, the Big Three began to improve their quality after losing substantial market share. The Japanese countered with a huge effort to learn more about the voice of the customer. The word "quality" appeared in the advertising slogan of nearly every car company at the 1997 Auto Show.

DATE: January 10-19, 1998

SPONSOR: DADA

BUILDING: Cobo Hall

ADMISSION: $8.00 for adults
$4.00 for children 12 and under
Free for children 12 and under accompanied by an adult
$4.00 for senior citizens

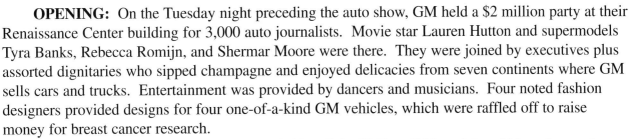

OPENING: On the Tuesday night preceding the auto show, GM held a $2 million party at their Renaissance Center building for 3,000 auto journalists. Movie star Lauren Hutton and supermodels Tyra Banks, Rebecca Romijn, and Shermar Moore were there. They were joined by executives plus assorted dignitaries who sipped champagne and enjoyed delicacies from seven continents where GM sells cars and trucks. Entertainment was provided by dancers and musicians. Four noted fashion designers provided designs for four one-of-a-kind GM vehicles, which were raffled off to raise money for breast cancer research.

The annual black-tie charity event was held at Cobo Hall on Friday night. Although attendance was up, there was more room to party. Previously, people gathered around the popular displays, while other areas were almost empty. Tables, serving 5,000 bottles of champagne, were moved from high traffic aisles to less-crowded areas to spread people out. The display space, which spilled from the Hall into the Arena, was expanded from 700,000 sq. ft. to 703,500. Nearly 97% of the $250 ticket price for 17,000 people was donated to ten children's charities.

INSIDE THE SHOW: More than 700 cars and trucks from 45 manufacturers were on display, including 60 North-American introductions of vehicles that included premieres of redesigned or totally new models scheduled to reach the showrooms later in the year. Also included were 35 futuristic concept cars representing the latest innovations in automotive design and engineering. On hand and taking notes were 5,700 journalists from more than 60 countries.

The 1998 show required 14 million tons of steel, wood, and material compared to 3 million in 1989. It was four times the size in terms of displays using double and triple decks. At least 50% of the displays were new, with an average cost between $4 and $5 million. For example, Lincoln-Mercury had an 18-ft.-high waterfall that communicated a "sense of class and elegance." Initially, Lincoln-Mercury officials checked the display out in the warehouse and decided they didn't like the color of the slate on the back wall, nor did they like the lights used to play off the water. After being fixed and delivered to the show and fabricated, plumbers were needed to fix leaks.

Robert Eaton, Chairman of Chrysler Corp., held up a sack and told a room full of journalists that the sack contained the only carryover parts used for the new Jeep Grand Cherokee. He said most of the 127 parts were mostly small fasteners. Audi AG, pursuing what it called an "un-SUV strategy," unveiled its "all-road quattro" concept vehicle. Actor Paul Hogan made an appearance at a Subaru event, unveiling the latest variation on its sport-utility hybrids, an Outback version of the Legacy sedan.

A Chrysler Jeep shown in the setting of Sedona, Arizona.

Raytheon Aircraft was the manufacturer of the Jaguar Special Edition airplanes. The first production model was based on the Beech King Air C90B, shown in the photograph. A convention center door was widened and the plane's wings were removed then rebolted.

NOTE: So-called light trucks were outselling cars for the first time in history. One study showed that fuel economy ranked 35th on the list of attributes important to truck buyers.

DATE: January 9-18, 1999

BUILDING: DADA

LOCATION: Cobo Hall

ADMISSION: $9.00 for adults
Free for children 12 and under accompanied by an adult
$4.00 for senior citizens

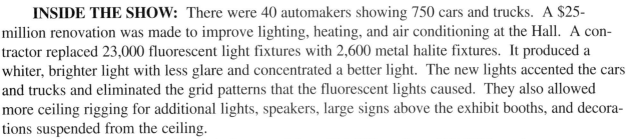

INSIDE THE SHOW: There were 40 automakers showing 750 cars and trucks. A $25-million renovation was made to improve lighting, heating, and air conditioning at the Hall. A contractor replaced 23,000 fluorescent light fixtures with 2,600 metal halite fixtures. It produced a whiter, brighter light with less glare and concentrated a better light. The new lights accented the cars and trucks and eliminated the grid patterns that the fluorescent lights caused. They also allowed more ceiling rigging for additional lights, speakers, large signs above the exhibit booths, and decorations suspended from the ceiling.

The floor space was effectively increased from 700,000 sq. ft. to 800,000 by using two-story exhibits. In 1997, there was one double-deck exhibit in the 30-ft.-high hall, and in 1998 there were

An example of the two-story displays which resulted from the show starting to outgrow Cobo Hall.

four. There were 20 for the 1999 show, creating a "city within a city." Designers called it Detroit's first "vertical" auto show. Some displays had elevators to better serve people with disabilities. In the last three weeks of December, more than 1,400 construction workers worked around the clock to assemble 40 automakers' exhibits.

The Ford Motor Co.'s double-deck display featured a grand staircase as its centerpiece. The display required 200 tons of structural steel, 6,000 sq. ft. of European beechwood, 2,800 sq. ft. of rusted metal used in the truck area, and eight tractor-trailer truckloads of plywood. It had 101,600 sq. ft. of space over the two levels. It also boasted an amphitheater with 350 seats and 75 video screens.

Swedish automaker Saab hired an ice carver and set 60,000 lb. of ice into a glass floor to give its display a frosty, Nordic look. Nearly every exhibit featured computers that connected viewers to the manufacturer's internet site. For the first time, aromatherapy was popular too: Like rival Subaru, Nissan lured viewers to its stand with an "espresso-making" machine that emitted a coffee fragrance. The 1999 auto show displays—minus the cars—cost over $100 million.

Appendix
William Metzger

William E. Metzger was born in Peru, Illinois, on September 30, 1868. His parents were Ernest F. of Frankfort-on-the-Main, Germany, and Maria (Bosley) Metzger of Ohio. Ernest F. Metzger came to America in 1859 when he was 14 years old. The family lived in Ann Arbor, Michigan, where "Billy" attended a German school for one year. The family moved on to Detroit where he graduated from high school in 1884. He went to work as a clerk for Hudson & Symington, where his father was a partner. Hudson had two stores at the time, J.L. Hudson sold clothing, and down the block, Hudson & Symington sold furniture and carpets.

While Bill made $8.00 per week selling furniture, he became interested in bicycles. In 1889, he began working at night to start a bicycle business, and gradually started selling them. It was a treat in those days to see Bill come proudly down Woodward Avenue riding a 52-in.-wheel bike, the large wheel in the front and a small wheel in the rear. Bill was the first one in Detroit to realize the dawning years was to be those when the whole world took to wheels. Eventually, he participated in bicycle racing and became a member of the Detroit Wheelmen. "Speed is the thing," he declared, and as events proved, Bill was right.

Before the late 1870s, blacksmiths and carriage makers sold bicycles, and the bikes were typically imported from England. Bicycle manufacturing started in earnest in the U.S.A. around 1880. By 1895, Detroit had many bicycle shops, and even small communities had shops. By the late 1890s department stores began selling bikes at cut-rate prices, driving many of the small stores out of business. The shops that did stay in business turned to selling horseless carriages and motorcycles in the early 1900s.

In 1891, Bill Metzger and Stanley Huber opened a bicycle shop at 13 Grand River, between Woodward and Griswold. Stanley B. Huber came to Detroit in 1891 to open a store after being a partner in a bicycle shop in Louisville, Kentucky, since 1883. Business went well and in 1894 they

View looking north on Woodward Avenue from Campus Martius (military camp). The Hudson & Symington furniture store is located at the far left. The Civil War statue is in the foreground on the right. (Reprinted with permission of the State Archives of Michigan, Lansing)

265

The Huber & Metzger bicycle shop located at 13 Grand River Avenue.

expanded next door to No. 15. Business was so good that Bill took on Remington typewriters and a line of cash registers to use for the bicycle business cash-flow transactions, while at the same time selling cash registers for extra profit.

Bill combined his retail business with the wholesaling of bicycles, making annual trips to all parts of the United States in the interest of the wholesaling business. Of necessity, he was a close student of the bicycle trade press, and in early 1895 he learned that a horseless carriage show would be held outside London in the fall. Bill was already familiar with the experiments of Gottlieb Daimler and Karl Benz of Germany who both created their own gasoline-powered horseless carriages in 1885. He decided to take a trip to Europe and see for himself. He sold his interest in the shop to Stanley Huber. The partners split up, with Huber keeping the shop for a couple of years longer. Then in 1898 Huber became manager of the Detroit Cereal & Nut Food Company, which sold Battle Creek Sanitarium Health Foods (the original name of the Kellogg Company).

Upon Bill Metzger's return to Detroit, he exclaimed: "It will revolutionize transportation" and "I'm going to get into the game in earnest." He summarily purchased a small quantity of electric vehicles, which became the first motor vehicles ever offered for sale in Detroit. In 1898 he opened up the first retail automobile store in Detroit in the old Biddle House. He became the first "independent" auto dealer in Detroit, and probably the U.S.A. Bill was the first dealer to realize that people were not buying machines, they were buying transportation. He emphasized service and parts to keep vehicles operating and became the owner of the first "accessory" store. Just before Christmas, he hung a sign in his store window that read: MANY A MAN WOULD RATHER HAVE A NEW SET OF SPARK PLUGS FOR HIS CAR THAN WILD NECKTIES.

While preparing for an interview during his later years, he wanted a cigar. An attache asked him if he wanted a mild one or a strong one and he replied: "A strong one, the mild ones are always breaking in my pockets." Later, he was asked if he attended college. He said his alma mater was "Rah,

266

rah, rah, H.F.S." "What college does H.F.S. stand for?" "Hudson's Furniture Store," was the reply. I went through high school and then to the "College of Work."

Frank Duryea is seated on the right side of the Duryea carriage at the first "automobile" race in the U.S.A., held in Chicago in 1895.

The first "automobile" made in Detroit. Charles Brady King, seated on the right side of the photo, and Oliver Barthel at Capitol Park in Detroit. The vehicle's first public drive took place on March 6, 1896. The photograph was taken in November 1896.

Index

White, Rollin 102
White Sewing Machine Co. 9, 12, 15, 16, 19, 21, 26, 28
    Steam Carriage 9
Will Ste. Claire 106
William F.V. Nueman & Co. 33
Willow Run factory 148
Willys 88, 135, 153
    Bermuda 156
    Overland 73, 74
    six 116
Willys-Knight 98, 110
Willys-Overland Knight 94
Wilmot, Walter 45
Winton, Alexander 9, 71
Winton 12, 15, 19
    gasoline car 12
Wittbold, George 143
Wolverine 19, 21
Wolverine Auto Club 52
Women, influence on design 204, 252
Women, percent of car-buying market 251
Woods electric 19
World War I 73, 79, 81, 88
World War II 145, 147, 148, 172

Y

Yale 21
Young and Miller 21
Yugo 240
Yugo GV 238
Yuppies 235, 240

Z

Zeckendorf, A.L. 88